Love Signs

P. Khurrana is a celebrity in the field of Astrology, Numerology and Vastu. He is a popular columnist, prolific author and an ardent devotee of Lord Shiva. He appears on various TV channels and is often consulted for *mahurat* of Bollywood films. He is an adviser to many politicians, actors and business tycoons.

Others titles by the Author:

- The Tarot Power
- The Power of Planets
- The Essence of Astrology
- Sun Signs
- Tarot- Love & Sex - A Guide to an Intimate Relationship
- Power of Mantra and Yantra
- Horoscope 2007

Love Signs

P. Khurrana

RUPA

Published by
Rupa Publications India Pvt. Ltd 2007
7/16, Ansari Road, Daryaganj
New Delhi 110002

Sales centres:
Allahabad Bengaluru Chennai
Hyderabad Jaipur Kathmandu
Kolkata Mumbai

Copyright © P. Khurrana 2007

All rights reserved.
No part of this publication may be reproduced, transmitted, or stored in a retrieval system, in any form or by any means, electronic, mechanical, photocopying, recording or otherwise, without the prior permission of the publisher.

ISBN: 978-81-291-1083-1

Fourth impression 2018

10 9 8 7 6 5 4

Typeset by River's Edge Graphics

Printed at Saurabh Printers Pvt. Ltd, Noida

This book is sold subject to the condition that it shall not,
by way of trade or otherwise, be lent, resold, hired out, or otherwise circulated,
without the publisher's prior consent, in any form of binding or
cover other than that in which it is published.

Contents

Preface	*ix*
Power to Improve Love Relationship	*xi*
Introduction	1
Aries–The Ram	3
How to Recognise Aries	3
Career and Finance	4
Health and Food	5
Your Love Life	5
Your Sex Life	8
Compatibility	10
Taurus–The Bull	31
How to Recognise Taurus	31
Career and Finance	32
Health and Food	33
Your Love Life	34
Your Sex Life	36
Compatibility	38
Gemini–The Twins	62
How to Recognise Gemini	62
Career and Finance	63
Health and Food	64
Your Love Life	64
Your Sex Life	67
Compatibility	68

Cancer–The Crab — 89
How to Recognise Cancer — 89
Career and Finance — 90
Health and Food — 91
Your Love Life — 92
Your Sex Life — 94
Compatibility — 96

Leo–The Lion — 117
How to Recognise Leo — 117
Career and Finance — 118
Health and Food — 119
Your Love Life — 120
Your Sex Life — 122
Compatibility — 124

Virgo–The Virgin — 147
How to Recognise Virgo — 147
Career and Finance — 148
Health and Food — 149
Your Love Life — 149
Your Sex Life — 152
Compatibility — 154

Libra–The Scales — 175
How to Recognise Libra — 175
Career and Finance — 176
Health and Food — 177
Your Love Live — 177
Your Sex Life — 180
Compatibility — 182

Scorpio–The Scorpion   204
   How to Recognise Scorpio   204
   Career and Finance   205
   Health and Food   206
   Your Love Life   207
   Your Sex Life   210
   Compatibility   211

Sagittarius–The Archer   233
   How to Recognise Sagittarius   233
   Career and Finance   234
   Health and Food   235
   Your Love Life   236
   Your Sex Life   239
   Compatibility   240

Capricorn–The Goat   265
   How to Recognise Capricorn   265
   Career and Finance   266
   Health and Food   267
   Your Love Life   268
   Your Sex Life   270
   Compatibility   272

Aquarius–The Water Bearer   294
   How to Recognise Aquarius   294
   Career and Finance   295
   Health and Food   296
   Your Love Life   296
   Your Sex Life   299
   Compatibility   300

Pisces–The Fish   323
How to Recognise Pisces   323
Career and Finance   324
Health and Food   325
Your Love Life   325
Your Sex Life   328
Compatibility   330

Preface

Love is an emotion that every single being on the face of the Earth wishes for. The concept of Love is a much debated topic in the fields of religion and science. The definition of Love would vary for different people in different perspectives. There are people who would love their country and give their lives for it, others for their lover or spouse, still others for their families and then, there are those, who would sacrifice everything for the love of their Guru or God. An emotion that has transcended generations and ages, love is indeed the most enduring of all sentiments.

This particular book is concerned with the love life and balanced relationships of husbands and wives. Ever since, man and woman first started living together, the level of expectations from each other increased meteorically. After spending considerable time with numerous couples, I decided upon penning down a book on LOVE SIGNS to illustrate the fact that via the modern astrological techniques, it is possible for men and women to create an atmosphere of compatibility and empathy with another, irrespective of Sun Signs.

While the varied books on Love Signs, shed light on the psychological and physical compatibility, this book would propel partners towards achieving complete sexual fulfillment and intense romantic liaisons.

When I read the numerous letters that I get from the young boys and girls who have either taken personal counseling or attended my seminars, telling me that the information they received helped them and that they are now enjoying wonderful relationships, my heart fills with warmth, sensing the love that flows from the letters and I consider myself as being loved by one and all.

The emotion of sincere love has no replacement. Love is one of the most fascinating and intriguing of all emotions. Every single culture and country has had a tradition of everlasting and true love. Whether it is Romeo-Juliet, Heer-Ranjha or Sheeri-Farhad, love has existed since time immemorial and would continue to do so. It is, indeed, the be all and end all of one's life. Love is an illuminating and enriching experience. It is a delicate warmth radiated by the Supreme Being and that is the reason why this particular emotion is thought of as heavenly, sacred and inspirational. Eternal and lasting love can be created by accepting and comprehending the distinct and vague differences with our partner and strengthening the similarities. Nearly every single individual at one point of time or the other interprets the emotion he/she feels as Love. Great things have been achieved in the name of love and ironically, offences are also, committed in the name of the same emotion. To be in love with anything or anyone, is definitely the destiny of every person on earth.

The relationship of men and women is, indeed, influenced strongly by astrology. Your Sun Sign would tell about your love and sex life while Venus and Mars would throw light on your compatibility with your partner. This book will determine the inscrutability of the intense love affair and help in establishing a harmonious relationship with your partner or spouse. It would answer questions such as what is your sexual type, what opinion does your partner hold of you, if your sexual and emotional wants are balanced and so on. It would be, definitely, the right advisor for a healthy and fulfilling love life.

If at any point in your life you feel you need help please do not hesitate to contact me at, Hotel Shivalikview, Chandigarh. Ph : (0172) 2703018, 2712280, 9810349900, 09819807558.

P. Khurrana

Power to Improve Love Relationship

There is no doubt about the fact that the stars have an undeniable influence on us and our personae. If there are some skeptics amongst you, who feel otherwise, I shall encourage you to read on further and help me dispel your doubts.

Is it not a fact that on dreary, cloudy days, when the Sun hides from us, we feel sad and low?

How can one explain the influence of the Moon in the tidal phenomena? How can one explain it when talking about the menses of women?

What is the reason for our personalities being so different from each other? Simply that all of us have been impacted, in distinct manners, by the state of the heavens at the moment of our birth.

You may still think that all this is a mere fad and that life is not affected by luck or unlucky stars. Well, life is impacted. Every Sun Sign has a particular weakness or two and this can be reversed into strength by utilising lucky numbers, days, colours, gems and crystals. All of these further enhance the intuitive and perceptive abilities of the individual. These cures are used for fortune and I have met many men and women who are keenly interested in working upon their love life by using any of these treatments. This book has a dedicated chapter, 'Zodiac Zone' for individual signs to enhance and improve their relationships by adhering to the conventions laid down therein.

As of now, I would want you to concentrate on the use of the crystal.

All the things in the Universe are interrelated and dependent upon each other. Humans, plants and animals are all, intricately linked to each other. Moreover, the planet Earth has an energy field which has an influence on everything that pervades the planet. Every crystal has a powerful storehouse of energy which gets transmitted to the individual who is wearing it. A crystal may be used for the solution of problems and the healing of the body. Suitable crystals can be given and recommended to overcome particular problems or problematic times.

When buying a crystal, ensure that it is four and a half carats or more. It should be clear, without any cracks or discolorations, and be of a deep, rich hue rather than an indistinguishable one. You should take the crystal in your hand and try to feel the vibration you receive. If it is warm one, the crystal is right for you. Moreover, you should wrap the stone in muslin and tie it on your arm for seven days. In the event of any positive indication or occurrence, you should surely buy the crystal.

Thereafter, the crystal should be washed and soaked for at least an hour in a mixture of raw milk, honey, sugar and ghee. Also, add a few rose petals to the mixture. Light incense close to the crystal and keep it near your person. Wearing it in a ring or pendant is what you could do while a larger sized crystal could be placed in your bedroom.

Venus and Mars in Your Sun Sign

Astrological study commenced way before man started to keep a record of his history or before the invention of a system of writing. The earliest astrological artifacts discovered show scratches on bones recording the phases of the moon and these are from an era way ahead of the one when man first learned to write.

Since time immemorial, the planets Venus and Mars have been thought to have tremendous influence. This is clear from the cautious efforts of early astrologers to document the impact of the two planets on mankind. Many hundred years later, the positions of the two planets were circumspectly illustrated in the personal horoscope. The vivid, immaculate planet Venus stands for the tender influence of the soul in our life. Venus brings about pure, tranquil, unsullied love and influences strongly our approach towards romance and the philosophical aspect of love. The planet is mild, warm, rich, benevolent, attractive and even, negative. It symbolises love, camaraderie, enjoyment, and the art involved in love. It is forever enticing and appealing. Sun Signs affected by Venus are always warm, beautiful, energetic and attractive. They prosper through the other sex and are essentially dedicated and affectionate people.

On the other hand, we have Mars, which influences the physical dimension. It influences our mental and physical strength and our ability to survive and endure. This planet is also, closely related to the libido of men and women. It rules our physical strength and sexuality. It bestows the person with a good body, constitution and an intense libido. The entire person of the native shows his/her sex appeal, a strong mannerism and allure for the opposite sex. The planet shows us a man who is attractive to women instantly, mainly on the basis of looks. While women would be attracted, other men would find him aggressive and revengeful. If Mars is on the Ascendant, the man will always be over-romantic or have an adoring temperament. It shows the incessant flow of love even after marriage. As far as women are concerned,

Mars would make them highly sexual and hence, they would either have passionate affairs or marriages. This planet would also, give an inclination for a marriage into money or power. In mid-heaven, the power of the planet is violent and could result in disgrace or infidelity or trouble through opposite sex and superficial, meaningless love affairs.

To put it in brief, those who have the planets Venus and Mars placed strongly would be in a better position to demonstrate their sexuality and their love. If either of the two-love or sex-is not given the appropriate outlet, there could be immense inner turmoil and trouble. All this could be removed by channelising the influence of Venus and Mars in a positive manner. It is a sincere request to my readers not to let this powerful emotion go awry or it would mar your relationship forever. You have the ability to lead your love and sex lives in a harmonious and fulfilling fashion after using the advice of the astrologer and following curative therapies, which I have endeavored to expound upon in the Chapter of Compatibility between the Sun Signs.

Introduction

One may define one's sun sign as that sign of the Zodiac which was occupied by the Sun when one was born. The world of astrological literature is filled with a plethora of books that explain the significance of Sun Signs. These books touch merely the surface of the science and give us but a glance at the intriguing yet general characteristics associated with the individual and his personality. Our book goes deeper and shows you how the planets – Venus and Mars, in conjunction with your Sun Sign, impact your approach to love and sex.

If you want to get a comprehensive look at your temperament, what is needed is a birth-chart or a natal horoscope. This particular chart would give the details of the particular position of all the planets, and not just the Sun, at the time of your birth. This implies that if the Sun was placed in one of the twelve signs and hence, made you a Cancer or Gemini, the other planets were also, placed in different signs. Various facets of your nature and personality are determined by each planet and therefore, Venus and Mars determine your romantic and sexual outlooks respectively.

The question, 'What's your Sun Sign?', is often used as an icebreaker in many conversations and once, the answer is given, leads into animated discussions about the characteristics of that particular sign. For instance, is you are a Sagittarius by your Sun Sign, you should be a confident, energetic and independent person. Yet if Venus was in Libra when you were born, you would be a submissive and sticky partner- something that is alien to the Sagittarius nature.

There is no doubt about the fact that the science of astrology could influence your thought patterns and your romantic behaviour. It can also, give you some unique and interesting facts about your partner and your relationships. At the same time, one must keep in mind that while it cannot dictate to you who you should love and who you shouldn't, it can definitely guide and assist you in making the right choice.

This means that when you are attracted towards someone, astrology would be able to give you a detailed look at his/her nature and attitude. It would also, be able to tell you about some unpleasant traits that your companion may be attempting to hide.

There are innumerable occasions when astrologers are consulted and asked to counsel those in love or those thinking about a relationship. This extremely critical aspect of astrological science is called Synastry. It consists of making a detailed comparison of the birth charts of both the partners. The birth charts depict the exact position of the planets at the moment and place of the individual's birth. By deciphering the charts individually and then, in comparison with each other, an astrologer would be able to evaluate the compatibility of the partners and also, earmark potential problem areas and strong points.

Here, it would be worthwhile to dispel one longstanding myth that certain signs are incompatible with some others. This is just not true. Whatever maybe your Sun Sign, you could well enjoy a successful and blissful relationship with a person of any other Sun Sign.

Aries—The Ram
(21st March – 20th April)
The Sign of the Pioneer or Warrior

How to Recognise Aries

Aries is known as the pioneer of the Zodiac, and Arians like to be first. Those who have this as their Sun Sign are generally uncomplicated in their attitude to life. They plan straightforwardly and convince the rest of us that there are no complications in what they suggest.

Arians are passionate by nature, and their enthusiasm for sex and the sheer enjoyment of it is communicated to their partners, who, if sympathetic to Arian needs, will get a great deal of pleasure from the relationship. Arians have a considerable reserve of emotion which surfaces readily, and in a very positive way. They make really lively parents, and as their children get older, they do not generally have too much difficulty in coping with the generation gap. Physical exercise is extremely important to them, and sport, or any activity which makes demands on their physical energy, is excellent for them. Like their emotional level, their physical energy level is high, and needs plenty of positive expression. Arians will spare nothing in expressing their natural enthusiasm, and at least once in their lives will take some action which would prove extremely daunting to other less assertive people, hence their reputation for bravery. They are motivated to achieve a great deal. Since Aries is a Fire sign, they have enormous **warmth**, which is endearing to those who like lively, positive, extrovert types.

Arian children will often feign laziness at school, because they are bored, and simply will not get involved in any subject that really does not interest them. They will cut out, drift off and think about their real interests, while the teacher fights a losing battle. It is, therefore, important for the parents of Sun or Rising-sign Arians to nurture any interest that the young Arian expresses, and to make a special effort to keep his or her initial enthusiasm stirring, perhaps by gradually encouraging the child to take up ever more daunting challenges.

The Arian body-area is the head. Arians either get an above-average number of headaches, or none at all and the cause of such headaches is usually either eye-strain or a minor kidney disorder. Their tendency to cut and burn themselves is considerable, because they are often unduly hasty and rather careless when handling sharp tools or hot dishes. Knocks and cuts to the head are often common.

Career and Finance

Arians are not totally financially oriented as a rule, and despite the very great need for money they will not be satisfied by a good salary if interest and enthusiasm in the daily work is lacking. Generally, a quiet, tense atmosphere will not be agreeable and most Arians would be happier in a noisy workshop, typing pool, factory, garage or busy department store than in some office in which a small group of people arrive every morning on the dot of nine, hang up their coats, make the same comments about the weather, and sit down at their desks not to raise their eyes until coffee time. All much too dull for the active Arian. If Arians make a career in such professions as the law or real estate they should see to it that they are the ones doing battle in court, showing and persuading people to buy new property, and so on, leaving as much of the contract-writing and routine jobs to others as possible. Arians represent action, not, generally speaking. Stodgy detail, in which they may tend rather dangerously to cut corners.

Health and Food

You will be endowed with a splendid constitution and great vitality. You would recover quickly from any illness. Your greatest danger will come from accidents of all kinds, especially those caused by firearms, fires, explosions, street or road dangers. Normally you suffer from these diseases like cuts, wounds, soar eyes, boils, burns, blood pressure, piles, sores, itches, fractures, urinary complaints, jaundice, oozing blood, tumours, epilepsy.

You will also have a liability for high blood pressure, heart disease and apoplexy.

Suggested Food Options:
- Potato
- Carrot
- Onion
- Apple
- Brain Food
- Fish
- Avoid Tomato & Red Meat

Your Love Life

First Decan of Aries : March 21st to March 30

The overpowering emotion of love is an incessantly essential influence in your life owing to an abundance of zest and enthusiasm in your own expressive temperament. Whatever you say and do reflects the passionate glow which is alight and bright in your very active romantic life. Love fills your entire persona with warmth and vigour.

However, plunging headlong into the alliance of matrimony is not suitable. You are attracted towards various people from diverse walks of life and there is no doubt about the fact that you would need sufficient amount of time before you make your final choice about your life partner. If you give yourself this time, you would be highly pleased and satisfied with your mate. Since you would be extremely social and quite the crowd-puller, you do not need to fear that you wouldn't be given enough choice as time passes by.

Though you are highly independent and self-reliant, the influence of your beloved would be calming and soothing for you. You would be completely content doing what your partner wants you to do and may give up your dominating influence for your loved one. In fact, you may even face the danger of becoming too passive and submissive, however, many people may not tell you that since you do not take criticism easily.

Undoubtedly, you would discover the path to faithful and sincere love which would fill your life with satisfaction and happiness. Moreover, you belong to the rare breed of people who would love with all the warmth and loyalty they possess within themselves.

Second Decan of Aries: March 31st to April 9

An explorer and adventurer, it is indeed difficult, if not impossible for you to settle down in one place for long. You feel that there is a lot that has to be discovered and hence, you look for the same qualities in your partner as well. It would do you good to find such a partner who would appreciate your quest for the novel and unknown. It would bore you extremely if you are married to one who would remain stagnant.

Your beloved should also, appreciate and value your vast circle of friends. For you, your social life is just as significant and important as your own individual life. Therefore, it would be essential for your partner to enjoy socialising and mingling with a diverse group of people. While personal, individual qualities are important, these attributes are equally important for you.

More demonstrative, you are one of those who would show your emotions than merely talk about them. Also, you are the kind who likes to be natural and unprompted about showing your affections. Despite the fact that you may not express your love in lofty speech, you do enjoy hearing from your beloved about how much your love means to him and what is the influence that it has over him.

For you, conviction in your partner is of absolute importance. Though your love may be immensely strong and firm, yet if at any point of time, you feel that the trust between the two of you is lacking, you would lose faith in your relationship and the love would die out.

Third Decan of Aries: April 10 to April 20

Though you are extremely emotional, you do have complete control over yourself and would always carry yourself with immense grace and dignity. You would demonstrate your emotions lavishly when in a satisfying and happy relationship.

However, you must be careful that you do not let anyone take advantage of you and hurt you. Use your good judgment to stay away from people with wrong intentions and those who might exploit the goodness of your nature.

For you it is essential that your love be reciprocated and that your beloved responds with the same fervor that you emanate. Your sensitive nature needs to feel love in your relationship else, you would sense dryness in your relationship with your partner.

When you are loved with sincerity and warmth, you would derive maximum pleasure out of it and would bask in the radiance of the affection. This would also, motivate you to do well in all your professional endeavours. As long as there is complete (even silent) trust within your relationship, all would be well in your world.

When loved and cared for, you put your best foot forward and play the social host with élan and finesse. Your home would be filled with happiness and contentment. Your state of bliss would make you the object of admiration for all those who know you.

Your Sex Life

First Decan, Mars-ruled: March 21 to 30 March

Your approach to sex is just as straightforward and spontaneous as it is with all other things. Though your sex drive is strong and vigorous, you tend to lose interest if other aspects of your life are not equally satisfying. In perfect situations, though, you are sexually active and do not hesitate to make the first move. You would also, be decidedly impatient and would throw yourself completely into the mood and situation. However, you might be a little selfish and give your own satisfaction more importance. You would be totally involved and would not appreciate distractions of any sort.

Second Decan, sub-ruled by the Sun: March 31 to April 9

You view sex as an essential part of life's wonderful exploration. You tend to categorise love and sex together, rather than bearing in mind that the latter could be a distinct or individual experience. Despite the fact that you have the fundamental Arian qualities of spontaneity and edginess, you also possess poise and the capability to sustain a balanced outlook in your approach towards sex. Because of this, you are in a better position to be in charge of your urges when they might propel you towards something that might spell trouble. Though you do have a strong sex drive, however, for you your emotions and feelings play a stronger role in deciding your sexual behaviour.

Third Decan, sub-ruled by Jupiter: April 10 to 20 April

You possess the essential Aries attributes of assertiveness and plentiful sexual liveliness; moreover you are a benevolent soul which does play a positive role in your sex life. You have the aptitude to generate an atmosphere of cheerful repose. This also, happens to be an attribute that you display in various other aspects of life along with sex. For you the sexual act must be preceded by good food, drink, music and intelligent tête-à-tête. All these are things that you relish and enjoy immensely. You are fond of letting others partake of these activities and hence, you might find yourself surrounded with a variety of sexual mates.

Aries Celebrities

Birth Date	Star	Vocation
2 April	Ajay Devgan	Actor
7 April	Pt Ravi Shankar	Musician
16 April	Lara Dutta	Actress
21 March	Rani Mukherjee	Film Star
21 March	Bismillah Khan	Musician

Compatibility

ARIES & ARIES

Fire Sign Ruled by Mars	Fire Sign Ruled by Mars
• Energetic	• Energetic
• Sexy	• Sexy
• Enthusiastic	• Enthusiastic
• Impulsive	• Impulsive
• Strong	• Strong
• Sincere	• Sincere
• Bossy	• Bossy

An Aries and Aries relationship is quite hunky-dory to begin with yet unfortunately, this is a relationship that doesn't have a happy ending. The reason is simply that when you add fire to fire-it leads to a bigger fire. Ruled by the planet Mars, when two of this particular sign get together, the outcome can be pretty fiery. However, this can also, have a positive impact because the two Arians would have a high level of honesty and protectiveness with one another. Since the two would need the same things out of a relationship, they would be able to create a world of happiness and joy. If both the partners have the right attitude, this is, indeed, a workable relationship and it would enrich their lives with plenty of independence, security, sympathy and acceptance. Just that one would need to maintain a highly rational and balanced approach, since this sign is an extreme and would either love strongly or hate deeply. Hence, if both the partners are determined to make the relationship work, they would need to adapt and understand each other profoundly. Fire with fire is a compatible combination, although it produces a volatile, exciting and sometimes stressful atmosphere. Peace, quiet and relaxation will be difficult to achieve.

If both people try to rule the roost or compete, disputes and tension will result. When necessary, each will defend the other. Your arch enemy—boredom will seldom arise in this duo because you both like to be active. There will be seldom any deception pretence or hypocrisy. They provide protection to each other. These two are capable of reaching the far heavens of happiness, since they both require essentially the same thing out of love & sex.

Astro Advice
o Wear Coral of four ratti
o Avoid wearing red while meeting

ARIES & TAURUS

Fire Sign *Earth Sign*
Ruled by Mars *Ruled by Venus*

- Energetic
- Sexy
- Enthusiastic
- Impulsive
- Fickle
- Impatient

- Steadfast
- Systematic
- Artistic
- Patient
- Kind-hearted and loving
- Sensual

Aries is a sign that is known for its energetic, dominating, spontaneous nature. It is also, a sign that is fond of talking and looking at the brighter side of things. Arians love to have an exciting and interesting life and are slightly impatient when it comes to getting the outcomes of their efforts.

Taureans, on the other hand, are known for their reticent, realistic, self-reliant temperament which has a tendency to be slightly negative. They desire security, seclusion and also, need plenty of relaxation and peacefulness in order to make life a smooth and easy journey. Strikingly different, these two can complement each other quite well. While idealistic Aries can show the solid Taurean her dreams, the practical Taurus can show Aries the unrealistic nature of some of those dreams and together they can achieve a lot in life. However, freedom-loving Aries can be quite abrupt and sever all relationships with the slightly possessive Taurean at a moment's notice.

The Taurean approaches love with the same realistic approach as he would anything else. Yet he would be profoundly tender and romantic about his love, even if he doesn't really care to display it with flamboyance. This could tend to give the Arian a mistaken notion about the Taurean's romantic inclinations. Therefore, whenever the Taurean would show his or her affection, it would be a pleasant surprise to the Arian. At the same time, though, there could be a few difficulties in this relationship, especially with the physical aspect. The Taurean approaches sex as an activity essential for the accomplishment of certain purposes while the Aries looks at sex as a form of release in all aspects. This difference in attitude would need to be met mid way so as to allow complete satisfaction for both the partners.

Astro Advice
o Wear a Diamond of two carats
o Woman should wear pink

ARIES & GEMINI

| Fire Sign | Air Sign |
| Ruled by Mars | Ruled by Mercury |

- Energetic
- Enjoys challenges
- Charming
- Sexy
- Enthusiastic
- Impulsive

- Restless
- Clever
- Changeable
- Expressive
- Witty
- Erratic

These two signs share similar gifts for persuasiveness, aestheticism and imagination. They enjoy living life fully and have a casual outlook towards amassing either immense power or wealth.

Essentially, both Aries & Gemini are straightforward, yet strangely, enough they tend to forget where the line between truthfulness and trickery exists. Whether they wish to be naive or unaware is something they need to work out on their own. What is important is that both of them are equally adept at selling their own images as they are at selling any material object. While Gemini is logical, intelligent and somewhat cynical, Aries finds it difficult to distinguish between the real and the fake most of the time. Only on being hurt a couple of times, would the Arian be able to differentiate and learn.

Ruled by the planet Mercury, the Gemini is gifted with a sharp brain that is forever at work behind the serene and graceful façade however Aries would take things as they come and happily get used to whatever is the pace of life. Both the signs do have a tendency to do some amount of wishful thinking.

They could very well do so but they would need to ensure that the base of their dreams is solid and stable else everything would come crashing to Earth. If the two get together and exhibit endurance and determination, nothing would be impossible for these intelligent and creative souls. They would also, enjoy a lot of synchrony in their lives and even in their sex life, they would feel as if they share one soul. Hence, if they manage to deal with the minor differences, they would be wonderful together.

Aries is courageous, vivid, gracious and passionate while Gemini is absolutely charismatic, multitalented and impulsive. Truly, they would make an appealing and ideal pair. One that could well, be the object of envy for many.

Astro Advice
o Avoid all intoxicants and non-vegetarian food
o Your lucky stones are Pukhraj and Emerald

ARIES & CANCER

Fire Sign *Water Sign*
Ruled by Mars *Ruled by Moon*

- Strong
- Fickle
- Confident

- Nourishing
- Sensitive
- Lazy

- Diligent
- Romantic
- Impatient
- Self-centered
- Ambitious
- Kind

The Arian is not only fond of but also, needs to win at everything. What the Arian also, enjoys doing is to be at the head of everything. And what about Cancer? Well, though the shy crab might conceal his desire to win, it certainly can not be ignored. One should never overlook the fact that it is the fundamental sign of control and management. Now, it does create a slightly sticky situation when you have two people who wish to be on top. One would obviously have to be the follower. While this may seem an unsolvable problem, it does have a solution. The solution being that the two could easily walk together, hand in hand, in tandem with each other. That way, there wouldn't ever be a leader and follower equation. This is what cooperation is all about. While the quiet Cancerians might become morose and quieter than ever when their feelings are treated harshly, the fiery Aries should not imagine them to be passive and servile. They would handle things with peace, tolerance and privacy. Hence, they wouldn't stay quiet forever. Just that their way of handling things would be different from the aggressive ways of the Arian.

Although, Aries and Cancer have dissimilar inspirations, aims and perspectives on life, they do have the capacity to enhance the quality of life for one another. Since both have a lot of righteousness in their own selves, they would be able to impart a fair amount to the other and hence, develop and better the life of their partner. Since this is a Fire-Water combination, both would have a feeling that they could very easily finish the other. Despite all these superficial differences, the two would be able to enjoy a relationship filled with trust, hope, love and sympathy for one another.

Astro Advice

o The man should wear pearl and women should wear coral.
o Avoid long drives

ARIES & LEO

Fire Sign
Ruled by Mars

- Energetic
- Loyal
- Sexy
- Enthusiastic
- Impulsive
- Go-Getter
- Enjoys Challenges

Fire Sign
Ruled by Sun

- Proud
- Self-confident
- Arrogant
- Energetic
- Glory Seeker
- Warm-hearted
- Egocentric

The Arian is a topper, a frontrunner- unquestionably, a winner. Whether it is their profession, relationships, business, the Arians would need to come out first in the run and that is what drives them to do their very best.

On the other hand, we have the Leos who do not believe in squandering their precious time and efforts in attempting to win. This is a group of people who do not need to vie with others for top honours. They consider themselves inherently finer and better than everybody else. Hence, by default, they become the best in everything that they do, whether it has to do with relationship, work or any other aspect of life. They were born to be at the top without having to try for it. The only issue being that how could two people be at the top.

One would need to consider the situation with a great deal of finesse and tact. Since two people vying for top honours wouldn't be able to enjoy a healthy relationship, one would need to sacrifice a little. The Leo has an innate and ingrained desire to rule and if the Aries understands and accepts this fact, then everything would be hunky-dory. And the relationship would be a dream. However, there is the possibility that the Aries might not quite agree with this since Aries, too, is ruled by a desire to win and achieve. That is when trouble would start to brew. Only when both partners would understand that one cannot always win and allow the other to be ahead at times, would the relationship be a little less turbulent.

The relationship between an Aries and a Leo may, in all likelihood, be an affectionate and brilliant one yet there are quite a few chances that it would also, create regular tempests centering around the emotions and self of these two fiery individuals. Both produce a strong and intense physical tremor in each other and this is strengthened by the frequent emotional encouragement that they give each other. Sexually, as well, they could be brilliant together since they would both combine love and passion and would create wonderful things together. Both Aries and Leo tend to treat love like a blessing and would strive hard to tend for and protect one another with the power of their love and affection.

Astro Advice

- Man should wear Pukhraj and woman should wear Ruby.
- Avoid wearing pink while going out for dinner.

ARIES & VIRGO

 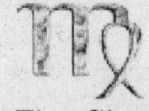

| *Fire Sign* | *Fire Sign* |
| Ruled by Mars | Ruled by Mercury |

- Energetic
- Sexy
- Enthusiastic
- Impulsive
- Youthful
- Confident

- Exact
- Methodical
- Discriminating
- Intelligent
- Expressive
- Analytical

The Arian would always make the first move based on their instincts and not on the facts before them. On the contrary, we have the Virgos who would, in characteristic manner, be completely pragmatic and realistic in their approach. Even though, the drives and attitudes may be dissimilar, both the signs are alike in many aspects. They would both not refrain from helping out others and would have a natural inclination towards wholesomeness in whatever they undertake. They move in harmony with one another towards their dreams of creativity and beauty. Moreover, both the signs would have the highest comfort level with each other and would be able to tell each other things they wouldn't even dream of telling anyone else in the world.

Since the Virgos can be highly methodical and proponents of intelligibility, Aries would at times, consider them hard to please and icy. Moreover, the spontaneity of the Arian and the inability to alter situations may cause the Virgo to be displeased with them, yet the Virgo wouldn't be vocal about the displeasure and all this might lead to misinterpretations and confusions between the two.

However, Aries and Virgo can enjoy a satisfying relationship, if there is a favourable aspect between the Sun and the Moon in their charts. When the two realise that they are capable of creating happiness, they would be pleasantly surprised. Both can learn a lot from each other. The methodical yet creative Virgo can teach the impulsive Aries to stop and appreciate the beauty in the little joys of nature and Life.

Physically, there would be a vague sort of delight and fascination between them. Irrespective of their inherent attraction for each other in passionate affairs, there will always be ambiguity as far as the level of emotional security in the relationship is concerned.

When the relationship faces stormy weather, it would be filled with disappointments and disapprovals and both the partners would move away from each other to search for peace and calmness, instead of talking things over and making them better together. This would be one of the most harmful things that they could do. On the brighter side, though, both Aries and Virgo have the ability to renew the relationship each time it loses some freshness and flavour. In any case, it would be nothing short of a miracle if this relationship would last forever, especially since both wouldn't wish to communicate with each other with candour and love together.

Astro Advice

o Man should wear Coral and women should wear Emerald.
o Saturday and Tuesdays are auspicious for outing.

ARIES & LIBRA

Fire Sign
Ruled by Mars
- Charming
- Romantic
- Crude
- Sadistic
- Adventurous
- Optimistic

Air Sign
Ruled by Venus
- Harmonious
- Selfish
- Hospitable
- Reasonable
- Fastidious
- Escapist

This is indeed, an interesting equation, since fire has an inherent closeness with air, yet both are opposite to each other in the zodiac, and therefore, they could both attract and keep away from one another. At the start of the relationship, there is a high degree of attraction–physical or emotional between the two. However, in situations of disagreements, Aries would often gain the upper hand while Libra would feel emotionally drained and would walk away from the situation. While, most of the time, Libra would maintain a steady and calm attitude, if fiery Aries becomes too bossy or domineering, there could be real fireworks. Libra gives the Aries bravery and a more objective and liberal motivation while Aries enthuses the Libran to become more decisive and firm with regards to his goals and aims.

In physical matters, Libra would depend on the feeling of romance and would have fun in love even when the relationship would culminate in marriage. He or she would, however, want his partner to reciprocate and therefore, Aries should be ready to be game for a long prelude to the actual act. This could range from a beautiful, candle lit dinner to a surprise vacation. What is important is that the magic should stay alive. When the relationship loses its thrill, Libra would become remote and disinterested. It is essential that any dreams that Libra has about Aries should be left as they are. Aries would need to keep up wooing the Libran with beautiful gifts and surprises. Once these minor adjustments are made, it would be smooth sailing for both.

For most part of the times, Libra would be the calming and soothing presence in this relationship, yet when the Arian pushiness becomes more than what he/she could possibly take, it would lead to trouble. Both would need to work together and learn to adapt to each other without trying to put the other one down. Since the Aries actually would value the Libran fairness and logic, he/she would try to top it. But what Aries needs to understand is that for the relationship to work, they would need to function as one unit and not rivals.

Astro Advice

o Man Should avoid material disruptions and focus on his beloved.
o Women should dress up in full white Sari with a golden border.

ARIES & SCORPIO

 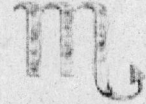

Fire Sign
Ruled by Mars

Water Sign
Ruled by Mars

- Headstrong
- Enjoys challenges

- Over-sexed
- Magnetic

- Confident
- Brash
- Hot-tempered
- Go-getter
- Survivors
- Boastful
- Obsessed
- Dynamic

The fire-water alliance is, indeed, one which is filled with potential for both good and bad. Since both these signs are ruled by the planet Mars, there would exist a reciprocal recognition of the positive points of each other. While straightforward Aries wouldn't really be too aware and even, appreciative of the hidden ways of Scorpio, this partnership would benefit from their fondness for working as a team, as long as they agree upon the goals that they wish to achieve. Scorpio adds value to the relationship by his/her immense dedication and principled temperament. At the same time, these two would also, have the ability to ruin one another. Aries might show an inclination to become unusually quiet and subdued in difficult times. However, during more pleasant times, the Scorpio would be able to give energy to the relationship as long as he/she maintains a balanced and liberal attitude towards the Aries' casual and amiable outlook.

While the Scorpio is not the sort to bother too much about appearances, the Aries can be quite conceited about their own as well as their partners' look. Capable and brave, the Aries would value Scorpio's smooth, affectionate and somewhat erotic voice. While the journey of life with a Scorpio may not be a bed of roses, with time and patience, it would definitely be a mature and harmonious relationship.

When it comes to physical matters, the Scorpio's possessive temperament would become stifling at times for the liberal Arian. Scorpio has a high sex drive and is an extremely ardent lover and this would need to be accepted by the Aries, if problems are to be avoided. The physical magnetism between the two can be quite powerful and permanent. The combination of love with sex is something that both find mutually gratifying and personally exhilarating. Deep inside, the Aries is sincere, virginal and childlike and in the same way, Scorpio is unique, alluring and inexplicable. They would definitely have the ability to build with each other a relationship filled with conviction and clemency.

Astro Advice
o Focus on good habits and avoid intoxication.
o Maintain diet and fitness routines.

ARIES & SAGITTARIUS

Fire Sign *Ruled by Mars*	*Fire Sign* *Ruled by Jupiter*
• Strong	• Honest
• Zestful	• Restless
• Adventurous	• Forthright
• Independent	• Earnest
• Youthful	• Selfish
• Energetic	• Immoral

While two fire signs wouldn't exactly negate each other, they would need to give each other a fair amount of independence and space. Aries values the archer's positive approach and truthfulness while Sagittarius also, motivates the high-energy Aries. It is indeed, a relationship which has a high level of enthusiasm and activity, hence the levels of calm and restfulness are relatively lower. Both wouldn't quite appreciate being pushed around. Aside from this, they would have lots more in common. They would enjoy being occupied-physically and mentally. That would give them a lot of joy. Though they might have the usual tiffs and spats, the Sagittarius character would always be touched by the straightforward attitude of Aries and similarly, the Archer would be able to show the Ram the importance of being affectionate and sympathetic impulsively.

A free soul, Sagittarius feels completely at home and at peace with himself when he is involved in more than one affair at a time and the Aries would need to deal with this. He would also, be quite a performer in bed and would always be able to satisfy the Arian. Hence, this particular aspect of their relationship would be both amazing and pleasing. They adapt to each other sexually almost, instinctively. Their ardour is tempered with their profound love for each other. They would be tender towards each other and hence, their relationship would be close and loving.

The two signs share quite a few traits and hence, are quite compatible. For instance, both have a fair degree of optimism and also, a liking to passionately argue out their point. Hence, the attraction between them would be nearly instantaneous. Generous, confident and amicable, the affection would never cool, since they share a common enthusiasm for novelty and innovation. Their tendency to get involved with a cause also, brings them closer to each other.

Both Aries and Sagittarius know that cooperation and mutual give and take is the ideal approach to take care of all arguments and squabbles. Hence, this understanding enables them to accomplish a unique synchrony in emotional, sexual and mental matters.

Astro Advice
o Men should trust their beloved
o Woman should wear dresses with stripes or checks.
o Wear a Coral of five carat

ARIES & CAPRICORN

Fire Sign *Ruled by Mars*	*Earth Sign* *Ruled by Saturn*
• Weak	• Stable
• Charming	• Over-Critical
• Hostile	• Determined
• Trail-blazing	• Limited
• Fickle	• Social-climber
• Over-confident	• Ambitious

Blending fire with earth can be quite a demanding composition, more so, since the ruling planets Mars and Saturn, respectively, bestow contrasting characteristics on the two. While Aries' planet, Mars makes it impulsive, raring to go and burning with energy; Capricorn's ruler Saturn is vigilant, solemn, sedate and purposeful. Capricorn likes to be prepared for the future and can easily wait for results to show. However, Aries is restless and would need to see immediate results. The two would need to practice a great deal of patience and ensure that their differences don't create resentments. Aries might often get subdued by the Capricorn and might feel that the latter lacks understanding. This however is not really true, since Capricorn is capable of showing a great deal of sympathy when they want to do so.

Sexually, Capricorn desires to be romanticised before the act itself and Aries would need to ensure that this aspect is catered to, else Capricorn would lose interest and sex could become bereft of magic and love. Even though the Capricorn does not have a strong sex drive, he does enjoy the experience and would feel hurt if he/she isn't accepted easily. When hurt, Capricorn would retreat and Aries would need to bide his/her time till the former is willing to emerge once again and join in physical expressions of love. Sexually, like emotionally, their ruling planets play a significant role. Aries is ruled by Mars-the planet of desire and sex, and hence would make the first move, frequently; Capricorn's planet is the steady Saturn which would give it the inclination to resist rather than reciprocate. Once these barriers are overcome and adjusted to, life would be relatively smoother and enjoyable for the two.

Capricorn would be pleasantly surprised and enchanted with the profundity of the love that he/she would receive and hence, this could play an important role in making their relationship rewarding, enduring and enjoyable.

Their sexual relationships would benefit greatly from paying heed to what they feel deep inside and by not repressing their desires and needs. This is true, especially for Capricorn who could spoil the spontaneity of the relationship by being too staid.

Take care, nourish and nurture your relationship with freshness and love and don't let the passions cool down. Only then would you be able to enjoy a mutually satisfying relationship that would stand the test of time.

Astro Advice
o Man should pursue surroundings by a positive force
o Let your beloved handle the situation himself; so do not interfere.

ARIES & AQUARIUS

 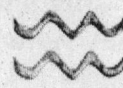

Fire Sign	Air Sign
Ruled by Mars	Ruled by Saturn
• Enjoys challenges	• Cowardly
• Reckless	• Truthful
• Bossy	• Sympathetic
• Optimistic	• Progressive
• Diligent	• Caring
• Adventurous	• Honest

While Fire and Air do tend to gel quite well with each other, the planets that rule them tend to create a huge amount of power and influence which would need to be dealt with in a positive manner.

The unique Aquarius would not ever want to put a wet blanket on the natural freedom and inventiveness of Aries, while Aries would welcome the presence of a companion in Aquarius. The innovative methods of the Aquarian would appeal to Aries, who in turn would appreciate anything with a touch of novelty. However, the erratic behaviour of the Aquarius could throw the Aries off and make him/her irritated. Both signs would, in any case, get along quite well simply because both are quite often misconstrued and think out of the box. There would be the occasional instances when Aquarius wouldn't be able to comprehend the Arian's fiery temper and the Arian would feel as if the Water bearer exists on a different planet. Yet, aside from these minor issues, the two would share an inimitable connection with each other.

Aquarians would hardly, if ever, overdo him/her in the sexual department. Primarily so, because they would be more involved in other activities and hence, would engage in sex only when they feel like, which could make them somewhat selfish in this area.

Fundamentally, the two signs share a lot of similarities and hence, would understand and respect each other greatly. While there could be fireworks since both can get somewhat forceful at times, the level of harmony would be much greater. Aries and Aquarius would be drawn towards each other because of their emotional and intellectual similarities. All this would ensure that the relationship is rewarding and beneficial to both the parties involved and the occasional tiffs would only add to the magic between the two. With time and practice, the two would learn how to create the beautiful music of love with each other. They do have the capacity to enrich each other's lives and would do so, once they overcome the minor hurdles in their path.

Astro Advice
o Women should wear a Coral of five carat
o Woman should show her nurturing nature and true feelings of love to her lover/husband.
o Man should wear a Black stone of four carat on the ring finger.

ARIES & PISCES

Fire Sign *Water Sign*
Ruled by Mars *Ruled by Neptune*
- Strong
- Enthusiastic
- Cowardly
- Deceptive

- Active
- Selfish
- Insensitive
- Hot-tempered
- Creative
- Trustworthy
- Guilt-ridden
- Escapist

Aries ruled by fiery Mars and Pisces ruled by watery Neptune are poles apart in temperament. So great would be the difference, that it would be extremely hard to find something that the two could possibly share. Optimistic, energetic Aries would not be able to understand the vague, mystifying character of Pisces who would further bother the Aries with his indecisiveness and pessimistic outlook.

They would be able to co-exist if they decide not to interfere with each other's attitude and outlook. There would be frequent heated arguments and cold wars, more so, when the blunt Arian would lose patience with the wily ways of the Piscean.

In physical matters, the fish is quite adjusting yet thin-skinned, which implies that he wouldn't be able to take any harshness in this aspect. He/she might display somewhat masochistic inclinations during sex by imagining that Aries is infidel. Yet these wouldn't be mentioned in the light of the day, since the fish would be quite scandalised by such talk. The fish would also, need to curb his need to be out of the house, socialising or drinking, which would only serve to make the Aries feel sad and exploited. On the whole, though, the two would enjoy a satisfying sexual relationship.

The partnership of Aries and Pisces is a gentle and pleasant one. Pisces would not be too opposing to Aries who in turn, would find them calming and soothing. The relationship would be gratifying for the two, if they learn to come to a common ground and adapt to each other's differences.

Astro Advice

- You are advised to keep porcelain figures of Venus and Jasmine in the south west corner of your bedroom.
- Man should wear a Yellow Sapphire of seven carat on the index finger
- Woman: it may be necessary to bend down to a stronger point of view.

Taurus–The Bull
(21st April – 21st May)
The Sign of the Builder or Producer

How to Recognise Taurus

Taureans, to function properly, need to live their lives in the knowledge that they have the security of a regular income and a stable emotional relationship. When this is achieved they are in the right position to achieve a great deal. Their most outstanding virtue is patience, they will plod very steadily onwards, and soon learn that short cuts are usually disastrous for them. Taureans need a steady, predictable routine, but the sort of rut in which they may get themselves will increase their sense of much-needed security and within its confines they will achieve much. But Taureans must also make something of an effort to break new ground, do new and different things and be open to the opinions of others in order to move with the times and to make sure that they are not missing out on life as it is actually being lived by other people. Visit a Taurean's home and you will relax on comfortable cushions, find the colours used in decoration pleasing and the place not lacking in beautiful things which will have cost the Taurean rather more than he or she can actually afford. This might seem superficial, but these outward expressions form an important part of the whole Taurean motivation. Possessions to the Taurean are very important. In fact, possessiveness is the major Taurean fault. The two go together. Taureans love to own beautiful things, and they really do need to be aware that their partner is not an extension of this basic urge. The realisation that no one can actually be possessed by another can be a cause of real heartache to Taureans. The sooner they learn to adopt a self-analytical and critical attitude in their expression of love the better, as this can help them to express themselves in a less claustrophobic way towards their partners.

Most Taureans have a happy knack either of making money or doing a great deal with what they have. They combine this with the ability to build up their own businesses and often with the aid of a more adventurous partner achieve much. They also do extremely well in banking or working for large multinational companies, as their need for financial security is then taken care of, and they can express themselves in the knowledge that the regular pay-cheque will arrive when expected. The Taurean body-area is the throat; colds often begin here, with a sore throat or loss of voice. Taureans have the reputation of being the best looking people in the Zodiac, due partly to their ruling planet, which is Venus. But because most Taureans love rich food, with heavy sweet things being particular favourites, they have a tendency to put on weight. Also, they are often slow movers and do not burn up their additional calories very quickly. So, a conscious and continual check on the amount of food and wine they consume is essential if they are going to keep the good looks they had when they were young.

Career and Finance

Financial stability and a secure job are essential for Taureans, who need to be assured that the pay-cheque or pay-packet will arrive regularly and on time, so that they are able to plan their finances well ahead, budgeting for purchases, holidays and the education of their children with care, forethought and precision. Of course, many

Taureans find themselves in less financially stable professions, but when this happens they have the sense to plan as carefully as possible, making investments as and when they can in order to give themselves a sense of security.

It is important that the Taurean has the right atmosphere in which to work. A large, noisy open-plan office may well have to be tolerated, but the Taurean will work very hard to get out of that office and into a quiet corner in which to work alone, away from everyone else's chatter and rushing about. Whatever the chosen profession, these are the sort of conditions that are right for the rather slow but very sound and steady Taurean temperament. Taureans will work hard and will get through the work allocated to them, though they could well slow down in the afternoon after they have taken a client to lunch and had perhaps a little too much to eat to make for a productive afternoon's work.

Health and Food

You will start life with an excellent constitution, but owing to a tendency for luxury and good living, you will be inclined to 'dig your own grave with teeth'.

You will have a slender symmetrical form in your early years which you are likely to ruin as you advance in life by over indulgence in sweet stuffs or the good things of the table.

You will be liable to flattery, degeneration of the heart and a dropical condition in your later years, but such things are in your own power to control as you will. There may also be some tendency for delicacy relating to the lungs, bronchial tubes and throat.

Suggested Food Options:
- Almond
- Cabbage
- Egg Yolk
- Avoid non-vegetarian food, especially red meat
- Try to avoid sugar.

Your Love Life

First Decan of Taurus: April 21 to 30 April

For you the emotion of love is as spontaneous and innate as the very nature of Man himself. You view love with great seriousness and maturity since it does happen to be one of the most important aspects of life. Your sexuality is unfathomable and so is your admiration for this amazing emotion which possesses exquisiteness and splendour.

You may adore a loved one and be incredibly overprotective as though your partner were the most valuable thing in the whole world. That pretty much expresses how you feel about the emotion of love, itself. It does happen to be for you the most precious and valued. While you do need a sense of allure in your emotions, you also, need a sense of emotional refuge which only true love can provide you with throughout your life.

When it comes to matrimony, you would be highly sensible about the whole issue since you do want a partner who would be able to give you the immense loyalty and love that you require. You would enter this alliance only when you are sure that you have found the right person and feels that same way as you do about family, relationships and home. For you the genuineness of the emotion is most important and you do need to know that the feelings run deep. A shallow or superficial person would certainly not win any favors with you ever.

Second Decan of Taurus: May 1 to May 10

For you love tends to be for a person who is just as pragmatic as you and would listen to your dictates on budgeting and the right way to run a home. Not the kind to get swayed by mere infatuations, you would wait for the right person to come your way before you plunge into matrimony. You would value the wavelength that your partner and you share as much as the love and affection between the two of you.

Although usually, sensible, you may be attracted by someone sexually in a very strong manner. On the brighter side, you do realise that you are prone to making this mistake and therefore, spend considerable time scrutinising your current love's motives and inclinations before you decide to take it further.

When married, you would fill your married life with immense love and would keep on working on retaining the magic and spark within your partner and you. There is no doubt that for you a marriage is for keeps and you would work hard at making it perfect. A good parent and a wonderful partner, you would bring love, joy and warmth into the home and make it stay there over the ages.

Third Decan of Taurus: May 11 to May 21

Gifted with profound intellect, you would bring this profundity of emotions into your relationship as well. For you intelligence is just that you would not be able to love someone whose intellect you do not respect. Neither would you be the kind to indulge in immoral or distasteful affairs, for you would stand purely and in a dignified fashion in love and all other matters as well.

For you beauty exists in everything and especially in the emotion of love and affection. You seek this beauty and on finding it, cherish it deeply and sincerely. Though you would worship and adore your partner, there may be a streak of possessiveness as well and this needs to be guarded against. You would need to balance out everything so that you are able to love and respect your partner truly without stifling him or her completely.

Since looking for the right person and love appeal to you immensely, you might just spend a lot of time with other people till you come across the right partner. Having found your mate though, you would show disregard for anyone who might try to even flirt with you lightly. Your sense of loyalty and sincerity, indeed, is very high. When you enter the alliance of holy matrimony, you would be diligent and dutiful towards your family and would leave no stone unturned in building up a foundation of love, respect and happiness, making your family the object of admiration for everyone else in the society. As a parent, you would give your children plenty of affection and bring them up as achievers and winners.

Your Sex Life

First Decant, Venus ruled: April 21 to 30 April

Your approach to sex is spontaneous, natural and unaffected. This combination is quite appealing, alluring and enticing. To add to this, you are quite loving and caring, as well. On the other hand, your inclination to give and receive love does not essentially always end in sex; you are quite content with embraces, kisses, and physical closeness with the one you care about. Gifted with immense patience, you would hardly ever plunge into anything. You would follow a slow and steady pace with enough time given to each stage preceding the final act. It is essential for you that there be balance and equilibrium in your relationship. Arguments and tiffs would cause you to turn off sexual activities until everything has been resolved amicably.

Second Decan, sub-ruled by Mercury: May 1 to 10 May

Although you possess the fundamental Taurean traits of a profound sex drive and a lovingly demonstrative temperament, you are in reality quite balanced and stable in your approach towards sex. You have a sensible and pragmatic viewpoint of life in general, and this includes the matters related to sex. You are not the sort to get influenced and swayed by the heat of the moment and despite the fact that you do give this issue a great deal of thought, you are reasonably grounded and practical about the whole matter. You also are inclined to associate intellectual understanding, empathy and camaraderie with your spouse or mate in your image of a satisfying sexual relationship. You are understanding, unselfish, and would be influenced by the nature of the surroundings when you engage in any kind of sexual activity.

Third Decan, sub-ruled by Saturn: May 11 to 21 May

There might have been some sort of hesitation or even fear, associated with sex within you which maybe related to the past. Although you are a loving and caring individual, with profound sentiments, you are not the one to demonstrate these feelings freely and openly, especially through sex. You would give considerable thought to the implications involved and would then make a decision about it. You are faithful, have the ability for abstinence should the need arise, and could exercise restraint when it concerns sexual expression. You would find that your sex life does get better and finer with the passage of time and age.

Taurus Celebrities

Birth Date	Star	Vocation
7 May	Rabindra Nath Tagore	Literati
13 May	Sri Sri Ravi Shankar	Religious Thinker
15 May	Madhuri Dixit	Film Star
24 April	Sachin Tendulkar	Sports Star
26 April	Moushmi Chatterjee	Actress

Compatibility

TAURUS & ARIES

Earth Sign
Ruled by Venus
- Steadfast
- Systematic
- Artistic
- Patient
- Kind-hearted and loving
- Sensual

Fire Sign
Ruled by Mars
- Energetic
- Sexy
- Enthusiastic
- Impulsive
- Fickle
- Impatient

Aries is a sign that is known for its energetic, dominating, spontaneous nature. It is also, a sign that is fond of talking and looking at the brighter side of things. Arians love to have an exciting and interesting life and are slightly impatient when it comes to getting the outcomes of their efforts.

Taureans, on the other hand, are known for their reticent, realistic, self-reliant temperament which has a tendency to be slightly negative. They desire security, seclusion and also, need plenty of relaxation and peacefulness in order to make life a smooth and easy journey. Strikingly different, these two can complement each other quite well. While idealistic Aries can show the solid Taurean her dreams, the practical Taurus can show Aries the unrealistic nature of some of those dreams and together they can achieve a lot in life. However, freedom-loving Aries can be quite abrupt and sever all relationships with the slightly possessive Taurean at a moment's notice.

The Taurean approaches love with the same realistic approach as he would anything else. Yet, he would be profoundly tender and romantic about his love, even if he doesn't really care to display it with flamboyance. This could tend to give the Arian a mistaken notion about the Taurean's romantic inclinations. Therefore, whenever the Taurean would show his or her affection, it would be a pleasant surprise to the Arian. At the same time, though, there could be a few difficulties in this relationship, especially with the physical aspect. The Taurean approaches sex as an activity essential for the accomplishment of certain purposes while the Aries looks at sex as a form of release in all aspects. This difference in attitude would need to be met mid way so as to allow complete satisfaction for both the partners.

Astro Advice
o Wear a Diamond of two carats
o Woman should wear pink

TAURUS & TAURUS

Earth Sign
Ruled by Venus
- Honest
- Philosophical
- Suspicious
- Boring
- Selfish
- Possessive
- Kind

Earth Sign
Ruled by Venus
- Honest
- Philosophical
- Suspicious
- Boring
- Selfish
- Possessive
- Kind

The combination of two Earth signs results in the creation of a relationship that is steady, traditional and long-lasting since both the signs have the desire to keep the relationship going. On the other hand, it may also, result in the formation of a routine that seems somewhat dull and dreary. Sparks of envy and possessiveness would fly, however, when pushed too far. On the whole, though, since both would crave for stability and would play safe, the relationship would not have much excitement and vitality.

An Earth sign, ruled by the planet Venus, Taurus is symbolised by the Bull. An involvement between two bulls would have the calmness and warm comfort yet would also, fall into monotony with the passage of time. Since both wouldn't be too comfortable with the art of apologising, there could exist some discomfort when neither is willing to budge. Provided they don't boss the other one around too much, the relationship could overcome most odds and benefit from the mutual respect and also, the sense of humour that both partners would share.

Both the partners would be highly expressive about their sentiments and would always try to put their feelings into words. There would be occasions when their shared obstinacy would stand in their way of successful and productive communication.

At the same time, though, since both the partners would have the ability to benefit from their experience and share their aggravations, they would balance out other differences. The physical aspect of love is just as important for them as the emotional aspect and they would place it on the same level as they would place the intellectual and emotional compatibilities. Their planet Venus bestows on them warmth and emotional tenderness and they would exhibit the same during their sexual activities. The area of sex is one domain where they would hardly ever have any discord. Both sexes have a fascination for their lover's body, skin and hair. Both would also, have strength, patience and stability as their characteristic traits. Once they take care of minor differences, they would enjoy a relationship which would fulfill most of what they were looking for and give them a reason to love and care for their partner with all their heart and mind.

Astro Advice
- Man should wear a Diamond of one carat
- Women: soft manners and smiles are your greatest charm.

TAURUS & GEMINI

| Earth Sign | Air Sign |
| Ruled by Venus | Ruled by Mercury |

- Earthy
- Generous
- Tolerant
- Musical
- Over cautious
- Materialistic

- Shallow
- Conversational
- Adaptable
- Selfish
- Artistic
- Open-minded

Taurus is an exceedingly Earthy sign whereas Gemini is the most airy of all. While Taurus is steady and sedate, Gemini is impatient, unpredictable and highly fickle. On the surface of it, they do seem like two opposites and a successful union seems somewhat doubtful. Taurus can get a little perturbed by Gemini's need for novelty at all times and vice-versa. Hence, it would be a Herculean task for a Taurean to win and keep a Gemini forever.

What the Taurean actually wants is the Geminian ability to be liberated and carefree most of the time. Nevertheless, the cautious Taurean temperament makes him wary of Gemini's wonderful art of using language to his advantage. For his/her part, Gemini finds it difficult to understand what would make the Taurean more malleable, emotionally and mentally. The stable, pragmatic Taurean is often unnerved by the quickness of the Gemini and his fondness for taking the easy way out. Yet, if the Bull is sure about his feelings and wishes to engage in a long and fruitful association with the airy Gemini, he/she would not rest until the relationship attains stability and social approval. When a Taurean is involved romantically, he/she would lose all rationale under the influence of the newfound wonders of love and preoccupation with the other senses. The serious minded Taurean is, indeed, the kind who would not only promise undying love but also, deliver that promise. Loyalty, devotion and steadfastness are some of the Taurean's prominent virtues. The problem exists only in comprehending the fickle Gemini whose moods and temperaments modify themselves constantly.

Taureans are intense, passionate and even, erotic in sexual matters. For Gemini, sex is yet another exciting adventure to be embarked upon. While both are interested in the physical aspect of their romance, the issues of temperamental Gemini and obstinate Taurean would remain the same and would need to be resolved so as to ensure a satisfying sex life.

Taurus desires fulfillment and satisfaction from his/her lover and in exchange would give one hundred percent of his/her own involvement. Gemini, on the other hand, would be spontaneous and even casual about sex and would seem preoccupied to the Taurean. The mind of the Gemini is, usually, filled with a thousand intriguing pictures but what the Taurean would want and appreciate would be the Gemini to be just as involved as he/she is in the relationship at all levels. In order for the relationship to be mutually satisfying, both the partners would need to adjust and find the middle ground with each other.

Astro Advice
o Man should wear thin bracelet or gold ring.
o Woman should use bright colour nail polish while going to meet their beloved.

TAURUS & CANCER

Earth Sign
Ruled by Venus
- Good taste
- Fruitful
- Staid
- Pig-headed
- Lazy
- Tenacious

Water Sign
Ruled by Moon
- Moody
- Tender
- Imaginative
- Tearful
- Fertile
- Demanding

The inherent attraction between the elements of Earth and Water results in a relationship that would have many things in common. Both the signs value and appreciate sentiments and the overpowering emotion of love. Moreover, Taureans revel in the protectiveness and warmth that the Cancerians relish giving to their loved ones. Essentially traditional in their outlook, there is little possibility that there would be any sort of discord caused by opposing viewpoints such. Rational conversations and exercising practicality would benefit both when the sentimentalism becomes a bit too much to handle.

Aside from certain trivial dissimilarities, both these signs have an uncanny amount of resemblances. Both enjoy food and money, and would want people to value them. However, when it comes to moodiness, Cancer would definitely take precedence in this case. The temperamental attitude of the crab is something that the Bull just cannot comprehend. On the whole, though, both Taurus and Cancer would bask in the calmness of their environments and would adjust easily with one another. As they would normally, get along easily, there would hardly ever be any volatile debates or heated exchanges. They would function beautifully together even in professional interactions and their concerted attempts would result in success, more often than not. Their inherent peacefulness imparts a wonderful sense of balance and tranquility.

Although this does seem like a remarkable relationship and, indeed, it is in many ways, it wouldn't always be a bed of roses. There would be certain hurdles which would need to be overcome and managed tactfully. The realistic, steady Taurean might not have much patience with the rosy creativity of the Cancer.

Sexually, the relationship would be close to perfect. While Cancerian would be intensely emotional, warm and loving, Taurus would relish these attributes and add to the passion and emotion. They would be able to merge well with each other and produce a relationship that would be fulfilling in all aspects. The strong sense of protection that the Taurean would give would fill Cancerian's need for tender loving. The crab would find it difficult to turn down the petition of love when offered in such a warm and loving manner by the Bull. On the whole, except for severe afflictions in the birth charts, both would enjoy a sexual relationship that would be gratifying and fulfilling for both the partners at all points of time.

Astro Advice

o Man should focus on diet and exercise.
o Man should refrain from telling a lie which can create problems.

TAURUS & LEO

Earth Sign	*Fire Sign*
Ruled by Venus	*Ruled by Sun*
• Fertile	• Romantic
• Possessive	• Hospitable
• Practical	• Glory-seeking
• Obstinate	• Rude
• Steadfast	• Domineering
• Obedient	• Ambitious

The union of two equally dominating, obstinate signs is bound to head for troubled waters unless the parties learn to accommodate and adjust with one another. Taurus will be able to satisfy Leo's need for admiration and praise but Leo, mostly manages to lead the Bull, only reasonably so. Traditional Taurus tends to get a little worried by the flamboyant thoughts of the Lion, however, both would share a sense of pride in holding their ground, no matter what and would not appreciate public displays of their defeat or loss. That would be regarded as highly private by both the signs and they wouldn't share it with the world.

Although, Taurus wouldn't mind being led by Leo, for whom, this dominance would hold much importance, yet there would be instances when the Bull would revolt. Both the signs relish being able to protect and care for others. They would, also, enjoy splurging on presents and surprises for their beloved. Though the Taurean might never admit it, he/she would enjoy the intense protectiveness and deep love which Leo would display.

In fact, the faithful, devoted Taurean would crave for it. Basically, the Taurean does not have an inherent taste for romance and when in love, he/she takes time to flower. But once, they do blossom, Taureans are the most tender and steady of lovers and this steadfastness is something which the Lion needs to sate his/her fanciful, emotional desire to travel, mentally or physically.

Both the signs are extremely strong willed and hence, there would be plenty of fireworks between them. While Leo would be vociferous, Taurus would be equally unmoved and stoic. They would, however, be able to make up more often than not, without the lion having to sacrifice his pride. Mostly, a physical gesture of affection would be able to help them make up and come back to normal.

While Leo may be arrogant and standoffish with others, when with his/her lover, the Lion would be the warmest, most tender soul.

Their needs to touch and feel each others' skin, hair and bodies would help them to attain ideal sexual compatibility and would enable them to recreate the magic of their first meeting. This would add to the sparks in their relationship at present and they would be able to take it to greater heights than ever before.

While the obstinacy of the Taurean and the conceit of the Leo can drive them away from each other, if they learn to compromise, they would be able to create a wonderful relationship filled with warm, gentle love and care. Sexually, as well, they would be perfect together and the union would have all the rhythm and music in the world.

Astro Advice
o Man should wear a Ruby of six ratti
o Woman: do not compare your beloved with anyone.

TAURUS & VIRGO

Earth Sign
Ruled by Venus
- Long-suffering
- Tactile
- Artistic
- Kind
- Sensual
- Dull
- Nagging

Earth Sign
Ruled by Mercury
- Truthful
- Critical
- Frigid
- Sensible
- Neat
- Calculating
- Down to earth

The combination of the two Earth signs does indicate a high level of compatibility and similarities in traits such as common sense, realism and efficiency. At the same time, they are markedly different as far as their emotional temperaments are concerned. The composed and cool Virgo can feel somewhat stifled by the intensity and possessiveness of the Taurean. Since both eventually want to attain financial security and prosperity, they would try and smoothen things out between them.

As both are considerably serene and placid, there wouldn't be too many violent outbursts. Though they may not be the most romantic couple, their deep affection for each other would form a steady force in their lives. They aren't the ones who would waste their intense emotions on trivia. They are the sort who would easily go through life saturated in the bliss of the real wonders of the world and achieving concrete, real things. For Virgo, the emotion of love is one that would need to be given a lot of practice so that it becomes perfect. Both would strive to achieve that perfection in their relationship.

This would be a couple who would be able to listen to the unspoken words and endeavour to fulfill those needs which are not put into words. The closeness and understanding that they would share would be remarkable. The conversations that they would share would also, be ideal. The Taurean would be an absorbed listener and an intriguing talker while the Virgo would be sparkling and intelligent which would ensure that there wouldn't be a dull moment between the two.

Their ability to understand each other without speaking would be seen in their sexual relationship as well. The sober Taurus would enjoy being able to indulge in love making without being disturbed by words and mushy speeches. Virgo, on the other hand, would prefer silence simply because; he/she would not have much to say on the subject. It should not be thought that Virgo is cold or uninterested in sex. As a matter of fact, Virgo would be able to bring a great loveliness to the whole experience by merging sentimental warmth with physical desires. Moreover, Taurus would not be opposed to such an outlook, but would welcome it and therefore, the relationship that they would share would be rewarding and enjoyable for both of them. This pair has the ability to use delicate romance in tandem with well grounded realism and virtues of faithfulness to create a relationship that glows with the light of loyalty and true love.

Astro Advice
o Woman: do not hide anything from your beloved.
o Man should wear, a Diamond of one carat.

TAURUS & LIBRA

Earth Sign	*Air Sign*
Ruled by Venus	*Ruled by Venus*
• Glutton	• Harmonious
• Constructive	• Calculating
• Sensual	• Charming
• Generous	• Unbalanced
• Self-centered	• Outgoing
• Tolerant	• Moody

While the elements of Earth and Air have little in common, the ruling planet for both the signs-Venus produces a firm bond, that would thrive on shared love and liking for beautiful and comforting things. Both the signs value tranquility and synchrony and wouldn't create an atmosphere of disagreement and discord. Subtle Libra has the ability to adroitly manage the obstinate Taurus. Since both would want the pleasures of life, they would need a decent amount of money to run their household. On the whole, there wouldn't be many areas where these two would not be in accord with one another. For most part of the situation, they would learn to understand and appreciate the other's point of view.

The caring Taurus would not be the one to stir up a hornet's nest for trifling reasons. And for his/her part, Libra would be appreciative of the Taurean's ability to stay peaceful and placid in the face of all the chaos around them. Even when they do argue, the pair would be able to resolve it within next to no time and would on the surface of it be the picture of peace and harmony.

Both are ruled by the planet Venus and hence, would have little cause for concern on the sexual front. The act of love would be preceded by arranging the right tempo, atmosphere and using their creativity to the max. They would transcend the merely physical aspect and attain mental, emotional and even, spiritual fulfillment through the act of loving each other.

The strong and forceful attraction between this couple would add intensity to the sexual aspect of their affection. Emotional and tender, they would be able to mix the sensuous with the comfort of love and attain complete satisfaction, therein. This is a union of selfless love with an inherent inquisitiveness about sexual matters and along with other attributes, would lead to a powerful relationship, fulfilling and enjoyable for the partners and socially, an example to all those who are close to them. The calmness of the Taurean would pacify the impatience which Libra would often, feel and bond them together in eternal, lasting affection.

Astro Advice
o Man: curb your habit of over spending.
o Woman: impress your beloved by giving small gifts.

TAURUS & SCORPIO

Earth Sign *Water Sign*
Ruled by Venus *Ruled by Mars*
- Good taste
- Tenacious
- Avaricious
- Magnetic
- Jealous
- Creative

- Slow
- Practical
- Persistent
- Greedy
- Positive
- Resourceful

Even though the element of Earth is well-matched with Water, the signs of Taurus and Scorpio are conflicting signs. To start with, in affairs of the heart, this conflict might result in attraction between the two, but with the passage of time, the emotion of love might give way to negative feelings unless the pair shares mutual interests and likings. Both have an inclination to be over domineering and hence, would need to trust each other implicitly. Since the strength of their emotions would be great, they would need to guard themselves against getting pulled into a whirlpool of emotional turmoil. When it comes to similarities, both would be distant with strangers and wouldn't be too great when it comes to communicating. They would believe in saying just what they have to in an unelaborated, simple, straightforward fashion.

Taurus and Scorpio would, both, have an unwavering confidence in their ability to judge the good from the bad and right from the wrong. When it comes to religion, they would either believe in God truly or doubt His existence. This is, indeed, a relationship that would have plenty of sparks flying considering how different yet alike the two are.

Realistic Taurus is certainly not irrational, erratic, impetuous or vague. Once the Bull has made up his/her mind that the Scorpion is the love of his life, there would be no looking back. Both would be equally faithful and devoted in their affections for each other.

While Taurus is ruled by Venus-the planet symbolising tranquility and love, Scorpio is ruled by Mars-the planet symbolising volatile passions and secrecy. The sexual attraction between the two would also, be filled with wondrous and unknown revelations. Scorpio would, also, regard the experience of sex as a sacred and spiritual quest and hence, satisfy the Taurean with tenderness and genuineness. The act of love is one of passion-emotional, mental and spiritual. Though they would gain much out of it, this wouldn't be a determining factor to sustain the relationship. Considerable compromises and changes would have to be made by both of them so as to live a life filled with admiration and deep love rather than with bitterness and anger.

Astro Advice

o Man should dress up in casual out fit but remember that strips will suit you.
o Woman should dress up in a traditional out fit with red bindi on her forehead.

TAURUS & SAGITTARIUS

Earth Sign *Ruled by Venus*	*Fire Sign* *Ruled by Jupiter*
• Good-taste	• Magnetic
• Earthy	• Immoral
• Reliable	• Optimistic
• Fruitful	• Lively
• Persistent	• Careless
• Kind	• Restless
• Honest	• Lawless

The alliance of Taurus and Sagittarius is indeed, one with marked differences. The earthy stability of the Taurean contrasts sharply with the fiery Sagittarius's need to be liberated and be on his/her own. The bull likes to be settled at one place whereas the archer wants nothing but to float about from place to place. Forever on the move, craving novelty and searching for the meaning of life in unknown places, the archer needs his/her space to flourish in. This would, in all likelihood, be quite unsettling for the stable, sedate Taurus. Yet, if the emotion that they feel is sincere and deep enough, they would be able to overcome all their difficulties and differences to create a lasting and loving bond.

The spontaneous, flighty Sagittarian may feel a little bogged down by the slow pace of the doctrinaire Taurus. The calmness of Taurus can at times, irk the cheerful and emotionally volatile archer. However, both of them would share a sharp intellect and be able to see through the veneer of people with ease and clarity. They would also, share a respect for honesty and straightforwardness. Moreover, if they work together they would be able to put together a neat packet and give each other the comforts of life.

The Sagittarius lover gives the Taurean all that he would want in his relationship-happiness, intelligence, imaginativeness and an astute business sense. The archer is also, incredibly faithful and devoted.

And if he gets all the love and attention that he wants, he would prove to be a strong, loyal and dedicated lover and life partner. The Taurean can complement the Sagittarian knack of dreaming up wild ideas by thinking them over and letting the Sagittarius see rationale before plunging headlong into anything. By lending the Sagittarius a patient ear, the Taurean would be giving him the respect and the attention that he so wants. The level-headedness and sensibility of the bull would be a happy foil for the impulsiveness of the archer.

To start with the two would be drawn to each other and the Sagittarius's directness would lead the Taurean to respond fully and with complete love and gentleness. Earthy and loving, the Taurus would put his/her feelings into words through the magic of touch and let the love flow through his/her gestures and caresses. He/she wouldn't be very communicative during the act of love and would try to express all the feelings through touch. However, for the Sagittarius, expression should be creative and dreamy, something that would add to the magic of the moment and give it greater depth.

The differences don't just end there. The Sagittarian enjoys a healthy debate and would never give up an opportunity to exercise and sharpen his wit. For the Taurean, on the other hand, this signifies mere wasting of time and energy. If they enter into marriage with each other, it would be filled with a combination of dedication and annoyance. Not the best thing, yet it would have its good moments as well. If the two manage to adjust well with each other and find their own unique rhythm, they would be able to create magic together.

Astro Advice
o Woman should wear modern clothes to impress her lover.
o Man should avoid fickle love for the sake of personal gains.

TAURUS & CAPRICORN

Earth Sign *Earth Sign*
Ruled by Venus *Ruled by Saturn*
- Bibulous
- Has temper
- Stable
- Depressive

- Fertile
- Tolerant
- Selfish
- Tamper

- Materialistic
- Trustworthy
- Gloomy
- Generous

This particular pairing is quite well-matched and attuned since the Taurean with his/her love of stability would value the Capricorn's realism, persistence and motivation. They would also, share attributes of patience, a certain level of orthodox values and most importantly, an adjustable attitude with an openness to share responsibilities. Since they would both place more emphasis on the deeper meanings and real pleasures of life rather than shallow ones, life could be a bit somber. However, their high level of compatibility would make-up and they would manage to have a fair amount of fun as well.

Irrespective of when these two decide to get together, what they would want from each other and themselves would nearly always be similar. Practical and astute, they would be perturbed only by their own internal fears and anxieties. Though they would have a deep yearning for love and attention, they would hardly ever voice their feelings. So strong is their mutual respect and love for each other, that even when they would have the occasional tiff, they would find it hard to stay annoyed with one another for long. They would reason out with each other and make up within next to no time. Satisfied and happy, indeed, their union is a special one.

These two seem to be able to steer their relationship in the right direction and hence, their love affair would be free of unpleasant bumps and obstacles. Their relationship would be marked with fidelity, trust and love-the three essential ingredients for any successful relationship. The Taurean's sense of humour and impressive voice would be one of the sources of attraction for the Capricorn.

Taurus because of his/her highly developed senses is, in a way, better equipped and more ready for the sexual part of the relationship. This would help him/her to express the physical gestures of affection in a more expressive and sensitive manner.

For Taurus, the emotion of love when expressed physically is a profound and strong one. This would propel Capricorn also, to be more liberal and passionate in his/her quest for gentle, warm expressions of love.

Regardless of whatever minor differences they may have, these two are sexually just as compatible as they are emotionally and intellectually. Both have the ability to rouse the other to the heights of passion and sensuality. Their sexual union would have a firm foundation in the emotion of love which would, therefore, make it more meaningful. Both during and after the act, they would share a unique feeling of companionship and warmth that would bring them closer than ever before. They are, indeed, lucky because they would have a love that would last till the sun sets forever in the distant horizon.

Astro Advice
o Man should respond vibrantly to the feelings and ideas of his beloved.
o Woman should wear a Blue Sapphire of five ratti on Saturday after Pran Pratishta (Prayer to Saturn)

TAURUS & AQUARIUS

 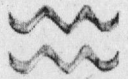

Earth Sign *Air Sign*
Ruled by Venus *Ruled by Saturn*

- Distrusting
- Philosophical
- Boring
- Artistic
- Slow
- Fruitful

- Honest
- Negative
- Critical
- Rebellious
- Cowardly
- Truthful

These two signs are two opposite poles and hence, have little in common with each other. Different in temperament, they would find it difficult to understand and adjust with one another. While the earthy Taurus would find it hard to accept Aquarius's erratic ways and desire for freedom along with openness to spread love and affection with all and sundry, the liberal Aquarian would find Taurus' inability to share love with everybody difficult to digest. For Taurus, feelings and emotions are meant to be shared only with those who hold any significance. Moreover, they would also, differ socially. The Aquarian would be able to make acquaintances if not friends in next to no time while for the Taurean it would take ages to be able to bond with another. Taurus is practical and realistic, taking in to account the present and preparing for the future while the Aquarian is just the opposite, living in an ideal world and more in the future than in the present. All things said and done, if the two want to make the relationship work, they would be able to do so only if they learn to communicate with one another and also, compromise and adjust with each other. If they do so, there is plenty that they could learn from each other and it would be an extremely enlightening experience for both of them. Talking things out and learning to deal with their differences would bring them closer emotionally and also, give them greater insight into each others' souls.

For the Taurus, love is an emotion that needs to be taken seriously and rarely if ever, would one find the Taurean plunging headlong into love. However for the Aquarian, love happens mostly at first sight. For the Taurean, profound, sincere love happens over a period of time and is the most beautiful, soul-touching emotion of all.

Since both are tightly wound bundles of energy, there would be quite a few turbulent scenes. Yet they also, have the capacity to brave the odds and forge a bond filled with gentleness and understanding. Sexually, they wouldn't be compatible unless they learn to satisfy the other's needs and merge their desires with their imagination to be able to achieve sexual compatibility.

Astro Advice
o Man should show his feelings by giving gifts and valentine cards.
o Woman should wear modern clothes to impress her lover.

TAURUS & PISCES

Earth Sign
Ruled by Venus
- Hospitable
- Tenacious

Water Sign
Ruled by Neptune
- Perceptive
- Broadminded

- Nagging
- Obstinate
- Kind
- Fruitful
- Loyal
- Dreamer
- Diffuse
- Drifting

This particular union of Earth with Water is a pleasantly satisfying one since the planets that rule the signs-Venus and Neptune are not in opposition to each other. They would enjoy a relationship filled with plenty of companionship, affection and a common love for the finer things in life. They would help to provide harmony to each other. The realist Taurus would be able to bring the dreamy Pisces back to Earth gently and firmly.

While the Piscean would display greater and more creative powers of making and spending money, it would be the steady Taurean who would be able to educate the Piscean about valuing money and learning through experience reality more so than anything else. It is not as if everything would be smooth sailing with the two of them, they would have their share of arguments and quarrels. However, their sense of humour would save the day and they would be able to make up with a good laugh over things. It is a fact that they are inevitably drawn together since they both tend to value and appreciate the same things, such as calmness and tranquility, with a slight danger of becoming prone to sadness and negativity.

This is one couple who would be able to offset each others' attributes perfectly. Sexually as well, they would have a high level of compatibility and would be able to give themselves to the other without any questions. Taurus would be able to give plenty to the tender, creative Pisces. The Taurean sense of peace, gentleness, soothing presence and warmly gentle expressions of love would fill the Piscean with wonder and awe. Both of them would enjoy the sensuality and passions of love making and would be able to let the other know their true feelings and emotions. This, in itself, would make their union a pleasurable and happy one.

Astro Advice
o Man should be wary of the beloved who suddenly presents you with unsolicited ideas for consideration. Try not to meet your beloved in casual wear.
o Woman should avoid junk food.

Gemini–The Twins
(22nd May – 21st June)
The Sign of the Artist or Inventor

How to Recognise Gemini

Perhaps the most dominant Geminian characteristic is versatility. Gemini will never be involved in only one specialist area of one subject and will never get stuck in a rut. If out of necessity he or she is forced into that position, they will suffer considerably not only from boredom (something which they come near to fearing) but more deeply psychologically, too. The ruling planet of Gemini, Mercury, gives them a powerful need to communicate at all levels and more often than not it will be Gemini who will speak up when something is wrong, will write to the newspapers or contribute to a 'phone-in' on radio or television. At a more personal level the need to communicate worries well to Geminians because they have the ability to build up an excellent rapport with their partners, so that brooding and discontent are kept at a minimum. An air of activity surrounds most Geminians. They always tend to be in a hurry, illustrated by their very distinctive, springy, fast walk. It is absolutely vital that from an early age Geminians should be helped to develop consistency of effort, because there is a strong tendency to be always moving on to some new interest or project, leaving a trail of unfinished tasks. While in many cases a little knowledge of a great many subjects can be of advantage to Geminians, it is good for them to have some kind of a structured framework in their interests, so that superficiality does not mar real progress. The Geminian body-area covers the shoulders, arms and hands-which are accident-prone. The lungs too are Gemini ruled, so coughs should not be ignored. There is also an accent on the nervous system, and it is up to Gemini to find a satisfactory outlet to counter tension and restlessness.

Career and Finance

Whatever the chosen career, it has to be the kind that keeps the lively Geminian on the go. It must be pretty demanding intellectually, but not so much as to worry them or oppress them. For instance, a Geminian would not enjoy collecting mountains of facts or putting together a lot of fussy detail to make a presentable report, or making a study in depth of one narrow area of a subject. That sort of thing can make Geminians restless, and in such situations they will cut corners-extremely cleverly, no doubt, so that it doesn't show. But should some more patient, painstaking mortal check up on them they might get into hot water. For instance, some Geminians find it surprisingly difficult to learn shorthand and will ingeniously devise their own individual system. This will be perfectly sound and reliable to them but could cause difficulties when someone else has to read it. This is one example of how Geminian ingenuity can create problems for them in the long run. Geminians can sell and make excellent 'reps' or commercial travellers. They are perfectly happy driving around in the company car making regular calls, hearing the latest news on the trade grapevine and often adding to it themselves. They are not particularly fussy about the sort of atmosphere they work in, though a totally formal office where everyone works quietly at the same sort of task day in and day out would be anathema to them. They don't mind having some kind of pattern in their working life, but a dreary and totally predictable routine is not for them.

Health and Food

Healthwise you will be inclined to be your own worst enemy. You will have an excellent constitution, but of the highly strung type. You will take too much out of yourself in every possible way. You will be prone to live on your nerves and crave for change and travel. In order to 'keep going' you will be liable at times to indulge in stimulants which will injure your digestive organs. As you will desist rules and regulations, you will not be inclined to be regular in your habits, but may eat at any time of the day and night and only sleep as and when you can.

In this way you are likely to break up the splendid constitution you would otherwise have. You will be liable to have trouble brought on by 'nerves,' twitching of the eyelids, some defect in the tongue or speech, blood disorders eczema and skin eruptions. Do not nibble at food, eat regularly and learn to relax.

Suggested Food Options:
- Red meat
- Fish
- Egg
- Plums
- Oranges
- Water
- Avoid smoking

Your Love Life

First Decan of Gemini: May 22 to May 31

Your complete character is overflowing with light allure, and many would be attracted by this as well as your articulate and fluent usage of the language which you would display when you want to attract someone's attention. But you may soon realise that your romantic behaviour will keep you occupied and even cater to the romance aspect of your life but it may not be pleasing for long as it will not be profound or meaningful.

For you the journey of life is like a pleasure trip and affairs of the heart, the best parts of this trip. You are most likely to spend a considerable amount of time travelling and moving around to various places and in all likelihood, would have many affairs along the way. Yet nothing would be serious, merely good natured flirtations. However, your attraction and appeal would be so strong that it would make even those you hurt forgive you with a smile.

It is essential that you adopt a more serious and stable approach towards love in your younger days, if you want a partner for your older days. If you keep moving on the same path, you would soon be lonely and desolate. You would need the warmth of a relationship and the loyal love of a companion at some time, so this is the right time for you to look for a mate with whom you can share all the sunsets of life.

Second Decan of Gemini: *June 1 to June 10*

Though you portray a lighthearted approach towards love, you do look for someone who would truly understand and respect you. Beneath the superficial casualness, you have quite a mature outlook on life and its dimensions and it could, take you quite some time till you find a partner who would match your ideals and values.

Since you have a charming personality, you do attract many lovers, yet you tend to rub the magic off from the romance with a highly practical mind. You tend to become disappointed easily and you do need to be careful that you don't become pessimistic and mocking in your approach towards love, since that is one thing which would keep this beautiful emotion away from your life forever.

When in love with someone, you do want to appreciate the complete personality of your mate. You do get influenced by not only the inner persona but also, the outer one. Though this may seem superficial, it does hold an important place in your life. Aside from the looks factor, you would also, want a sharp intelligence and a strong streak of humour in your partner. Only then would you be sufficiently entertained and motivated to hold on forever.

It is essential that you do not quit looking for the perfect partner. Do not give into hopelessness and disillusion. You would surely find your partner and would live happily with your ideals and values intact.

Third Decan of Gemini: June 11 to June 21

Carefree and casual, you do have a considerate side to your personality and would be able to ignore shortcomings in others as long as you are confident about their devotion and dedication towards your own self. What you truly desire in a partner is keen intellect and finely honed abilities and when you find such a person, you would leave no stone unturned in trying to woo his or her attention. However, you also, need to ensure that you would have your partner's complete loyalty before you give your heart over. Another thing that you need to take care of is your doubting nature. You would not be sure about your own decision and hence would doubt your partner. Try to have complete faith in your self and your partner and this would keep you light at heart as well.

It is important that you are absolutely honest with yourself about your feelings and this would help in reducing your fears about your relationship, therefore, laying the foundation for a strong and affectionate alliance.

Your Sex Life

First Decan, Mercury-ruled: May 22 to 31 May

Since you are, in all likelihood, the most imaginative and mind-oriented of the signs, sex for you would nearly always start from the mind. A thought, an idea, a memory, a word, an image, any or all of these are likely to bring about a sexual response in you. You would have an inherent curiosity about the topic and would experiment with it as well. Since feelings and sentiments would not always play a dominant role, you would want a partner who would be enjoyable to be with at all times and who would appreciate your humour and intellect.

Second Decan, sub-ruled by Venus: June 1 to 10 June

For you sex and romance go hand in hand and you would need the right kind of atmosphere before you engage in any sexual activity whatsoever. Naturally vibrant and passionate, you approach sex with your characteristic keenness and excitement. You do have the essential Geminian traits of good humour, intelligent conversation and a preference for new and novel things. Your rational approach and optimism determine your sexual behaviour to a very large extent.

Third Decan, sub-ruled by Aquarius: June 11 to 21 June

Usually, you are the sort who is erratic and impulsive and this reflects itself in your approach towards sex as well. Orthodox principles and/ or customary ideas and perceptions of sex do not hold much relevance for you and since you would be highly curious about sex from an early age onwards. You might even have some highly unusual experiences. Your actual sex drive may be sporadic, it could be incited by dreams and feelings as well as by individuals; you may experience highs and lows in your sexual behaviour quite often. You are also, not the kind whose feelings are aroused easily although you do often wonder what the future would hold for you. However, like your other interests, sex would continue to mingle with them and take centre stage now and then.

Gemini Celebrities

Birth Date	Star	Vocation
7 June	Mahesh Bhupathi	Sports Star
8 June	Shilpa Shetty	Actress
10 June	Prakash Padukone	Sports Star
16 June	Mithun Chakravarthi	Film Star
17 June	Leander Paes	Sports Star

Compatibility

GEMINI & ARIES

Air Sign	*Fire Sign*
Ruled by Mercury	*Ruled by Mars*

- Restless
- Clever
- Changeable
- Expressive
- Witty
- Erratic

- Energetic
- Enjoy challenges
- Charming
- Sexy
- Enthusiastic
- Impulsive

These two signs share similar gifts for persuasiveness, aestheticism and imagination. They enjoy living life fully and have a casual outlook towards amassing either immense power or wealth.

Essentially, both Aries & Gemini are straightforward, yet strangely, enough they tend to forget where the line between truthfulness and trickery exists. Whether they wish to be naïve or unaware is something they need to work out on their own. What is important is that both of them are equally adept at selling their own images as they are at selling any material object. While Gemini is logical, intelligent and somewhat cynical, Aries finds it difficult to distinguish between the real and the fake most of the time. Only on being hurt a couple of times, would the Arian be able to differentiate and learn.

Ruled by the planet Mercury, the Gemini is gifted with a sharp brain that is forever at work behind the serene and graceful façade. However, Aries would take things as they come and happily get used to whatever is the pace of life. Both the signs do have a tendency to do some amount of wishful thinking. They could very well do so but they would need to ensure that the base of their dreams is solid and stable else everything would come crashing to Earth. If the two get together and exhibit endurance and determination, nothing would be impossible for these intelligent and creative souls. They also, would enjoy a lot of synchrony in their lives and even in their sex life, they would feel as if they share one soul. Hence, if they manage to deal with the minor differences, they would be wonderful together.

Aries is courageous, vivid, gracious and passionate while Gemini is absolutely charismatic, multitalented and impulsive. Truly, they would make an appealing and ideal pair. One that could well, be the object of envy for many.

Astro Advice

o Women & men should avoid all intoxicants and non-vegetarian food.
o Man should wear Pukhraj of seven ratti in index finger on Thursday after Pran Pratishta (prayer to Jupiter).

GEMINI & TAURUS

Air Sign	Earth Sign
Ruled by Mercury	Ruled by Venus
• Easily bored	• Patient
• Expressive	• Over cautions
• Bright	• Materialistic
• Tempramental	• Generous
• Persuasine	• Tenacious

Taurus is an exceedingly Earthy sign whereas Gemini is the most airy of all. While Taurus is steady and sedate, Gemini is impatient, unpredictable and highly fickle. On the surface of it, they do seem like two opposites and a successful union seems somewhat doubtful. Taurus can get a little perturbed by Gemini's need for novelty at all times and vice-versa. Hence, it would be a Herculean task for a Taurean to win and keep a Gemini forever.

What the Taurean actually wants is the Geminian ability to be liberated and carefree most of the time. Nevertheless, the cautious Taurean temperament makes him wary of Gemini's wonderful art of using language to his advantage. For his/her part, Gemini finds it difficult to understand what would make the Taurean more malleable, emotionally and mentally. The stable, pragmatic Taurean is often unnerved by the quickness of the Gemini and his fondness for taking the easy way out. Yet if the Bull is sure about his feelings and wishes to engage in a long and fruitful association with the airy Gemini, he/she would not rest until the relationship attains stability and social approval. When a Taurean is involved romantically, he/she would lose all rationale under the influence of the newfound wonders of love and preoccupation with the other senses. The serious minded Taurean is, indeed, the kind who would not only promise undying love but also, deliver that promise. Loyalty, devotion and steadfastness are some of the Taurean's prominent virtues. The problem exists only in comprehending the fickle Gemini whose moods and temperaments modify themselves constantly.

Taureans are intense, passionate and even, erotic in sexual matters. For Gemini, sex is yet another exciting adventure to be embarked upon. While both are interested in the physical aspect of their romance, the issues of temperamental Gemini and obstinate Taurean would remain the same and would need to be resolved so as to ensure a satisfying sex life.

Taurus desires fulfillment and satisfaction from his/her lover and in exchange would give one hundred percent of his/her own involvement. Gemini, on the other hand, would be spontaneous and even casual about sex and would seem preoccupied to the Taurean. The mind of the Gemini is, usually, filled with a thousand intriguing pictures but what the Taurean would want and appreciate would be the Gemini to be just as involved as he/she is in the relationship at all levels. In order for the relationship to be mutually satisfying, both the partners would need to adjust and find the middle ground with each other.

Astro Advice
- Woman should wear Emerald of five ratti on Wednesday after Pran Pratishta (Prayer to Mercury)
- Man should wear Diamond of one carat on Friday after Pran Pratishta (Prayer to Venus).

GEMINI & GEMINI

Air Sign *Air Sign*
Ruled by Mercury *Ruled by Mercury*
- Youthful
- Conversational
- Artistic
- Friendly
- Easily-bored

- Youthful
- Conversational
- Artistic
- Friendly
- Easily-bored

This is one combination which would at all times, be highly entertaining. Air with Air could never be a monotonous union. Their relationship would be characterised by excitement, liveliness, a certain sense of chaos, novelty and plenty of talking. Moreover, they would share not only an emotional compatibility but also, an intellectual one and would be quite on the same wavelength as each other.

Ruled by Mercury and symbolised by twins, when two people of this sign get together, it is an interesting sight. However, they may have the tendency to stand in each others' paths since the way they would take would often be the same. At the same time, they would have a greater understanding of each other and would be able to accept one another's idiosyncrasies with greater ease. Together they would be able to achieve many great things and put the sum total of their intelligence and creativity to good use. This would enable them to scale great heights of emotional, material and intellectual success.

As far as the physical aspect of the relationship is concerned, they would be highly attuned to each others' needs and would be able to form a closer and more intimate bond than ever. They would be able to understand that sex would need to be as much a mental activity as a physical one. And hence, they would be able to keep the fire alive in their relationship eternally.

This relationship also, has the benefit that it would be marked with a refreshing sense of liberality and space. Relaxed and casual, the camaraderie between these two souls would always be a pleasure for them and for the people who know them. Their creativity, sensitivity and their ability to keep the magic alive would ensure that the relationship would always contain an element of newness and yet comfortable familiarity.

Astro Advice
o Man should be loyal and faithful towards his beloved.
o Woman dress up in pink or sky blue while going to meet your beloved.

GEMINI & CANCER

Air Sign	*Water Sign*
Ruled by Mercury	*Ruled by Moon*
• Ambitious	• Nourishing
• Imaginative	• Moody
• Bright	• Sensitive

- Teases
- Gossips
- Erratic
- Self-centered
- Helpless
- Tender

The blending of Air and Water is not the best of combinations. Especially, since, Gemini is more intellectually inclined while Cancer tends towards the emotional side of the personality. Moreover, for Gemini, there must always exist the element of novelty and change which somehow makes Cancer feel a little lost. Similarly, Cancer's reliance on sentiments and excessive emotionality would not have much of an impact on the relatively practical Gemini. To compound things further the ever busy Gemini might not always have the time to cater to Cancer's whims and fancies and the result would be that the latter would feel uncared for.

The two of them are relatively fluent conversationalists, have creative ideas and the tendency to indulge in public displays of affection and other emotions. Therefore, there is a considerable amount of similarity between the two.

Concerning their physical union, Gemini would approach the act of sex intellectually while for Cancer it would be a highly emotional act. This could give rise to some amount of misunderstandings as regards this area of the relationship. They would end up wanting different things at different times and this would result in dissatisfaction for both of them.

Personality wise, Gemini is overgenerous; gregarious and enjoys socialising and going out whereas Cancer is more of a home bird and fond of children and young people. Hence, it would be essential for them to define their areas and learn to meet each other mid way. As long as they can overcome their differences, they would be able to enjoy a relationship that would give both of them plenty of contentment. They would also, need to set their expectations right so as to avoid getting disappointed. They do have the ability to balance each other out with Gemini's gentleness proving to be a foil for Cancer's tender sexual temperament. Though it isn't an impossible relationship, it has its fair share of difficulties.

Astro Advice

o Man should wear Pearl of six ratti on Monday after Pran Pratishta (Prayer to Moon)
o Woman wear thin bracelet or gold chain.

GEMINI & LEO

Air Sign
Ruled by Mercury
- Open-minded
- Impulsive
- Intelligent
- Temperamental
- Restless
- Communicative

Fire Sign
Ruled by Sun
- Sunny
- Exhibitionist
- Vain
- Kind
- Jealous
- Delegates

The union of Air and Fire is an intriguing one, especially on an intellectual rather than emotional level. While Leo enjoys being in the limelight, Gemini would much rather spend time with others and this could make the Lion feel alienated. Also, Leo has the tendency to dominate which may stifle the free-spirited Gemini. However, the latter would appreciate Leo's generosity and ambitious nature. If they understand and appreciate each other's independence, this could be a wonderful relationship.

These two have an instinct about each other. Genuinely friendly, Leo might not be very appreciative of the Geminian fickleness and recklessness as far as life is concerned. For the laidback Leo, this rush through the journey of life is not the ideal thing. However, since Gemini is gifted with charisma and smoothness, he/she would be able to easily subdue the roaring Lion.

In matters of sex, as well, Gemini would puzzle the warm, loving Leo with his diverse preferences. However, Gemini's tendency to keep things inside can make him/her somewhat restrained in the physical expressions of love and it could stand in the way for both of them. The usually warm and caring Leo could see this aloof behaviour as a form of alienation and be put off by it.

Although Gemini may seem detached in physical expressions, he/she would have the ability to display incredible amounts of tact, allure and elegance in winning the Lion over. Leo, for his/her part would be the epitome of warm, overflowing affection, fiery passion and easy going sensuality.

For the benevolent Leo, love and sex go hand in hand and although he/she would be able to attract the normally distant Gemini, however wouldn't be able to make Gemini let go completely. That would be indeed, a difficult task. In contrast, Gemini's open attitude would be in accordance with what Leo appreciates in a relationship- the ability to be free yet feel possessed and cared for.

They would need to make their share of adjustments in order to enjoy a mutually satisfying and enriching relationship.

Astro Advice
o Woman should carry a bunch of flowers for her beloved to make him feel cherished.

o Man should wear Emerald of five ratti on Wednesday after Pan Pratishta (Prayer to Mercury).

GEMINI & VIRGO

 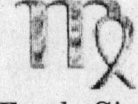

Air Sign	Earth Sign
Ruled by Mercury	Ruled by Mercury
• Shallow	• Organised
• Bright	• Voyeuristic
• Persuasive	• Busy
• Selfish	• Mean
• Unreliable	• Truthful

Despite the fact that Air and Earth have little in common, both Gemini and Virgo are ruled by the same planet-Mercury. And this factor can play quite a significant role in their relationship. Both are equally realistic and practical as far as emotions and sentiments are concerned. They would share interests in fields of business, social life and even intellectual concerns. The organised Virgo would not always agree with the whole host of schemes and ideas that the ever enthusiastic Gemini would throw around, simply because for Virgo, it is essential to be more focused and single-minded.

Gemini does have something that is mystifying and alluring for the shyer Virgo and this charm is at times, more than what they need to put a permanent seal on their relationship. A seal of constant novelty, mystery and thrill. Though they have their share of differences, the scales also tip in favour of the similarities. They have a unique intellect, an elegance of disposition and an inherent inquisitiveness. All of these would help them move through the journey called Life with happiness and ease.

In love, this is one couple who when the initial flush of romance wanes, would feel quite lost and even somewhat sad. They would use the power of language to either build or break the relationship and wouldn't just keep up an act for the sake of it. The relationship should always have some meaning for them. They can very easily use their similarities to adjust and adapt and find tranquility and contentment in each others' company.

Sexually, they would be drawn towards one another in the beginning. However, if Gemini feels intimidated in any manner, it would switch off the magnetism instantly. As far as Virgo is concerned, there would need to be plenty of actual expressions of love and tenderness which Virgo would surely reciprocate. This would give Gemini the sense of security which would lead to a lasting and reciprocally satisfying love and sex life.

Astro Advice
o Man : need to improve tolerance power.
o Woman : best to observe silence over heated discussions.

GEMINI & LIBRA

Air Sign
Ruled by Mercury
- Open minded
- Intelligent
- Teases
- Gossips
- Communicative

Air Sign
Ruled by Venus
- Charming
- Calculating
- Sociable
- Unrealistic
- Moderate

Similarity of element along with a combination of Mercury with Venus, the Gemini- Libra relationship is indeed, one of taste, aesthetics and intelligence. A shared love of all that is pleasing to the senses, sophisticated, educative, it would involve many long discussions by the eager Gemini and received eagerly by Libra. Libra, in fact, wouldn't like being alone so the interesting new ideas and company of Gemini would prove to be perfect.

This relationship would have the quality of being blindingly brilliant and painfully whirly. Both have the knack of being incredibly fickle-minded so it would be next to impossible for one to know what comes next. The bright Gemini would enjoy a puzzle and Libra would often be one for them, so they would always remain interested and intrigued. They would, however, be much happier with themselves and their relationship if they learn to experience and enjoy the emotions more rather than merely analyising them and rationalising.

The amalgamation of exquisiteness, refinement, charisma, common sense, astuteness, radiance and mutual adulation makes them quite an irresistible couple. Spontaneous Gemini often makes a hasty choice and this for a Libra is a taboo. Libra can take forever when it comes to making up his/her mind and can even procrastinate about it for ages. However, it goes without saying that both are light rational beings who exist more in the head than the heart.

Sexually, they would have quite a satisfying relationship, especially since Libra is an extremely competent and sensitive lover with a fine intellect and would be able to stimulate Gemini mentally and even verbally. Sex would, however, need to go hand in hand with love and romance and life would turn into a real joyride for the two of them. Although it would be difficult to understand their relationship, yet they would have enough in it for them to feel at ease inside themselves and their physical expressions of love would have something fragile and vaguely aloof about them.

Astro Advice

o Man should wear white stone of ten ratti on Monday after Pran Pratishta (Prayer to Moon)
o Woman should wear Emerald three ratti on Wednesday after Pran Pratishta (Prayer to Mercury).

GEMINI & SCORPIO

Air Sign *Ruled by Mercury*	*Water Sign* *Ruled by Mars*
• Open-minded	• Charming
• Adaptable	• Fanatical
• Charming	• Constructive
• Selfish	• Resourceful
• Fanciful	• Proud
• Sharp tounged	• Sincere

Extremely different, this is one relationship that would be made up of markedly opposite souls trying to battle it out together. Gemini with its element of Air, does not have the depth and passion of Scorpio, with its element of Water and would feel weighed down by such compelling and mesmerizing influences. Moreover, the freedom loving Gemini would feel suffocated by Scorpio's possessiveness.

Usually Gemini and Scorpio would never get together unless someone makes a deliberate effort of pairing them with each other. Their complete lack of similarities and shared interests doesn't really allow that. However, when they do get together, regardless of the differences, there is considerable dedication on the part of Scorpio and similar amount of mysterious fascination of the Gemini towards the scorpion and these qualities would enable to weave tender, vague dreams with each other and even work towards realising those dreams.

This union is a fine specimen of how a couple's sex life is affected by what happens beyond the four walls of the bedroom. They would definitely come closer to each other because of the act of love yet a nagging insecurity could lead to frequent tiffs due to which the intense Scorpio may find solace in alcohol and the like. However, if they are sure about their partner one hundred per cent, they would be fiercely passionate and profound when expressing themselves sexually. One must not overlook the fact that while Scorpio has a strong sex drive, for Gemini, sex is just yet another thing to be explored and not all that significant. Hence, it is Scorpio who would often play the wooer and pursuer. Gemini would be more influenced by the scorpion's intellect and charisma.

Astro Advice
o You both should need to develop faith in each other.
o Woman apply light colour mascara.

GEMINI & SAGITTARIUS

Air Sign
Ruled by Mercury
- Artistic
- Erratic

Fire Sign
Ruled by Jupiter
- Generous
- Disloyal

- Flirtatious
- Communicative
- Intelligent
- Optimistic
- Devoted
- Immoral

The combination of Air and fire is, indeed, an extremely exciting one however, not without its own set of flaws. As both these signs are in opposition to each other, they have the knack of being able to be drawn both towards and away from each other. Gemini would have its own individuality which would go well with the Sagittarius trait of wanting to be free and on their own. Since they are both inherently energetic and desire to lead eventful lives, they would keep themselves occupied with a multitude of interests and activities and hence, would have plenty to talk about.

Each time a Gemini and a Sagittarian enter a relationship, they normally follow one of the two modes of behaviour. They would either hero-worship one another and try and inculcate the qualities of the other one or they would feel insecure and jealous about the other's admirable characteristics. It is only due to the fact that they feel, and rightly so, that the other one has the attributes that they would like in their personality. So they would either work on developing those or they would resent their presence. However, since both are good communicators with each other, they would often be able to talk things out and realise that although they are markedly different, they have their own unique similarities and these would see them through all the difficult days.

They share a particular intellectual bonding which makes a good base for the culmination of their relationship in the act of love. They would make good use of their expressive eyes and other gestures to begin the physical expression of their love.

Both would enjoy a sex life that would be characterised by its adaptability and the constant element of novelty. This would make it highly interesting and fascinating for both the partners. Their desire to be reckless, adventurous, and flamboyant balances out any differences that they may have. The archer is mystified by the twins' sophistication and elegance and together, their mutual admiration for each other would ensure that their relationship is forever filled with an intense physical attraction. Since both also want to become more like the other one, they would endeavour constantly to grow and keep an element of change alive in the relationship.

The only potential drawback that their love as well as sex life could face would be the emotions of envy and temperamental swings taking over every now and then. They should learn to avoid these and be more adjusting with one another so as to be perfectly compatible.

Astro Advice

o Woman should share responsibilities of her lover.
o Man should avoid fickle love.

GEMINI & CAPRICORN

 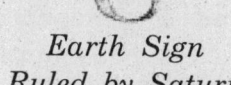

Air Sign
Ruled by Mercury
- Artistic
- Intellectual
- Communicative
- Open-minded
- Ego-tripping
- Teases

Earth Sign
Ruled by Saturn
- Generous
- Stable
- Patient
- Reliable
- Over-critical
- Greedy

Even though the elements of air and earth lack many similarities from one another, they still have the ability to give each other a sense of fulfillment. The youthfulness of Gemini complements the maturity of the Capricorn and they would spend many happy moments together as long as they learn to let each other know their thoughts and ideas verbally. There would be times when they would argue and debate, especially when Gemini would want to quit from something while Capricorn would want to take it through till the end. Moreover, the stable and balanced Capricorn would find it hard to comprehend the erratic, emotionally excitable temperament of Gemini. Yet, more often than not, they would be able to give each other a lot of mental and emotional satisfaction by their unique types of common sense and even, material gifts.

Theirs is a relationship that would be marked by their ability to accommodate and adapt. Somber but tender Capricorn would have the ability to soothe and direct the reckless, impulsive Gemini. He/she would have the capacity to give Gemini a place to seek refuge in and fill their souls with a feeling of tranquility.

As far as the physical aspect of the relationship goes, they would be able to bring the intuitive understanding of one another into this particular domain as well. It is not as if their sex life would be filled with fireworks, it would be more like a warm winter fire. For them, sex would be more a means of relaxing than anything else. Not the sort to be emotionally demanding they would enjoy feelings of companionship and bonding during sex.

Being able to express themselves sexually is critical and important for them and the relationship, particularly since both would attract and tempt each other infinitesimally. Although these two signs are considered to be quite cool emotionally, however, they do have a considerable amount of warmth concealed within them and at more than one level; this relationship has the quality of being rock solid and enduring.

It is indeed, a wonderful relationship and would have plenty of good moments to hold onto as warm memories.

Astro Advice
o Man : to impress your beloved show your good sense.
o Woman : wear any sort of dress with matching head accessory.

GEMINI & AQUARIUS

 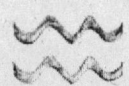

Air Sign	*Air Sign*
Ruled by Mercury	*Ruled by Saturn*
• Ambitious	• Honest
• Imaginative	• Forthright
• Bright	• Erratic
• Impulsive	• Cowardly
• Temperamental	• Caring

Although the combination of Air with Air is well-matched yet the planets that rule them-Mercury and Saturn endow them with diametrically opposite temperaments and thought processes. It would be this constant element of change and differences that would make the relationship enjoyable and appealing. The freedom-loving Gemini would be able to get accustomed to Aquarius's aloofness and unconventional behaviour and would also, be inspired by his/her innovativeness and uniqueness.

Despite the differences that their respective planets bestow them with, Gemini and Aquarius are usually quite compatible with one another. They have more or less the same way of looking at things, issues and opinions. They are not disturbed by each others' idiosyncrasies and variable moods. Together they can be entertaining, amusing and even, thought provokingly deep.

They have the habit of being either a wonderful source of happiness or an irritatingly complex enigma for others, yet for each other they would be plain, simple, easy to read books. The areas they would need to tread with care would be the fact that both are equally complicated and although fits of rage would be rare, there could be plenty of arguing and heated debates. On the whole, this is one pair with an exceedingly strong compatibility. With relatively few areas of concern, they would sail through life and togetherness blissfully. They would make a good amount of money, however, even if they happen to lose it, they wouldn't be terribly perturbed. Their shared likes and dislikes in movies, books, travel, spiritualism and even animals would ensure that they always have something to talk about and discuss.

Since both of them would have a diverse range of interests and hobbies to keep them busy, they would often not feel the need to engage in sexual activities as often as others. Gemini might feel the lack at times, but on the whole, both would be occupied and engaged in a host of other things and wouldn't even realise that there is something missing.

Sexually, they wouldn't give a lot of importance to the act of loving. At the same time, they wouldn't neglect it altogether. It is just something that they would accept as being part of a relationship and deal with it. They would enjoy it whenever they indulge in it. It would be like everything else in their relationship- enigmatic, exhilarating, and elating. So entertaining is this pair that even the wrong moves they would make would be highly enjoyable.

They would be able to achieve better and more sexual satisfaction if Venus and Mars in their horoscopes are heavily afflicted. This is one relationship, where even if the partners do have some doubts about their sexual compatibility, as long as they are together, their sex life would be fantastic even if occasional.

Astro Advice

o Man should wear Black Stone of eight ratti on Saturday after Pran Pratishta (Prayer to Saturn)
o Woman should trust her beloved.

GEMINI & PISCES

| Air Sign | Water Sign |
| Ruled by Mercury | Ruled by Neptune |

- Youthful
- Humorous
- Conversational
- Sharp-tounged
- Distracted

- Cowards
- Compassionate
- Unreliable
- Apathetic
- Lazy

Glaring differences in the temperaments and attitudes of the two signs only confirms the influence that the difference in their elements exercises. While Gemini is decisive, analytical, realistic and inclined to think with the head, Pisces is fickle, vague, and thin-skinned and leads with the heart. However, they are quite adjusting by nature and would be quite patient with one another and even if they don't really understand each other they would not be critical of the other one.

Even if there may not always be smooth sailing with the two of them, it is possible for them to live happily, as long as they continue to make whatever minor adjustments are needed. If Gemini learns to communicate more expressively and Pisces learns to be a good listener, they would be quite content with each other. While Gemini would need someone who would value them, Pisces would want to feel wanted. So, if they learn to satisfy their individual expectations in the best possible way, they could well be happy and peaceful in this particular union.

As far as their sexual aspect of the relationship is concerned, they would be quite satisfied with it. Since both of them would want the emotional aspect of their relationship to be a part of the sexual expression. Also, both would be equally open to introducing newness in the relationship, so that monotony doesn't set in. Gemini's unconventional approach to sex would be appealing to the highly creative imagination of the fish. These two would also, share plenty of other likes and dislikes. Quite a good number of them make proficient lovers who admire loveliness and the finer aspects of life. At the same time, since both Air and Water do not really feel the need for sexual expression as strongly as other elements, this aspect might lack real meaning for them.

Theirs is a union which would have many happy moments. Their lives would move together and although there would be plenty of love, yet physically, it would be bereft of real warmth and closeness. It would have many other good things that would make up for this particular aspect.

Astro Advice

- Men should wear yellow sapphire of six carat in index finger on Thursday after Pran Pratishta (after prayer to Jupiter)
- Women should use light colour lipstick and hair combed back in a bun.

Cancer–The Crab
(June 22 – July 22)
The Sign of the Prophet or Teacher

How to Recognise Cancer

Challenge a Cancerian and at once you will see his or her natural self-defence system come into play. The need to protect themselves and their loved ones is an extremely basicinstict with people of this Sun-sign. Used positively it is marvellously helpful, but sometimes it can result in their becoming too easily annoyed, so that a slight 'huffiness' is displayed at the mildest opposition. The need to protect and look after others is second nature, and indeed usually emerges at an early age; children of this sign are good at looking after wild birds or any creature that has been injured, and it is an excellent thing for them to do. Cancerians are extremely tenacious and hard-working once they have decided on a course of action, whether it relates to a life-long career or interest or to some minor domestic task or project. The tendency to hoard is very strong, so much so that it is very easy for Cancerians to fill their homes with clutter, of which it is almost impossible to rid themselves. The instinct and intuition of the Cancerian is second to none, and is something that should be developed and used to the full. When a Cancerian 'feels' that something is going to happen, or instinctively 'knows' what decision to make, the chances of their being right are very high indeed. Cancerians are unfortunately terribly prone to worry, and it is no good whatsoever to tell them to stop it. To counter this they should follow their instinct and learn to put no psychological barriers between whatever is bothering them and this marvellous source of strength.

The Cancerian emotional level is very high, and needs constructive channelling. Much emotion will be spent on lovers and children-no generalisation where Cancer is concerned. They also have an extremely powerful imagination, and this too needs careful consideration and control. The Cancerian with no creative or positive outlet for these resources will find that they tend to become dominant. If any member of the family is late home, for instance, imagination will insist that disaster has struck, and there will be irrational worry-the children's train has plummeted over a cliff, the car has crashed... Cancerians should use their imaginations, but in a creative way, perhaps by making beautiful things, telling bed-time stories to the children (and maybe going on to write them down), or becoming involved in some aspect of history or collecting-the past is very much alive for most Cancerians. The Cancerian body-area is the chest. This can be vulnerable area, but as most Cancerians are prone to worry this too can affect their health-mostly causing digestive problems, which may in themselves be a signal of worry before the subject consciously realises that this is creeping up on him or her.

Career and Finance

Cancerians can usually settle into almost any working environment, either because they are adaptable enough not to be-stifled by the atmosphere, or because their natural Cancerian protective shell comes to their aid in uncongenial surroundings, enabling them to ward off anything which might distress them too much. Cancerians should be very careful that their tendency to worry does not become an integral part of their working day. It is as easy for them to worry about their careers as any other important part of their lives. Of course it is not possible to tell them just to 'stop worrying': it is up to them to find the right approach to the problem. Most Cancerians, like all of us, have to settle down into some kind of daily routine, which can, of course, grow dreary. But Cancer, a Water sign much influenced by the sea, will very much identify with the ebbing and flowing motion of the tides, and maybe this kind of regularity will be in someway a form of strength to them. Yet they must be able to express their changing moods, and their liking for change. How? Every individual must, of course, work this out for themselves. Many will find themselves able to arrange their working day to reflect changing moods, provided all the work gets done satisfactorily. Those who cannot must simply accommodate themselves to the routine, ignoring passing whims and feelings-as their colleagues must do!

Health and Food

You will be extremely sensitive to your surroundings; if these are fortunately to your liking you will probably get through life without much trouble. If, on the contrary, you are forced to live under depressing or unhappy conditions, you will be liable to suffer a great deal from bodily ill. In other words, with you it will be largely a question of the effect of 'mind over matter.' The general tendency will be for almost unaccountable pains and cramps in the internal organs. There will be some likelihood of tumours, lesions and adhesions in connection with the intestines.

Suggested Food Options:
- Fish
- Potatoes
- Water Melon
- Melon
- Mushroom
- Avoid pastries, cakes & Junk food

Your Love Life

First Decan of Cancer: *June* 22 to *July* 1

A sentimental person, you hold on to your romantic thoughts and keep them safe with you to be looked over in leisure. Your feelings and sentiments are extremely important for you and would have so much strength in them that they can often adversely affect your mental health. You have the habit of remembering fond moments shared with your beloved and keep every single experience- good or bad, happy or sad, in your mind' storehouse. It would do you good, however, to let go of a few disturbing experiences. This would help you feel lighter at heart and give you greater room for happier thoughts.

You revel and bask in the warmth of your family. Relationships, kith and kin hold a dear place in your heart and your own family would hold centre stage in your life. If married, you would focus all your attention and energy on your partner and your children.

Not the one to poke your nose into the affairs of other people, you would gladly go about life minding your own business and living peacefully. However, this does not mean that you wouldn't be concerned about society; you would have a keen interest in the social circuit related to your own self, your spouse and your children, since these are the most valued for you.

You fill the atmosphere around you with immense thoughtfulness and tenderness. You would graciously overlook all the shortcomings in your partner and children and would, also, desire similar dedication and devotion from your partner and offspring.

Second Decan of Cancer: *July* 2 to *July* 11

What makes you really happy is making others happy and you would do so gladly for friends and family. You would be genuinely interested in what is going on in the life of your family members and would try to fulfil the desires of your near and dear ones. Friends would, also, not be treated any differently. You would be generous and dignified even when others would try to take you for granted.

You are of a sensitive temperament so much so that even the slightest contempt in someone's tone can hurt you deeply. When married, you would need a partner who would value and cherish you and also, have a high level of consideration and kindness of spirit. You would always take special care to look your best since you like to please your partner by making an extra effort.

Being partly ruled by Pluto, you would have the desire to feel secure and well loved in your relationship. Creative and fluent, you would express your love with great finesse and beauty. You would be demonstrative in your romantic behaviour and would warmly and generously assure your beloved about your love for him or her. You, also, feel that this would increase the stability and emotionality of your relationship.

You seek peace and contentment in your marriage and would like to hear your partner express his love for you as well. This would make a difference to the level of tranquility and emotional security in your relationship.

Third Decan of Cancer: *July* 12 *to July* 23

What you absolutely adore is the feeling that others are dependent upon you and this would inspire you to work harder than ever to give every single luxury and fulfill every want of your family members. You, also, like to be valued and commended for the same. Other than that, you are the most simple and easy individual to be with.

It gives you great joy to see your loved ones winning accolades in society. Whether it is your spouse or your children, you would devote your time and attention in ensuring that they do well in their respective fields and that others admire them and in the process, you.

Giving and caring, you value your partner for the person he or she is. And would want that even they treat you like a distinct individual. You would need complete trust and faith in your relationship. Your mate must be exceedingly faithful and devoted with absolutely no scope for any suspicions. Thoughtful and compassionate, you would desire similar behaviour from your family and strongly feel that the happiness in a marriage is infinite when both the partners respect and honour each other as individuals and not take each other for granted.

What you truly enjoy are the quiet moments that you share with your spouse and would spend endless hours in each other's company without quite feeling the need for anyone else. Your social life would also consist of your partner, you and a few old friends. In this manner you would be able to give expression to your love for your partner in the most honest and genuine way. Your marriage would always have the spark of romance alive if you would continue the same way, giving you eternal marital bliss.

Your Sex Life

First Decan, Moon ruled: June 22 to July 1

Ruled by the Moon, your sexual behaviour would be deeply and significantly influenced by your feelings that run deep and you would have a strong emotional temperament. You would show your need for emotional and financial security in your sex life and this highly emotional nature would often lead you to get deeply involved with a sexual mate. You do need a great deal of love, pampering and the constant assurance that the bond that you share has a deeper meaning attached to it. Though you would have a keen interest in sex and would enjoy it, the satisfaction would be dependent upon your varying moods and temperaments. You are essentially an emotional individual and this reflects in your sexual behaviour.

Second Decan, sub-ruled by Pluto: July 2 to 11 July

Born in this decan, you would have a highly charged emotional temperament, stronger and more profound than your other counterparts. You would also, have a slightly forceful approach towards issues related to sex. You would also, unfortunately, have the tendency to use sexual behaviour as an instrument to accomplish other motives and would need to refrain from doing so, since by this you would be selfishly using people. What would help you would be to use your deep emotions and dominant streak to find a partner who would be able to bring you happiness and contentment with his own emotional temperament.

Third Decan, sub-ruled by Neptune: July 12 to 23 July

For you, sex is essential and also, idealistic. What you seek and desire is a wonderful combination of emotional fantasies with profound happiness. Some of you may have a dominant streak, however, for the rest, you would be swayed by your feelings and would tend to view partners through rose-tinted glasses. You would also, have an intense pining for the perfect partner along with an actual want to express your affection physically and therefore, what you would need to achieve would be a delicate balance between the two. That is what would help you eventually to have and enjoy a satisfying, rewarding and harmonious sexual life.

Cancer Celebrities

Birth Date	Star	Vocation
1 July	Pt Hariprasad Chaurasia	Musician
8 July	Dimple Kapadia	Film Star
8 July	Sourav Ganguly	Sports Star
10 July	Sunil Gavaskar	Sports Star
18 July	Priyanka Chopra	Film Star

Compatibility

CANCER & ARIES

Water Sign
Ruled by Moon
- Nourishing
- Sensitive
- Self-centered
- Romantic
- Lazy

Fire Sign
Ruled by Mars
- Strong
- Confident
- Fickle
- Impatient
- Diligent

The Arian not only is fond of but also, needs to win at everything. What the Arian also, enjoys doing is to be at the head of everything. And what about Cancer? Well, though the shy crab might conceal his desire to win, it certainly cannot be ignored. One should never overlook the fact that it is the fundamental sign of control and management. Now it does create a slightly sticky situation when you have two people who wish to be on top. One would obviously have to be the follower. While this may seem an unsolvable problem, it does have a solution. The solution being that the two could easily walk together, hand in hand, in tandem with each other. That way, there wouldn't ever be a leader and follower equation. This is what cooperation is all about. While the quiet Cancerians might become morose and quieter than ever when their feelings are treated harshly, the fiery Aries should not imagine them to be passive and servile. They would handle things with peace, tolerance and privacy. Hence, they wouldn't stay quiet forever. Just that their way of handling things would be different from the aggressive ways of the Arian.

Although, Aries and Cancer have dissimilar inspirations, aims and perspectives on life, they do have the capacity to enhance the quality of life for one another. Since both have a lot of righteousness in their own selves, they would be able to impart a fair amount to the other and hence, develop and better the life of their partner. Since this is a Fire-Water combination, both would have a feeling that they could very easily finish the other. Despite all these superficial differences, the two would be able to enjoy a relationship filled with trust, hope, love and sympathy for one another.

Astro Advice
o The man should wear pearl and women should wear coral.
o Avoid long drives.

CANCER & TAURUS

Water Sign *Earth Sign*
Ruled by Moon *Ruled by Venus*
- Moody
- Tender

- Good-taste
- Fruitful

- Imaginative
- Tearful
- Fertile
- Demanding
- Staid
- Pig-headed
- Lazy
- Tenacious

The inherent attraction between the elements of Earth and Water results in a relationship that would have many things in common. Both the signs value and appreciate sentiments and the overpowering emotion of love. Moreover, Taureans revel in the protectiveness and warmth that the Cancerians relish giving to their loved ones. Essentially traditional in their outlook, there is little possibility that there would be any sort of discord caused by opposing viewpoints or such. Rational conversations and exercising practicality would benefit both when the sentimentalism becomes a bit too much to handle.

Aside from certain trivial dissimilarities, both these signs have an uncanny amount of resemblances. Both enjoy food and money, and would want people to value them. However, when it comes to moodiness, Cancer would definitely take precedence in this case. The temperamental attitude of the crab is something that the Bull just cannot comprehend. On the whole, though, both Taurus and Cancer would bask in the calmness of their environments and would adjust easily with one another. As they would normally, get along easily, there would hardly ever be any volatile debates or heated exchanges. They would function beautifully together even in professional interactions and their concerted attempts would result in success, more often than not. Their inherent peacefulness imparts a wonderful sense of balance and tranquility.

Although this does seem like a remarkable relationship and, indeed, it is in many ways, it wouldn't always be a bed of roses. There would be certain hurdles which would need to be overcome and managed tactfully. The realistic, steady Taurean might not have much patience with the rosy creativity of the Cancer.

Sexually, the relationship would be close to perfect. While Cancerian would be intensely emotional, warm and loving, Taurus would relish these attributes and add to the passion and emotion. They would be able to merge well with each other and produce a relationship that would be fulfilling in all aspects. The strong sense of protection that the Taurean would give would fill Cancerian's need for tender loving. The crab would find it difficult to turn down the petition of love when offered in such a warm and loving manner by the Bull. On the whole, except for severe afflictions in the birth charts, both would enjoy a sexual relationship that would be gratifying and fulfilling for both the partners at all points of time.

Astro Advice
o Man should focus on diet & exercise.
o Man : refrain from telling a lie it can create problems.

CANCER & GEMINI

Water Sign	Air Sign
Ruled by Moon	Ruled by Mercury
• Nourishing	• Ambitious
• Moody	• Imaginative
• Sensitive	• Bright
• Self-centered	• Easy-going
• Gossips	• Teases
• Tender	• Erratic

The blending of Air and Water is not the best of combinations. Especially, since, Gemini is more intellectually inclined while Cancer tends towards the emotional side of the personality. Moreover, for Gemini, there must always exist the element of novelty and change which somehow makes Cancer feel a little lost. Similarly, Cancer's reliance on sentiments and excessive emotionality would not have much of an impact on the relatively practical Gemini. To compound things further the ever busy Gemini might not always have the time to cater to Cancer's whims and fancies and the result would be that the latter would feel uncared for.

The two of them are relatively fluent conversationalists, have creative ideas and the tendency to indulge in public displays of affection and other emotions. Therefore, there is a considerable amount of similarity between the two.

Concerning their physical union, Gemini would approach the act of sex intellectually while for Cancer it would be a highly emotional act. This could give rise to some amount of misunderstandings as regards this area of the relationship. They would end up wanting different things at different times and this would result in dissatisfaction for both of them.

Personality wise, Gemini is overgenerous; gregarious and enjoys socialising and going out whereas Cancer is more of a home bird and fond of children and young people. Hence, it would be essential for them to define their areas and learn to meet each other mid way. As long as they can overcome their differences, they would be able to enjoy a relationship that would give both of them plenty of contentment. They would also, need to set their expectations right so as to avoid getting disappointed. They do have the ability to balance each other out with Gemini's gentleness proving to be a foil for Cancer's tender sexual temperament. Though it isn't an impossible relationship, it has its fair share of difficulties.

Astro Advice
o Man should wear Pearl of six ratti on Monday after Pran Pratishta (Prayer to Moon)
o Woman wear thin bracelet or gold chain.

CANCER & CANCER

Water Sign *Ruled by Moon*	*Water Sign* *Ruled by Moon*
• Moody	• Moody
• Self-centered	• Self-centered
• Maternal	• Maternal
• Loyal	• Loyal
• Tender	• Tender

The element of Water for Cancer gives them a highly emotional temperament. When two Cancerians decide to get together, one could easily expect a relationship in which emotions would dominate and play a critical role. This relationship could have both good and bad consequences. Both of them would be considerate, tender and understanding and therefore, would be able to comprehend what the other person is feeling. However, the very emotions that help them could also, play confusing roles at times.

Cancerians together would be able to empathise with each other and feel the way the other feels, provided they have the same wavelength. Although, they seem hesitant and shy, they are incredibly determined about what they want from life and when in a difficult situation, can show immense strength of character. Two Cancerians would always have something to talk about, joke, cry, or whine about. They have the qualities of chivalry, tenderness, wisdom, tranquility, honesty. On the flip side, they also, have the attributes of being closed and mysterious. Tempted by money and good food, they would have a great deal of things that they would enjoy doing together such as doing up and re-doing up their place, travel to exotic places, sing and listen to others' music, and even, sob in each others' arms.

Sexually, they tend to try and have the other one initiate the act. Attracted by the softer aspects of romance, such as mood, lighting, music, they sexual behaviour would often be influenced by all of these. They would also, need complete emotional satisfaction in order for their sexual lives to be equally satisfying. Since both are equally fond of financial stability and security, they have good opportunities of becoming rich together. It is a relationship that would give them both plenty of fulfillment and emotional security and warmth. These are the very things that would make the two Cancers happy and content with their respective lives.

Overall, a balanced union which would enrich and help them both immensely.

Astro Advice
o For men it is suggested that you carry a bunch of roses or white Lilly to your beloved. To make him/her feel cherished.
o Woman should be practical and reliable. Do not be over emotional.

CANCER & LEO

Water Sign
Ruled by Moon
- Nourishing
- Oversensitive
- Patient
- Selfish
- Timid

Fire Sign
Ruled by Sun
- Romantic
- Thoughtful
- Bossy
- Vain
- Oversexed

Irrespective of the fact that the elements of Water and Fire don't really suit each other well, the ruling planets of Moon and Sun would be quite well-matched and this would enable a Cancer-Leo relationship to be solid and stable. While the quieter Cancer might submit to the stronger Leo, he/she would admire the Lion and that is something which Leo would be really happy with.

Together Cancer and Leo can either make or break each other. Money could often be a bone of contention between them, and whenever there would be any tiff between them, it could have both good and bad repercussions. Good in the sense, that it could motivate Leo to strive for even higher accomplishments. Considering their suitability for each other, Cancer with its intuitiveness and determination can show the dominant Leo how to achieve what they want to.

The crab is a sweet, gentle being however the fiery Leo can quite singe Cancer's peaceful and profound emotions. When a Cancerian has to bear the egotistical requirements of Leo, he/she would endure it, however, would become quite touchy and short-tempered. They would have the ability to hurt each other, at times, without meaning to do so. Ironically, they would also, appreciate and think highly of each other.

Although they might fall in love instantaneously, with time, there could be a decrease in the intensity. The important thing being that they learn to combine their starkly different dispositions in as fine a manner as possible. Physically, they would be a great deal of intimacy between the two, especially since Cancer is evocatively reciprocal and Leo is incredibly warm and loving. Their passions would be accompanied with a tenderness and sensitivity that would give their sexual expressions greater meaning.

Even though, the relationship would have its share of sad moments, the happiness would come when both would make up with love and tenderness. The intensity of their individual emotions, affection and mutual respect would make the relationship a pleasant and delightful one.

Perception, compassion and their respective gifts would be the foundation for closeness and confidence between these two different yet similar souls.

Astro Advice

o Man : spend money wisely on your beloved.
o Woman should learn to be cheerful while going to meet her beloved.

CANCER & VIRGO

Water Sign *Earth Sign*
Ruled by Moon *Ruled by Mercury*
- Fertile
- Sincere
- Far-sighted
- Demanding

- Selfish
- Slavish
- Hypochondriac
- Frigid
- Forceful
- Practical

Since the elements of Water and Earth are indeed, well-matched, the relationship would be one which would have many advantages to it. Cancer would give it plenty of genuine affection, devotion and tenderness and would sincerely value Virgo's meticulous nature and diligence. The tolerant Cancer would be able to deal with most of Virgo's eccentricities. For instance, Virgo would want everything to be done in as ideal a fashion as possible and would want time and attention given to each and every minute detail.

Since Cancer gets hurts really quickly, the ever critical Virgo would need to refrain from nitpicking and think about shy Cancer's feelings and sentiment. For Cancer it would be beneficial if he/she remembers that unlike themselves, Virgo is not the sort to indulge in too much display of affection. For Virgo, subtlety is quintessential.

When they join forces, Cancer and Virgo can bring to life some of the greatest and strongest vibes-emotional, physical and intellectual. They are industrious and would enjoy keeping themselves occupied. Moreover, both of them are also, quite gentle and loving, so one would find the protective Virgo support and shield sensitive Cancer and the affectionate Cancer creating a haven of warmth and love for Virgo.

From the physical aspect, Cancer and Virgo follow a quiet music of their own. They have their own unique sense of romance and love and they would communicate the same to the other. Since both would enjoy making their partner happy, the relationship would see many happy and glorious moments of love and affection. They would ensure that they make each other feel emotionally safe and wanted.

The act of love for both of them is an intensely emotional one and they would take to it with naturalness and sincere warmth. Even though sex would have quite a minor position in their love life, they would treat it with a healthy attitude and a genuine interest, ensuring that it brings happiness and greater intimacy into their steady relationship.

Astro Advice
o Women should dress up in a traditional outfit and put on a red bindi.
o Man should wear pearl of five ratti on Monday after Pran Pratishta (Prayer to Moon).

CANCER & LIBRA

Water Sign	Air Sign
Ruled by Moon	Ruled by Venus
• Shrewd	• Harmonious
• King	• Escapist
• Thrifty	• Moody
• Helpless	• Loyal
• Masochistic	• Balanced

In spite of the fact that the elements of Water and Air are not in great harmony with one another, the planets that rule the signs- Moon and Venus, respectively are quite compatible and balance well together. Sensitive Cancer can bruise easily however; Libra is relatively calm and placid and would hardly ever hurt Cancer intentionally. Moreover, Libra would enjoy Cancer's warm affection at times, may take him/her for granted. Also, since Libra is indeed, more balanced in outlook than Cancer, he/she might find Cancer extremely over-emotional.

This is an appealing and yet, demanding relationship. Both would need to comprehend and empathise with the other and that in itself would be a formidable task to accomplish. However, they should keep the end goal in mind and work towards it with perseverance and fortitude. Even though they are characteristically different from each other, yet they have the ability to be a wonderful couple together. With time and experience, they would learn to value each other and from then onwards, the relationship would a beautiful and expressive one. The composed Libra would be patient and understanding of Cancer yet wouldn't really go below the surface and see what lies beneath. That is something that Libra would need to develop- a deeper understanding of the seemingly hard-shelled but actually soft Cancer.

Finances would be yet another area where the two would not be able to see eye to eye. While the Cancerian would want money to gain a sense of security, the Libran would consider money earned to be money spent. While Cancer would gain maximum happiness from staying at home and keeping it warm and well-maintained, Libra would rather be out and about and socialise as much as possible. If they learn to balance their similarities and their differences in a seamless fashion, it would be a near-perfect relationship. However, if the differences crop up time and again, the stress would tell on both Cancer and Libra's mental health.

Together these two would enjoy uncovering new and fascinating things about the world and about one another. Their sex life would be understated and subtle, with good use of elements of romance, long forgotten by others. Although it might take ages for them to sort out their differences, yet in the end, it would be worth the effort and the time.

Astro Advice

o Man should wear white stone of seven ratti on Friday after Pran Pratishta (Prayer to Venus)
o Woman should wear Pearl of five ratti on Monday after Pran Pratishta (Prayer to Moon).

CANCER & SCORPIO

 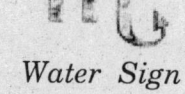

Water Sign *Water Sign*
Ruled by Moon *Ruled by Mars*

- Ambitious
- Protective
- Loving
- Tenacious
- Retiring

- Magnetic
- Greedy
- Power tripping
- Healers
- Courageous

Although the element Water is common for both, yet compatibility might not exist naturally within this relationship. Particularly, during times of arguments and disagreements, one would find that emotions would run high and disturb the equilibrium that existed during peaceful times. Since the element of Water would give both the signs high emotionality, this would come into play more during the difficult times. However, when everything would be fine, this would be a fantastic team and would show each other great understanding, trust and respect.

The attraction between the two might be instant and nearly magnetic, especially for Cancer. Though this might seem like an unlikely relationship, more often than not, it has a happy ending. Both are intuitive and would have many qualities-good and bad, in common. Their profound understanding of each other would result in the formation of a strong support system for both of them.

Both, Cancer and Scorpio are fiercely devoted, intense and infinitely tender, hence, when they come together, the relationship radiates warmth, affection and security. The challenging Scorpio enjoys pulling the Cancerian leg a little and the easy going Cancer enjoys matching the Scorpio's steady gaze for as long as possible. Fun, tender and affectionate, that is precisely what this relationship would be.

However, it is not as if everything would always be hunky-dory. There can be times when the temperamental, exacting Cancerian can throw a tantrum or when intense, passionate Scorpio can be too focused on his/her own idea of love. That is when disagreements could occur and throw a spanner in the works. Scorpio would need to show greater understanding of gentle Cancer and Cancer would need to be more empathetic of Scorpio and his/her views and ideas.

As far as the sexual aspect of the relationship is concerned, Scorpio would definitely be more passionate than Cancer, who in turn, would be romantic and whimsical about love. This blend would create a blissful union which would have a mutual attraction and an encouraging note in it. Both would endeavour to fill the sexual union with gentleness and softness which would make it truly an act of love. Their deep-seated passion gives them a devotion to love akin to spiritual zeal. This particular bond would create beautiful things if both love and sex go hand in hand and the usual adjustments are made without any ado.

Astro Advice
o Both should understand each others feelings.
o Woman should be confident while speaking.

CANCER & SAGITTARIUS

Water Sign	Fire Sign
Ruled by Moon	Ruled by Jupiter
• Secure	• Honest
• Good-memory	• Open
• Sympathetic	• Careless
• Depressive	• Indulgent
• Unambitious	• Trusting

The blend of Water with Fire displays the stark contrast in the temperaments of the two signs. Unless the relationship is characterised by perfect communication, it is a difficult alliance with many challenges. While Cancer is a home bird, the archer is a complete extrovert with one foot always on the move. Moreover, Sagittarius has a high level of emotional, physical and intellectual independence and this can make the naturally timid Cancerian somewhat more anxious. Cancer has the desire to hold on while this would make the freedom loving Sagittarius feel stifled and claustrophobic.

However, it is not as if all is lost. Both have plenty in common and this is a relationship that would have many advantages for both, more so for Cancer. Because Cancer can inculcate the trait of being emotionally stronger and self-confident, while the Sagittarian can learn to appreciate the empathetic and gentleness of the Cancer. Together they can produce some brilliant ideas and do plenty of logical thinking. There could be a difference of opinion as far as money is concerned, yet as with everything else, they would manage to sort this one out as well.

The inquisitive Sagittarian would be intrigued by the mystery that Cancer would hold for him/her and also, be attracted by the powerful yet subtle sex appeal of the crab. And these factors would compel the normally ebullient archer to conduct himself/herself in an unusually calm and sedate fashion.

The crab would show his/her love in an understated yet erotic fashion and would give himself/herself to Sagittarius who would, return the feelings with equal ardour and passion. Sexually, they would be in harmony with each other and would carry their goodness of nature with them into their sexual union. Their genuineness, honesty and sensitivity would make their sex life a warm and fulfilling one. The gentleness and deep love of the Cancerian holds a promise of happiness for the Sagittarian and this would surely be an alliance of love and bliss.

Astro Advice
o Woman should wear yellow Sapphire of five ratti on Thursday after Pran Pratishta (Prayer to Jupiter)
o Man should wear pearl of seven ratti on Monday after Pran Pratishta (Prayer to Moon).

CANCER & CAPRICORN

Water Sign *Earth Sign*
Ruled by Moon *Ruled by Saturn*
- Self-pitying
- Secure
- Social-climber
- Manipulator

- Tearful
- Cloying
- Helpless
- Limited
- Ambitious
- Materialistic

While the elements of Water and Earth are indeed, compatible, the positioning of the signs in the Zodiac is such that they can not only be harmonising but also opponents to each other. The thin-skinned Cancer may feel wounded and uncared for if Capricorn is too ambitious and power-driven. While Cancer would appreciate and value the Capricorn's conscientiousness and dependability however, he/she would want Capricorn to be more emotional and warm since this would make a tremendous difference to the crab.

They have their share of similarities. Both are crusty outside but soft and mellow inside. They have a depth of emotion and would always like to be at the front. However, one of them would have to make more adjustments than the other and in all likelihood, it would be Cancer. Their similarities in conjunction with their differences would create a union that would be strong and supporting. It is a well-known fact that Cancer craves and seeks someone who would take care of his/her needs-emotional, mental and material. Therefore, the Capricorn is perfect because he/she is a motivated, prosperous, somewhat orthodox and slightly dominating go-getter. Initially, Cancer would give into Capricorn's authority for the sake of tranquility, however, at the end, it would be beneficial for both of them. The reticent Cancer would be alluring and maybe a little too possessive while the Goat would be careful, genuine and protective. Together they would be sincere and wise about everything that they do.

Sexually as well, they would be sensitive and sensuous and even candidly erotic. The devotion and strength of Capricorn would motivate the Cancerian to be innovative and imaginative sexually. They would be as earnest about their sex life as they are with everything else. Deep, enriching and enlivening, they would give meaning and insight to their love and sex lives at all times.

Astro Advice
o Man should wear Blue Sapphire of six ratti on Saturday after Pran Pratishta (Prayer to Saturn)
o Woman : try to sort out differences of opinion.

CANCER & AQUARIUS

Water Sign	*Air Sign*
Ruled by Moon	*Ruled by Saturn*
• Lazy	• Honest
• Fertile	• Impractical
• Good-memory	• Erratic
• Dramatic	• Cowardly
• Helpless	• Loyal

The elements of Water and Air as well as the ruling planets- Moon and Saturn have a great deal of differences. The emotional temperament and possessiveness of Cancer can stifle and smother the liberal and independent Aquarius. The water bearer is an aloof, impersonal lover who would radiate his/her love to the entire world rather than confine it to one single person.

While Cancer finds Aquarius intriguing and Aquarius finds Cancer cooperative, the two have very little in common, as far as personality traits are concerned. Cancer doesn't like the straightforward nature of the Aquarian while the latter doesn't really appreciate the

Cancerian habit of sulking. Together they would be highly volatile. The emotional Cancer would experience and express all the emotions under the sun but the practical Aquarian would muse about the essentiality of those emotions and the reasons for them. There could be times when they could get on each others' nerves and need to be away from one another so that the distance could make the heart grow fonder. However, if they are willing to adjust and make compromises, they would find happiness and love in each others' arms. The determination of the crab would win over the Aquarian while the idealism of the water bearer would strike a chord with the Cancerian.

Physically, the relationship would be quite harmonious. Cancer would have to tempt Aquarius, so that the latter doesn't get occupied with one of his varied interests. Intellectual stimulation works best with Aquarius. Both would use the power of gestures and eyes to communicate their feelings. Their sexual union would indeed be charged and dynamic which would enhance the quality of their relationship as well.

Astro Advice
o Man : do not be in the grip of false hopes.
o Woman : you need to take care of your body & health.

CANCER & PISCES

Water Sign
Ruled by Moon
- Depressive
- Nourishing

Water Sign
Ruled by Neptune
- Guilt
- Philosophical

CANCER

- Secure
- Maternal
- Cloying
- Ambitionless
- Confused
- Escapist

The joining of Water with Water symbolises a high level of emotionality, since Water is linked with sentiments and emotions. Therefore, the feeling aspect would always have dominance over reason and logic in this relationship. Pragmatism might get overlooked and even neglected. The intensity of emotions would bring you closer and increase the level of intimacy in your relationship without you making a conscious attempt. Both of you are incredibly romantic and yearn to be cared for and made a fuss of.

This is one alliance where everything would nearly always be peaceful and composed. Their sympathy and understanding for one another is nearly instantaneous. They have more similarities of character than differences. Both of them are equally temperamental, fickle, enigmatic and insightful. The one area where they could be differences would be finances and even here, adjustments and conciliations could be effected.

Since the crab is more overprotective, he/she would try to influence the fish into adapting more. Moreover, Cancer also, enjoys holding onto yesterdays and yesteryears. However, since Pisces is considerably more adjusting and is also, an incredibly good listener, therefore, there would be many happy days together. This is in many more ways than one an elegant and blessed couple. Their differences are few and far between and the similarities make the journey a pleasant and enjoyable one.

Sexually the creativity of this couple would be at its height and they would use their intense love for each other to enhance and liven up their sex life. The element of romance would play a dominant role as would their individual imaginations. A satisfying sex life would only strengthen their already strong and dynamic relationship.

This is in nearly every way a perfect relationship. Physically, emotionally, mentally, Cancer and Pisces have a togetherness that is profound and at the same time, inspiring. Their life with each other would be full of intense love and sensitive love making signifying an ideal understanding, a perfect union.

Astro Advice
o Men: don't forget to carry pack of chocolates with you.
o Women: should remember that your beloved believes in Spartan simplicity.

Leo–The Lion
(July 23–August 23)
The Sign of the King or President

How to Recognise Leo

Leo, the lion, the king of the jungle, must of necessity have his or her own individual kingdom-whether it is larger or small. The ability of people with this Sun-sign to organise their own lives and the lives of others is paramount, as is their ability to lead. There is no doubt about it, a really flourishing Leo will make the most of this potential, sometimes stretching ability too far. There will be great satisfaction in inspiring others to make more of themselves, too, and in trying to impress upon them that the development of and concentration on talent is the best way to ensure a fulfilled and rewarding life. Leos get as much out of life as possible, and will always do things in as big a way as possible-spending more money than they should-sometimes simply to show off. While magnanimous, Leos are often accused of bossiness-and not without reason. Inwardly they know that they are capable of organising other people's lives far better than those others themselves, and find it quite difficult not to interfere. While there is a certain enjoyment in being 'boss', it is also true to say that Leos will be willing slaves to someone whom they admire and respect. They need to be in a position of prominence themselves, however, if they are really to shine. There is a natural sense of drama in every Leo Sun-sign, and they revel in it. They should not, however, just go in for making a fuss, creating scenes in public, but should use their dramatic sense to bring inspiration, light and colour into other people's lives. They should use this sense to set an example to those they come into contact with, and if they see that someone has improved their lifestyle, attitude, or any sphere of their life, then this will make Leo very happy, for every Leo believes that life is for the living, and to be enjoyed to the full. And they will work hard to achieve their ambitions, too, whether personal or career oriented.

Enthusiasm and a positive, fiery emotion are very much part of the Leo personality, and are expressed vividly in the attitude towards sex and emotional relationships. Leos can inspire their partners to greater achievement, and will do much to make marriage and permanent relationships work well, but must certainly be careful not to dominate their partners too determinedly. Their real strength lies in positive support and the continuing development of their own and their loved ones' individual interests. Leos make lively enthusiastic parents, encouraging their children to keep busy both in and out of school. They tend to expect too much from them, and must be very careful indeed to allow them to develop along their own individual lines and not to over-influence them, especially where the choice of career is concerned. The Leo body-area is the back. Many Leos have long straight backs and walk very well, but do tend to suffer from backache from time to time. Leo also rules the heart, so the circulation should be watched-especially during cold weather, which most Leos do not like at all. It is quite common for Leos to have a real lion's mane of hair, and, also rather lion-like, they usually have small waists.

Career and Finance

Leos like to do things properly; they hate amateurism, and in whatever they choose to do they will achieve a high standard. This trait is nowhere more obvious than in their careers, and in the search for perfection they set an example to other, less exacting folk. They strive for the best. A Leo girl working in a bakery, for instance, will arrange her cakes beautifully every morning, and she'll be noticed by her employers, in time will be manager-and woe betide any underlings who leave messy crumbs or splodges of whipped cream on the display units! The Leo secretary will run her boss's working life and be far more the head of their department than he is. She will not only want, but need to work well, and in doing so will express her potential to the full.

Scope of choice of career for Leos is very wide, and they have a place in many areas of life. The nature of the work itself is less important than the opportunities for self-expression within the job. This is of greater importance to Leos than to most Zodiac types. Although quite willing to knuckle under and perform all sorts of tasks, working conditions are of great importance, as are the kind of people they have to work under, and their attitudes: for they will not suffer fools gladly, and certainly won't want to be bossed by them. Nor will they tolerate a situation where they and their workmates can't speak up and make suggestion for the improvement of working condition.

Health and Food

In your childhood and early years you will be liable to have many minor illness, especially fevers, rheumatism, inflammation of the blood, carbuncles, boils etc. But as you become older you will grow out of such that problems and become healthy and vigorous.

The spirit, the heart and many a times the eyes are weak health areas. Do not tax your nerves and your reserves of energy. Sometimes the solar-plexus can malfunction.

Suggested Food Options:
- Lemons
- Coconut
- Litchi
- Honey
- Green vegetables
- Avoid Red Meat

Your Love Life

First Decan of Leo: July 24 to August 2

Expressive and dramatic, you would put your feelings for your loved one into beautiful words and would desire similar attention from your partner. However, you shouldn't be too rigid about this since not everyone would have the flair or the liking for such expressive forms of declaring one's sentiments.

You are a sincere and persistent lover with a tendency to be easily moved by the green-eyed monster at times. You need constant reassurance that your loved one loves you the same way and though you do not show it that often, you are terribly sensitive and are actually quite concerned about your love life.

What you want to do is fill the environs around you with immense affection and let the world see how much you care for your partner. You enjoy the feeling of being in love and more than anything enjoy the frills and fancies of romance. If your partner is even remotely distant with you, you tend to become morose and depressed. However, you would be your cheerful self, once back to normal. Yet you are certainly not the kind to be taken for granted for long and if you feel that you aren't being valued, you would look elsewhere for the attention and affection that your heart craves for.

It is essential, though, that you don't ask for too much attention, since it can be quite wearisome for any individual. Try not to be in the limelight at all times, be more generous and altruistic, learn to find happiness in quiet moments and this would give you greater joy and contentment than any material gifts that money could buy.

Second Decan of Leo: August 3 to August 12

Warm and impulsive, you tend to plunge headlong into relationships. You would benefit from giving careful thought to your affairs. More so, since for you, home and family are essential and integral to happiness. Irrespective of the wealth and name that you may earn, your family would always come first in line and therefore, it is important that you spend considerable time in choosing the right partner to set up that family with.

You are a benevolent soul and enjoy giving a great deal of happiness to your kith and kin. You also, thrive on the appreciation that you get from them and in the absence of support and praise; your happiness can get darkened by the dull clouds of sadness. You need to know that you are valued and appreciated by those for whom you work so hard.

Your relationship must be solid and stable, with trust and faith as its foundation. Your partner must give you the same amount of love, if not more then you shower him or her with. Intuitive and intelligent, you perceive any danger to your romance well before it becomes imminent. There should be constant warmth and love in your relationship for it to thrive and flourish.

It is important for you that there be no closed doors or hidden secrets. Affection and trust must co-exist and your partner and you must be able to work together on making your relationship more enriched and hence, everlasting.

Third Decan of Leo : August 13 to August 23

You are guided by your insightfulness as you look for the right person to share your hopes, dreams and life with. You are not the kind to fritter away your emotions on the wrong person. Though, you may come across as standoffish and proud, people need to realise that it is only your way of keeping your distance till the time is right, for you to decide who to choose as your partner for life.

You completely understand the importance of the relationship of marriage and will never underestimate it. you would leave no stone unturned in ensuring that your marriage be really an eternal alliance. You would in all likelihood, be drawn towards someone who comes from a social and economic background similar to your own. Aside from this, you would want your partner to be intelligent, good looking and charming. The factors of devotion, sincerity and trust would also, need to be met.

There is no doubt about the fact that you would be a steadfast lover and would want the same from your partner. You would need to respect and care for your partner the same way you want to be cared for. It is also, imperative that in your efforts to make your marriage last forever, you do not become passive. Remain as enthusiastic and spontaneous as you always were, remembering that love is nothing but give and take, sharing and caring. Once you are assured that your relationship has all of these, you would stop worrying about the nitty-gritty and learn to take things in a more relaxed fashion.

Your Sex Life

First Decan, Sun-ruled : July 24 to August 2

For you sex, more than anything else, should be an expression of good, old fashioned love. If it is anything other than that, it would not bring you much happiness or contentment. Frivolous sexual behaviour is really not your cup of tea, however, if your life lacks real meaningful love, you might indulge in the same to make up for the lack of something better. Keen and intelligent, you do have a strong sex drive and may even place your own pleasure above your partner's. However, if you are in a loving and caring relationship, you would work on this and ensure that the relationship is truly harmonious. You do have a strong streak of self-confidence and assurance and harsh words of denigration or scorn can hurt your pride deeply and this would have an immediate and immense affect on your sex drive and make you lose interest at once.

Second Decan, sub-ruled by Jupiter: August 3 to 13 August

Generous and caring, you would leave no stone unturned to make your beloved feel special and wanted. You would flood them with gifts, warmth and love. Your generosity would be the same in your sexual behaviour. You do possess the essential Leonine qualities of focusing completely on something and when it is sex, you would give it the same unwavering attention and would make use of the immense sexual energy that you have within you. Your sex life is brightened and sharpened by your natural enjoyment for life and a cheerful temperament. Though you sincerely would want to be with one partner for ever, there are strong chances that you may have quite a few partners to amuse yourself with till the time you find the perfect mate.

Third Decan, sub-ruled by Mars: August 14 to 23 August

You may face some difficulties in your sex life, particularly so if other aspects of your life are not moving ahead smoothly enough. Though you do have a strong sex drive and may be receptive to varied sexual motivations, you tend to be somewhat self-centered in your approach. You are also, influenced positively and negatively by what is happening in other areas of your life- home, career, social life, et al. Naturally spontaneous, you move from one sexual alliance to another with alarming rapidity. You would need to be more selfless and also, more stable with regards to your sexual behaviour.

Leo Celebrities

Birth Date	Star	Vocation
5 August	Kajol	Film Star
6 August	Manoj Night Shyamalan	Writer, Director
16 August	Saif Ali Khan	Film Star
20 August	Narayana Murthy	Industrialist
29 July	JRD Tata	Industrialist

Compatibility

LEO & ARIES

Fire Sign
Ruled by Sun
- Self-confident
- Arrogant

Fire Sign
Ruled by Mars
- Loyal
- Sexy

- Energetic
- Glory-seeker
- Warm-hearted
- Egocentric
- Enthusiastic
- Impulsive
- Go Getter
- Enjoys Challenges

The Arian is a topper, a frontrunner-unquestionably, a winner. Whether it is their profession, relationships, business, the Arians would need to come out first in the run and that is what drives them to do their very best.

On the other hand, we have the Leos who do not believe in squandering their precious time and efforts in attempting to win. This is a group of people who do not need to vie with others for top honors. They consider themselves inherently finer and better than everybody else. Hence, by default, they become the best in everything that they do, whether it has to do with relationship, work or any other aspect of life. They were born to be at the top without having to try for it. The only issue being that how could two people be at the top.

One would need to consider the situation with a great deal of finesse and tact. Since two people vying for top honours wouldn't be able to enjoy a healthy relationship, one would need to sacrifice a little. The Leo has an innate and ingrained desire to rule and if the Aries understands and accepts this fact, then everything would be hunky-dory. And the relationship would be a dream. However, there is the possibility that the Aries might not quite agree with this since Aries, too, is ruled by a desire to win and achieve. That is when trouble would start to brew. Only when both partners would understand that one cannot always win and allow the other to be ahead at times, would the relationship be a little less turbulent.

The relationship between an Aries and a Leo may, in all likelihood, be an affectionate and brilliant one yet there are quite a few chances that it would also, create regular tempests centering around the emotions and self of these two fiery individuals. Both produce a strong and intense physical tremor in each other and this is strengthened by the frequent emotional encouragement that they give each other. Sexually, as well, they could be brilliant together since they would both combine love and passion and would create wonderful things together. Both Aries and Leo tend to treat love like a blessing and would strive hard to tend for and protect one another with the power of their love and affection.

Astro Advice

o Man should wear pukhraj and woman should wear Ruby.
o Avoid wearing pink while going out for dinner.

LEO & TAURUS

Fire Sign	*Earth Sign*
Ruled by Sun	*Ruled by Venus*
• Romantic	• Fertile
• Hospitable	• Possessive
• Glory seeker	• Practical
• Rude	• Obstinate
• Domineering	• Steadfast
• Ambitious	• Obedient

The union of two equally dominating, obstinate signs is bound to head for troubled waters unless the parties learn to accommodate and adjust with one another. Taurus is able to satisfy Leo's need for admiration and praise, though most of the times, Leo manages to lead the Bull, but only reasonably so. Traditional Taurus tends to get a little worried by the flamboyant thoughts of the Lion, however, both would share a sense of pride in holding their ground, no matter what and would not appreciate public displays of their defeat or loss. That would be regarded as highly private by both the signs and they wouldn't share it with the world.

Although, Taurus wouldn't mind being led by Leo, for whom, this dominance would hold much importance, yet there would be instances when the Bull would revolt. Both the signs relish being able to protect and care for others. They would, also, enjoy splurging on presents and surprises for their beloved. Though the Taurean might never admit it, he/she would enjoy the intense protectiveness and deep love which Leo would display. In fact, the faithful, devoted Taurean would crave for it. Basically, the Taurean does not have an inherent taste for romance and when in love, he/she takes time to flower. But once, they do blossom, Taureans are the most tender and steady of lovers and this steadfastness is something which the Lion needs to sate his/her fanciful, emotional desire to travel, mentally or physically.

Both the signs are extremely strong willed and hence, there would be plenty of fireworks between them. While Leo would be vociferous, Taurus would be equally unmoved and stoic. They would, however, be able to make up more often than not, without the lion having to sacrifice his pride. Mostly a physical gesture of affection would be able to help them make up and come back to normal.

While Leo may be arrogant and standoffish with others, when with his/her lover, the Lion would be the warmest, most tender soul.

Their needs to touch and feel each others' skin, hair and bodies would help them to attain ideal sexual compatibility and would enable them to recreate the magic of their first meeting. This would add to the sparks in their relationship at present and they would be able to take it to greater heights than ever before.

While the obstinacy of the Taurean and the conceit of the Leo can drive them away from each other, if they learn to compromise, they would be able to create a wonderful relationship filled with warm, gentle love and care. Sexually, as well, they would be perfect together and the union would have all the rhythm and music in the world.

Astro Advice
o Man: should wear Ruby of six ratti
o Woman: don't compare your beloved with anyone.

LEO & GEMINI

Fire Sign
Ruled by Sun
- Sunny
- Exhibitionist
- Vain
- Kind
- Jealous
- Delegates

Air Sign
Ruled by Mercury
- Open-minded
- Impulsive
- Intelligent
- Temperamental
- Restless
- Communicative

The union of Air and Fire is an intriguing one, especially on an intellectual rather than emotional level. While Leo enjoys being in the limelight, Gemini would much rather spend time with others and this could make the Lion feel alienated. Also, Leo has the tendency to dominate which may stifle the free-spirited Gemini. However, the latter would appreciate Leo's generosity and ambitious nature. If they understand and appreciate each other's independence, this could be a wonderful relationship.

These two have an instinct about each other. Genuinely friendly, Leo might not be very appreciative of the Geminian fickleness and recklessness as far as life is concerned. For the laidback Leo, this rush through the journey of life is not the ideal thing. However, since Gemini is gifted with charisma and smoothness, he/she would be able to easily subdue the roaring Lion.

In matters of sex, as well, Gemini would puzzle the warm, loving Leo with his diverse preferences. However, Gemini's tendency to keep things inside can make him/her somewhat restrained in the physical expressions of love and it could stand in the way for both of them. The usually warm and caring Leo could see this aloof behaviour as a form of alienation and be put off by it.

Although Gemini may seem detached in physical expressions, he/she would have the ability to display incredible amounts of tact, allure and elegance in winning the Lion over. Leo, for his/her part would be the epitome of warm, overflowing affection, fiery passion and easy going sensuality.

For the benevolent Leo, love and sex go hand in hand and although he/she would be able to attract the normally distant Gemini, however wouldn't be able to make Gemini let go completely. That would be indeed, a difficult task. In contrast, Gemini's open attitude would be in accordance with what Leo appreciates in a relationship-the ability to be free yet feel possessed and cared for.

They would need to make their share of adjustments in order to enjoy a mutually satisfying and enriching relationship.

Astro Advice
o Woman : carry bunch of flowers to show that you cherish your beloved.
o Man should wear Emerald of five ratti on Wednesday after Pan Pratishta (Prayer to Mercury).

LEO & CANCER

Fire Sign *Water Sign*
Ruled by Sun *Ruled by Moon*
- Romantic
- Thoughtful
- Bossy
- Vain
- Oversexed

- Nourishing
- Oversensitive
- Patient
- Selfish
- Timid

Irrespective of the fact that the elements of Water and Fire don't really suit each other well, the ruling planets of Moon and Sun would be quite well-matched and this would enable a Cancer-Leo relationship to be solid and stable. While the quieter Cancer might submit to the stronger Leo, he/she would admire the Lion and that is something which Leo would be really happy with.

Together Cancer and Leo can either make or break each other. Money could often be a bone of contention between them, and whenever there would be any tiff between them, it could have both good and bad repercussions. Good in the sense, that it could motivate Leo to strive for even higher accomplishments. Considering their suitability for each other, Cancer with its intuitiveness and determination can show the dominant Leo how to achieve what they want to.

The crab is a sweet, gentle being however the fiery Leo can quite singe Cancer's peaceful and profound emotions. When a Cancerian has to bear the egotistical requirements of Leo, he/she would endure it however would become quite touchy and short-tempered. They would have the ability to hurt each other, at times, without meaning to do so. Ironically, they would also, appreciate and think highly of each other.

Although they might fall in love instantaneously, with time, there could be a decrease in the intensity. The important thing being that they learn to combine their starkly different dispositions in as fine a manner as possible. Physically, they would be a great deal of intimacy between the two, especially since Cancer is evocatively reciprocal and Leo is incredibly warm and loving. Their passions would be accompanied with a tenderness and sensitivity that would give their sexual expressions greater meaning.

Even though, the relationship would have its share of sad moments, the happiness would come when both would make up with love and tenderness. The intensity of their individual emotions, affection and mutual respect would make the relationship a pleasant and delightful one.

Perception, compassion and their respective gifts would be the foundation for closeness and confidence between these two different yet similar souls.

Astro Advice

o Man : spend money wisely on your beloved.
o Woman : should learn to be cheerful while going to meet her beloved.

LEO & LEO

Fire Sign
Ruled by Sun
- Weak
- Cutting
- Domineering
- Ambitious
- Generous

Fire Sign
Ruled by Sun
- Superior
- Popular
- Decisive
- Petty
- Creative

The relationship of Fire with Fire can have both positive as well as negative repercussions. When two Leos come together they unite in themselves, a high level of positivism, determination, and even appreciation. They can create wonders together and display the very best of teamwork, adjustments and overcoming challenges. At the same time, they are equally capable of producing the biggest screaming match in town. Mostly though, these two vain souls manage to sort out their differences in an amicable fashion and live happily together.

It is for certain that Leos are, in quite a few ways, better than the rest of mankind. They are wise, dynamic, good-looking, benevolent, protective, devoted and completely endearing. Two Lions do manage to live together in companionship because they have a greater understanding of the Leo psyche. They know exactly how to deal with a fellow lion/lioness and hence, can create a comfortable atmosphere in the relationship.

Both the Leos would have their own common admiration, respect and loyalty towards one another and would be able to cater to their respective needs of recognition and appreciation. Yet the flaming Leonine temper would be seen whenever they clash. The conflicts would mainly arise due to a blow to the male Lion's pride. It could either be over money or over personal/professional achievements or even plain jealousy. As for a lioness, if she is not given the royal treatment that she so deserves, she would refrain from all romantic and sexual activity. Hence, we see that, if the necessary adjustments are made, they would create fireworks but if not, then there can be complete coldness. They would both have a powerful libido and many a quarrel would be patched up during or after the act of love. They have great potential. They would just need to take the right steps to realise it.

Astro Advice

o Man should wear Ruby of six ratti on Sunday after Pran Pratishta (Prayer to Sun)
o Woman should wear white stone of five ratti on Monday after Pran Pratishta (Prayer to Venus).

LEO & VIRGO

Fire Sign *Earth Sign*
Ruled by Sun *Ruled by Mercury*

- Flamboyant
- Petty

- Organised
- Fretful

- Proud
- Lazy
- Self-important
- Calculating
- Quick-tempered
- Down-to-earth

The combination of Fire with Earth results in a relationship that would see happy times only when both parties agree on adjusting and cooperating with one another. It does require that one of the two agrees to give in more often than the other. Once this is worked out, there is absolutely nothing that would not be possible for the two of you.

One may come across some rare Leo-Virgo couples who plunge into a relationship where one is completely dominant while the other is merely the doormat. While it is true that Leo is definitely more domineering and vain, Virgo is not all passive. When things get too much, the gentle Virgo can be quite firm and set in his/her ways. Loving Leo, with a bit of tact and sensitivity, would get a friend and a lover in Virgo. Moreover Virgo would also, be able to truly appreciate the Lion, something which the latter revels in.

As far as the sexual aspect of the relationship is concerned, there could be a few minor hitches, since the vivacious Leo would need to show his/her affection and emotions all the time and Virgo wouldn't be able to cope with it. For Virgo, involvement in work would take top priority and Leo would at times, feel somewhat neglected. Although Leo is a benevolent and giving soul, yet after a while he/she would want the affection to be reciprocated.

Hence, they would need to work out the balance so that both of them feel secure enough and their sex life doesn't become a drudgery and source of conflict.

Astro Advice

o Men should give proper attention to their beloved.
o Woman should wear Emerald of six ratti on Wednesday.

LEO & LIBRA

Fire Sign *Air Sign*
Ruled by Sun *Ruled by Venus*

- Responsible
- Glory-seeker
- Cutting
- Vital
- Popular

- Harmonious
- Graceful
- Moody
- Fair-minded
- Reasonable

The natural affinity of Fire and Air would have a bearing on this relationship which would, of course, have many good things about it. both Leo and Libra would have a common interest and liking for most of the finer things of life and would build many cheerful memories together. They would also, balance each other out. The level-headed Libra would help to keep the normally flashy and overgenerous Leo on an even keel.

The relationship would be a success mainly because there would be many channels of communication between the two. They would be friends and lovers, and hence, would share a natural and genuine bonding. They would take on life with all its ups and downs with vim and vigor. The usual development of understanding would have to be taken care of, though. The Leo would need to realise that when Libra wants to talk things out, he/she doesn't mean a yelling match. Similar adjustments would have to be made by Libra as well.

This is a relationship that could culminate in anything, from a strong friendship to a loving marriage or even, just a memorable affair. There is a great deal of common ground here so life seems much happier when they're together. They're both just and generous. Also, they have a fair amount of realism blended with their sunny optimism. Just that arrogant Leo's incessant demands might irk the sensitive Libra to the point of becoming really angry. Irrespective, Libra does admire Leo for all his/her good qualities- honesty, nerve, sense of humour and charisma. The adoring, stylish Leo will endearingly pay beautiful compliments to Libra which would heal any injury or hurt that the latter may have felt. With a smattering of tiffs, both would eventually realise that theirs is indeed a love that is meant to be. This is one relationship that can easily withstand the test of time.

Their compatibility extends to the sexual domain as well. The Lion is a sensuous and royal figure while the Libran is fascinating and enticing. Both make great lovers since they are expressive and emotional with each other. The intensity of their passions is well matched and their laidback approach would work wonders in this day of rush and haste. Each aspect of this relationship augurs well for both of them.

Astro Advice
o Men : you should not lack motivation, ambition, or drive to face the challenges.
o Women : you should sense the potential and look forward to what's ahead.

LEO & SCORPIO

 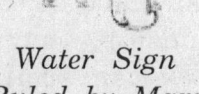

Fire Sign
Ruled by Sun
- Superior
- Leader
- Inexperienced
- Vital
- Jealous

Water Sign
Ruled by Mars
- Boastful
- Determined
- Venomous
- Revengeful
- Healers

The merging of Fire and Water along with the coming together of two strong and determined signs, would, indeed, result in a relationship that could become earthshaking. A consequence that can be avoided only if both agree to give each other their space and also, respect each others' individuality. If they learn to live and work together, these two can achieve great things and have great times in each others' company. Yet there would be times when the straightforward Leo would disagree with the secrecy, and craftiness that Scorpio would employ to achieve his/her means.

When it concerns things that they have in common, both Leo and Scorpio have a genuine, deep-seated mutual reverence. When they come together, they have their own unique intimacy and bonding. Perceptive Scorpio would intuitively know when proud Leo is injured or disturbed and would try to soothe and calm his/her frayed nerves. However, in a relationship that lacks this profound understanding, the charm may wear off sooner than expected and nothing would materialise out of the relationship.

While Leo is sunny, gregarious and extroverted, Scorpio is more worldly wise and philosophical, yet with a bit of understanding; they would balance each other and exist in perfect harmony. Money matters would pose a problem, since the Lion enjoys spending while for Scorpio that would be sacrilege. If they feel strongly about the relationship, they would be able to live happily forever. Leo can spoil Scorpio with an abundance of unconditional love while Scorpio can give Leo a sense of stability and steadfastness. Though the Lion may seem teasing in nature, he/she would be incredibly devoted to the Scorpion.

Sexually, they could have both good days and not-so-good days. There would be times when passions would rage high followed by days of detached coolness. Sporadic is probably the best way to describe its nature.

Astro Advice
o Man should wear Pearl of six ratti on Monday.
o Woman : avoid your stubborn nature.

LEO & SAGITTARIUS

Fire Sign
Ruled by Sun
- Extravagant
- Stubborn
- Charming
- Organised
- Materialistic

Fire Sign
Ruled by Jupiter
- Lawless
- Gambling
- Earnest
- Restless
- Tolerant

The alliance of two fire signs ruled by Sun and Jupiter respectively is, of course, a favourable one. Primarily, for the reason, that their planets endow them with advantageous characteristics, which make them into well-rounded personalities, who are naturally compatible with one another. Both of them are straightforward, benevolent and sincere and hence, can very easily complement each other. Free and liberal Sagittarius would chafe and sulk if Leo attempts to be more domineering or possessive than necessary. On the other hand, Leo would feel ignored if Sagittarius leads a carefree and footloose lifestyle.

This is, however, a relationship that would witness, probably some of the most memorable disagreements and confrontations. Most of the conflicts though would be quite amicable and genial in nature, without a hint of malice or spite. The smarter ones realise that there wouldn't ever be a consensus and so decide to go with the flow of events. Irrespective of what their individual thoughts might be, as long as these two are together they would radiate energy and enthusiasm all around. They would unknowingly fill their own and the lives of others' with cheerfulness, brightness and optimism.

The Lion would exercise his/her opinions with wisdom and thought which would enable the normally forthright Sagittarius to also, learn restraint and hence, develop him/her into a better person.

Since Leo needs quite a lot to be made happy and feel loved, the archer would be quite the one with gifts, flowers, compliments, and that works. He/she would be a devoted, warm and thoughtful lover who would endeavor in all earnestness to fill Leo's life with immense love and caring.

The emotion of love would be demonstrated sexually through gentle, subtle yet passionate acts of love. There would be a sophisticated air along with the sensual ambience when these two indulge in sexual relations. In fact, when they unite sexually, it is quite a transcending experience.

They are one of those rare partners who manage to merge their love and their desire for each other in the most beautiful manner. The Leo-Sagittarius couple is one that is created for the purpose of love and affection. They move through life with an essence of innocence and worldliness, romance and erotica, realism and fantasy and spread joy wherever they go.

Astro Advice
o Man : try to be warm and soft.
o Woman : carry bunch of flowers with you while going to meet your beloved.

LEO & CAPRICORN

Fire Sign *Ruled by Sun*	*Earth Sign* *Ruled by Saturn*
• Ambitious	• Narrow-minded
• Popular	• Neglectful
• Self-confident	• Earthy
• Restless	• Loyal
• Elitist	• Social climber

The glaring differences between the element of Fire and Earth are further enhanced when one considers the éclat of the Sun with the orthodoxy of Saturn. When in a long-term intimate relationship, there is always the risk that the ebullient Leo would feel restrained and controlled by Capricorn. On the other hand, Capricorn could well think that Leo is way too much a spendthrift or even, physically demonstrative. The differences don't just end there. Leo would want to live life to the hilt while the careful Capricorn would want to plan and chart out everything to the minutest detail. Since Capricorn is not the kind to show his/her feelings in public, there would be times when Leo would feel isolated, ignored and abandoned. The Lion under all circumstances needs to be lavished with attention, care and recognition.

Since these two are so different from one another, they have an inherent inquisitiveness about the other one. This can result in one of two things. Either they would make each other get all awkward and nervy or they could bond together and learn to use their differences to the best possible advantage. It is, indeed, possible that Leo would learn stability and emotional security from Capricorn while the latter could adopt the Lion's optimism and ambition.

However, in all likelihood, this would be quite a tumultuous relationship with a fair amount of ups and downs. Particularly, because, Capricorn would find it difficult to be drawn towards a leonine personality. It is a personality that thrives on appreciation, attention and the element of drama. Capricorn would always find such a persona to be proud, arrogant and egotistic while Leo would consider Capricorn to be detached, aloof and cold-hearted. At the bottom of it all though, the fact remains that Leo would be able to mould Capricorn as per his/her likings, yet he/she would need to work really hard for the same.

Sexually, they can be quite incompatible. However, it does rest on the aspects of the planets in their individual horoscopes. Incompatibility could result in detachments and even, breaking away of ties. At the same time, if the planets are placed favorably, the sexual relations could be quite passionate and enduring.

All in all, this is a relationship that does not really stand on rock solid ground. It has an infirm basis and that could be its undoing.

Astro Advice
o Man should wear Blue Sapphire of six ratti on Saturday after Pran Pratishta (Prayer to Saturn)
o Woman should wear Ruby of six ratti on Sunday after Pran Pratishta (Prayer to Sun).

LEO & AQUARIUS

 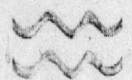

Fire Sign *Air Sign*
Ruled by Sun *Ruled by Saturn*
- Charming
- Responsible
- Generous
- Superior
- Weak

- Honest
- Cowardly
- Critical
- Progressive
- Fanatical

Regardless of the fact that Fire and Water have an inherent attraction, the signs of Leo and Aquarius are placed opposite to one another in the Zodiac charts. At the beginning there could be a powerful attraction which could later, turn into equally intense antagonism. Both, Leo and Aquarius, have set ideas, strong wills and are intensely indomitable. Therefore, if one of them doesn't learn to adjust and give way, there could be big problems on hand.

Since Leo needs validation and attention at all times, he/she would find it difficult to digest that Aquarius intends on spending a considerable amount of time and attention on people in general. It would be hard for the Lion to get accustomed to the idea of Aquarius being independent and even aloof. The unpredictable, erratic nature of Aquarius would never cease to puzzle and confuse Leo. This could lead to some misunderstandings which would need to be dealt with in a mature fashion with communication and rationality.

It is not as if both of them are starkly different. They do have a fair deal in common and would often have great times in each others' company. Both are fond of being surprised and are liberal in their thinking. They are both givers and protectors of the weak and needy. Most of the values they believe in are common. Hence they would manage to generate an atmosphere of optimism, goodness and ambition around them. Both of them are also, logical and intelligent beings who would consciously make an effort to develop qualities of gentleness, patience, meekness which would ensure that the relationship moves on the right track at all times.

There would be instances when the fixated nature of their signs would make them adopt contradictory stances in a discussion resulting in a stand-off. The pride of the Lion would confuse and even irk, the relatively fuss-free Aquarius. The indifference of Aquarius, on the other hand, coupled with his/her changeableness would make Leo display his/her fiery temper. This would be one of the times when a logical, calm discussion would just not be possible. It would be best to let time do its work and when they cool down, both would be able to analyse and reflect on their actions and words in a sensible manner.

Sexually, Leo would be the one to take dominance, since he/she would have a powerful sex drive and would be able to use it well to enrich the relationship. In this area, Aquarius would cede gracefully and admire the Lion's excellence. Their lovemaking would be preceded by sweet words, gestures and even, gifts to please. The entire atmosphere would be one of tranquility and bliss.

Although, their individual needs from the relationship differ, yet their sexual bonding would bring them much closer and would give their relationship a wonderfully, interesting dimension.

Astro Advice
o Both are suggested to avoid getting caught in the controversial issues.

LEO & PISCES

 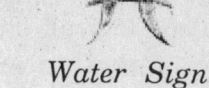

Fire Sign
Ruled by Sun
- Rude
- Creative
- Administrator
- Hospitable
- Loving

Water Sign
Ruled by Neptune
- Dreamers
- Guilt-ridden
- Philosophical
- Idealistic
- Romantic

The disparity between Fire and Water just goes to show how unlike Leo and Pisces are from each other. While Leo is straightforward, gregarious and candid, Pisces is vague, profound, mystifying and can be quite an enigma for most whom they come in contact with. Leo can never quite figure out what makes Pisces tick. However, Pisces does appreciate Leo and his/her characteristics such as perseverance and focus. Pisces frequently needs to be more planned and orderly and the Lion is the ideal teacher for the same.

As far as Pisces is concerned, he/she can fill Leo's life with a lot of gentleness and perceptiveness. And the Lion can further give Pisces a strong sense of security and stability. Yet for all the enrichment that they can do for each other, they lack the basic compatibility that is so essential for any successful relationship and they would, both, need to work really hard at bringing about any kind of equilibrium and synchrony in their lives. Once they learn to do that, they can focus on inspiring each other and helping one another towards self-development.

While Leo has a regal bearing and elegance, Pisces has an inherent philosophical superiority and this complements the leonine personality perfectly. Hence, with some work, they would be able to form a lasting and enduring relationship and give it their best.

There could be times when Leo would be unreasonable with the fish. However, Pisces would realise that eventually Leo would be a warm and companionable partner who would loyally and passionately protect and love. Sexually, there could be minor hitches. The mystery of Pisces could be too delicate to satisfy the Lion. On the other hand, the Lion could be too passionate and overbearing for the Fish. Their sexual relations would have their basis in a mutual admiration for each other more than anything else. And in order for sex to be there, the element of love must always be there.

When they overcome all their challenges, both would want to create an atmosphere of romance and sensuality preceding their lovemaking. Their intimacy would be characterised by plenty of tender, romantic moments. There does exist the possibility of envy creeping into the relationship since both have the capacity to tease and flirt. If they learn to get their expectations right from the relationship, they would attain a great deal of happiness. Leo would want to get generous amount of loving, appreciation and intense passion. Pisces would crave a fulfillment complete in all respects. Together, with compromises and adjustments, they would lead happy and delightful lives.

Astro Advice
o Men should show their feeling by giving gifts and cards.
o Women should wear yellow sapphire of six carat in their index finger.

Virgo–The Virgin
(August 24–September 23)
The Sign of the Craftsman or Critic

How to Recognise Virgo

Of all the twelve signs, Virgo is the busiest. Those who have it as their Sun- or Rising-sign will surround themselves with a great many tasks, so that their day is full of activity. It is very difficult indeed for them to relax totally-putting their feet up and doing nothing has no great appeal, so the best way for them to cut out is to move from work which is intellectually demanding to something that makes greater demands on their physical energy. Virgoan organising ability is not very strong, and sometimes a fair amount of time and energy is wasted because they do not allow themselves enough time to get tasks sorted out or executed in an orderly way. Here we have the critic of the Zodiac, and it is usual for Virgoans to work in a very analytical way on small details. They give marvellous support to 'front' men and women, making excellent secretaries and personal assistants, and usually enjoying that kind of role, rather than one which carries heavy responsibility. It is, alas, far too often the case that Virgoans are imposed upon. They have by nature a very strong sense of duty, and this can sometimes be carried to extremes, so that a young Virgoan woman will sacrifice her career to look after an ageing or sick mother, who will become more and more demanding of her and her time and energy. Because Virgoans like to live active and busy lives, they enjoy filling their out-of-work hours with & great many hobbies and interests. If they are at all artistically inclined, craft-work using natural materials-wool, clay, wood and so on-is particularly rewarding. They often have green fingers, and love tending gardens and potted plants. To ward off tension, demanding physical exercise is excellent for them, with walking, cycling and jogging being especially beneficial.

Career and Finance

Virgos like plenty of hustle and bustle and will make work if it's not there. In office a Virgo is quite likely to be seen clearing out a filing cabinet while everone else is having a coffee break.

The Virgo is an ideal secretary or personal assistant, and will do more than would be expected of someone else in that role. Once they know what is expected of them, Virgos are marvellously efficient: but they do have to be told exactly where they stand and precisely what they have to do. Once they have been given a precise briefing they will be away, and everyone else, from managing director to coffee-lady, can rest assured that they will always be there, running the whole set-up like a well-oiled machine, with Virgo wielding the oil-can, or if necessary carrying it for other less efficient types. A great many Virgos work in the media as the influence of Mercury, their ruling planet, gives them a strong urge to communicate. They excel as critics, investigative journalists and writers of all kinds-the number of Virgo novelists, for example, is much above average. They are happy in a school or college environment and enjoy teaching and lecturing as this offers a positive expression of their well-developed critical faculties. Among their students or employees they often have a reputation for being strict. But this apparent strictness is really a desire for efficiency-for the neat presentation of work and the smooth running of a timetable. An insistence on such things has probably earned many a Virgo somewhat undeserved reputation as a martine.

Health and Food

You live too much on your nerves. You are generally at high tension all the time and in consequence are subject to nervous break-downs.

You often have a twitching in some part of the face, a slight stammering in speech trouble with the nerves of the tongue and a tendency in advanced years towards paralysis or cramp of the lower limbs. As a rule you will be 'light sleepers' or suffer from insomnia and not get enough of rest and sleep.

Harmonious environment generally effects your life style. You should eat well and do some light exercises. The lungs, bowels, hips and feet come under troubled area.

Suggested Food Options:

- Lemon
- Almonds
- Grains
- Cheese
- Beef
- Lamb

Your Love Life

First Decan of Virgo: August 24 to September 2

You are born under the zodiac which has a reputation for most of its natives remaining single or unattached. This should in no way be interpreted as you not being emotional or interested in affairs of the heart. However, it does signify that you are wary of being emotional and would rather be ruled by your head than your heart. You do have the tendency of picking out shortcomings in relationships and love affairs around you which makes you nearly cynical about love itself. While you aren't cold at heart, your mind takes precedence and only when you are convinced about the sincerity of the feeling would you take another step. If you can avoid becoming overly distrustful about emotions, you would have a pleasant love life.

You do desire having someone to call your own, someone you would be able to rely on and talk to after long hours at work. Only when you would meet someone who appeals to your mind and your mental temperament would you start to consider marriage. Casual flings are certainly not your cup of tea. When married, you would be deeply interested in knowing all about your partner and making an effort to keep the home front nice and happy. If you face everything with an open mind, you would find that not only love but marriage, too, is an extremely enjoyable expedition which holds many interesting and quaint attributes within itself.

Second Decan of Virgo: September 3 to September 12

While you do have a sincere liking for people, you do, also, have extremely strong dislikes. You enjoy being admired and appreciated by members of the opposite sex, however, you have high standards and preferences and there is little chance that you would be swayed merely by sweet words and charm. In order to make a lasting impact on you, people would need to match up to your demanding preferences.

You would appreciate affection, high standards and intelligence, along with sexual attraction in people you meet, yet when the issue of marriage arises, you would be a bit inhibited and restrained. In all likelihood, you could have even decided to remain single, but would be open to altering that view provided you meet someone who you feel is ideal for you and is in keeping with your standards and values.

For you the emotion of love is something to be taken seriously and not fooled around with. Your loyalty and devotion would be unquestionable and in most cases, you would also, be quite overprotective and even controlling. You would be a perfectionist as far as your home is concerned and you would want everything to be beautiful and tidy, prim and proper. You would relish the experience of shopping for your home and doing it up with the help of your partner and it is important that your partner's tastes match your own. Marriage is something that you would treat with the utmost respect and you would give a hundred percent of yourself to your relationship. You would be happy with sharing your life with someone who matches you more intellectually than merely physically.

Third Decan of Virgo: September 13 to September 23

Those born under this decan of Virgo enjoy being the object of attention of all and sundry since they feel that they have the unique ability of helping others by bettering their quality of life and raising them to a higher standard. When you speak, your words reflect your thoughts and more often than not, hold advice in them. However, this has many advantages attached to it, especially when you are dealing with members of the opposite sex.

For you romance and your own sense of worth go hand in hand. When you feel that you are relied upon and needed, you tend to get involved romantically. This, however, is not a very strong foundation for love. It holds good only when the other person enjoys being dependent upon someone. Though, this may work out, it is quite possible that the emotion of love may not be present or that you may have to consciously seek it.

With age and experience, it is indeed, possible that you would marry and settle down in life. Though, there is a fair chance of this happening quite late in life. If, unfortunately, you have had an unpleasant early marriage failing, there is little chance that you would marry again. At the same time, you are quite the house proud person and would enjoy having a nice, comfortable home and be surrounded by people who really love and care for you.

It is extremely important that you exercise complete wisdom and control when choosing your partner for life. If you ignore your intuition or instinct, there are good chances that you would not be very happy for long. This would make you feel sorry about your choice and in turn, would transform you in to an ill-tempered, domineering and skeptical individual. Hence, you should take your time but never make a hasty decision. Let the light of love be a beacon and not blind you to reality. At the same time, remember to let the feeling be that you love to accept and not change the person you fell in love with.

Your Sex Life

First Decan, Mercury-ruled : August 24 to September 2

Although you do have a strong sex drive, you are mainly guided by your inherent wisdom and pragmatism when expressing yourself sexually. You are not the kind to be ruled only by your sex drive when in various situations. You have a restrain on yourself and this may lead people to assume that you are unapproachable. However, this is only you being on your guard and therefore, should not be interpreted as snobbery. When in the appropriate situations, you would be extremely responsive and participative in sexual behaviour. Nonetheless, there would always exist some sort of discipline and routine, even a kind of lack of naturalness, in most sexual situations.

Second Decan, sub-ruled by Saturn: September 3 to 13 September

For you consciousness and understanding about sex would have occurred later than for others in your peer group. Since your natural interests are more so towards intellectual and physical work, these sexual matters simply would have taken a back seat. It could also, be that certain inherent hesitations or the lack of sex stimuli are the reasons for your late sexual blooming. Once you reached sexual maturity, even then, it would always be relegated to the background with restraint and control taking first preference. For you sex would always be something to be enjoyed now and then and not something that you need.

Third Decan, sub-ruled by Venus: September 14 to 23 September

You posses the perfect blend of idealism and realism when expressing yourself sexually. When you express your viewpoints on sex or think about it subjectively, they are dreamily idealistic, yet when you indulge in sexual behaviour it is only after you have thought everything through. An inherent common sense and knowledge of the real world plays an important role in who you would pick as your sexual partner. You enjoy being in the right atmosphere for sex-soft lighting, background music, plush furnishings and the works. While you may be endowed with a powerful drive for sex, it is, indeed, dependent on factors other than that. Your realisation that material possessions make a difference would play a dominant role in your selection of a sexual partner.

Virgo Celebrities

Birth Date	Star	Vocation
8 September	Asha Bhonsale	Musician
9 September	Akshay Kumar	Film Star
16 September	M S Subbalakshmi	Musician
24 August	Rekha	Film Star
27 August	Mother Teresa	Social Reformer

Compatibility

VIRGO & ARIES

Earth Sign
Ruled by Mercury
- Exact
- Methodical
- Discriminating
- Intelligent
- Expressive
- Analytical

Fire Sign
Ruled by Mars
- Energetic
- Sexy
- Enthusiastic
- Impulsive
- Youthful
- Confident

The Arian would always make the first move based on their instincts and not on the facts before them. On the contrary, we have the Virgos who would, in characteristic manner, be completely pragmatic and realistic in their approach. Even though, the drives and attitudes may be dissimilar, both the signs are alike in many aspects. They would both not refrain from helping out others and would have a natural inclination towards wholesomeness in whatever they undertake. They move in harmony with one another towards their dreams of creativity and beauty. Moreover, both the signs would have the highest comfort level with each other and would be able to tell each other things they wouldn't even dream of telling anyone else in the world.

Since the Virgos can be highly methodical and proponents of intelligibility, Aries would at times, consider them hard to please & icy. Moreover, the spontaneity of the Arian and the inability to alter situations may cause the Virgo to be displeased with them, yet the Virgo wouldn't be vocal about the displeasure and all this might lead to misinterpretations and confusions between the two.

However, Aries and Virgo can enjoy a satisfying relationship, if there is a favorable aspect between the Sun and the Moon in their charts. When the two realise that they are capable of creating happiness, they would be pleasantly surprised. Both can learn a lot from each other. The methodical yet creative Virgo can teach the impulsive Aries to stop and appreciate the beauty in the little joys of nature and Life.

Physically, there would be a vague sort of delight and fascination between them. Irrespective of their inherent attraction for each other in passionate affairs, there will always be ambiguity as far as the level of emotional security in the relationship is concerned.

When the relationship faces stormy weather, it would be filled with disappointments & disapprovals and both the partners would move away from each other to search for peace and calmness, instead of talking things over and making them better together. This would be one of the most harmful things that they could do. On the brighter side, though, both Aries & Virgo have the ability to renew the relationship each time it loses some freshness and flavor. In any case, it would be nothing short of a miracle if this relationship would last forever, especially since both wouldn't wish to communicate with each other with candor and love together.

Astro Advice
o Man should wear Coral and women should wear Emerald.
o Saturday & Tuesdays are auspicious for outing.

VIRGO & TAURUS

Earth Sign *Ruled by Mercury*	*Earth Sign* *Ruled by Venus*
• Truthful	• Long-suffering
• Critical	• Tactile
• Frigid	• Artistic
• Sensible	• Kind
• Neat	• Sensual
• Calculating	• Dull
• Down-to-earth	• Nagging

The combination of the two Earth signs does indicate a high level of compatibility and similarities in traits such as common sense, realism and efficiency. At the same time, they are markedly different as far as their emotional temperaments are concerned. The composed and cool Virgo can feel somewhat stifled by the intensity and possessiveness of the Taurean. Since both eventually want to attain financial security and prosperity, they would try and smoothen things out between them.

As both are considerably serene and placid, there wouldn't be too many violent outbursts. Though they may not be the most romantic couple, their deep affection for each other would form a steady force in their lives. They aren't the ones who would waste their intense emotions on trivia. They are the sort who would easily go through life saturated in the bliss of the real wonders of the world and achieving concrete, real things. For Virgo, the emotion of love is one that would need to be given a lot of practice so that it becomes perfect. Both would strive to achieve that perfection in their relationship.

This would be a couple who would be able to listen to the unspoken words and endeavour to fulfill those needs which are not put into words. The closeness and understanding that they would share would be remarkable. The conversations that they would share would also, be ideal. The Taurean would be an absorbed listener and an intriguing talker while the Virgo would be sparkling and intelligent which would ensure that there wouldn't be a dull moment between the two.

Their ability to understand each other without speaking would be seen in their sexual relationship as well. The sober Taurus would enjoy being able to indulge in love making without being disturbed by words and mushy speeches. Virgo, on the other hand, would prefer silence simply because; he/she would not have much to say on the subject. It should not be thought that Virgo is cold or disinterested in sex. As a matter of fact, Virgo would be able to bring a great loveliness to the whole experience by merging sentimental warmth with physical desires. Moreover, Taurus would not be opposed to such an outlook, but would welcome it and therefore, the relationship that they would share would be rewarding and enjoyable for both of them. This pair has the ability to use delicate romance in tandem with well grounded realism and virtues of faithfulness to create a relationship that glows with the light of loyalty and true love.

Astro Advice
o Woman : do not hide anything from your beloved.
o Man should wear a Diamond of one carat.

VIRGO & GEMINI

Earth Sign
Ruled by Mercury
- Organised
- Voyeuristic
- Busy
- Mean
- Truthful

Air Sign
Ruled by Mercury
- Shallow
- Bright
- Persuasive
- Selfish
- Unreliable

Despite the fact that Air and Earth have little in common, both Gemini and Virgo are ruled by the same planet-Mercury. And this factor can play quite a significant role in their relationship. Both are equally realistic and practical as far as emotions and sentiments are concerned. They would share interests in fields of business, social life and even intellectual concerns. The organised Virgo would not always agree with the whole host of schemes and ideas that the ever enthusiastic Gemini would throw around, simply because for Virgo, it is essential to be more focused and single-minded.

Gemini does have something that is mystifying and alluring for the shyer Virgo and this charm is at times, more than what they need to put a permanent seal on their relationship. A seal of constant novelty, mystery and thrill. Though they have their share of differences, the scales also tip in favour of the similarities. They have a unique intellect, an elegance of disposition and an inherent inquisitiveness. All of these would help them move through the journey called Life with happiness and ease.

In love, this is one couple who when the initial flush of romance wanes, would feel quite lost and even somewhat sad. They would use the power of language to either build or break the relationship and wouldn't just keep up an act for the sake of it. The relationship should always have some meaning for them. They can very easily use their similarities to adjust and adapt and find tranquility and contentment in each others' company.

Sexually, they would be drawn towards one another in the beginning. However, if Gemini feels intimidated in any manner, it would switch off the magnetism instantly. As far as Virgo is concerned, there would need to be plenty of actual expressions of love and tenderness which Virgo would surely reciprocate. This would give Gemini the sense of security which would lead to a lasting and reciprocally satisfying love and sex life.

Astro Advice
o Man : there is a need to improve tolerance power.
o Woman : best to observe silence over heated discussions.

VIRGO & CANCER

Earth Sign *Water Sign*
Ruled by Mercury *Ruled by Moon*
- Far-sighted
- Demanding

- Fertile
- Sincere

- Frigid
- Forceful
- Practical
- Selfish
- Slavish
- Hypochondriac

Since the elements of Water and Earth are indeed, well-matched, the relationship would be one which would have many advantages to it. Cancer would give it plenty of genuine affection, devotion and tenderness and would sincerely value Virgo's meticulous nature and diligence. The tolerant Cancer would be able to deal with most of Virgo's eccentricities. For instance, Virgo would want everything to be done in as ideal a fashion as possible and would want time and attention given to each and every minute detail.

Since Cancer gets hurts really quickly, the ever critical Virgo would need to refrain from nitpicking and think about shy Cancer's feelings and sentiment. For Cancer it would be beneficial if he/she remembers that unlike themselves, Virgo is not the sort to indulge in too many displays of affection. For Virgo, subtlety is quintessential.

When they join forces, Cancer and Virgo can bring to life some of the greatest and strongest vibes-emotional, physical and intellectual. They are industrious and would enjoy keeping themselves occupied. Moreover, both of them are also, quite gentle and loving, so one would find the protective Virgo support and shield sensitive Cancer and the affectionate Cancer creating a haven of warmth and love for Virgo.

From the physical aspect, Cancer and Virgo follow a quiet music of their own. They have their own unique sense of romance and love and they would communicate the same to the other. Since both would enjoy making their partner happy, the relationship would see many happy and glorious moments of love and affection. They would ensure that they make each other feel emotionally safe and wanted.

The act of love for both of them is an intensely emotional one and they would take to it with naturalness and sincere warmth. Even though sex would have quite a minor position in their love life, they would treat it with a healthy attitude and a genuine interest, ensuring that it brings happiness and greater intimacy into their steady relationship.

Astro Advice

o Women should dress up in a traditional outfit and put on a red bindi.
o Man should wear pearl of five ratti on Monday after Pran Pratishta (Prayer to Moon).

VIRGO & LEO

Earth Sign	*fire Sign*
Ruled by Mercury	Ruled by Sun
• Organised	• Flamboyant
• Fretful	• Petty
• Calculating	• Proud
• Quick-tempered	• Lazy
• Down-to-earth	• Self-important

The combination of Fire with Earth results in a relationship that would see happy times only when both parties agree on adjusting and cooperating with one another. It does require that one of the two agrees to give in more often than the other. Once this is worked out, there is absolutely nothing that would not be possible for the two of you.

One may come across some rare Leo-Virgo couples who plunge into a relationship where one is completely dominant while the other is merely the doormat. While it is true that Leo is definitely more domineering and vain, Virgo is not all passive. When things get too much, the gentle Virgo can be quite firm and set in his/her ways. Loving Leo, with a bit of tact and sensitivity, would get a friend and a lover in Virgo. Moreover Virgo would also, be able to truly appreciate the Lion, something which the latter revels in.

As far as the sexual aspect of the relationship is concerned, there could be a few minor hitches, since the vivacious Leo would need to show his/her affection and emotions all the time and Virgo wouldn't be able to cope with it. For Virgo, involvement in work would take top priority and Leo would at times, feel somewhat neglected. Although Leo is a benevolent and giving soul, yet after a while he/she would want the affection to be reciprocated.

Hence, they would need to work out the balance so that both of them feel secure enough and their sex life doesn't become a drudgery and source of conflict.

Astro Advice
o Men should give proper to attention to their beloved.
o Woman should wear Emerald of six ratti on a Wednesday.

VIRGO & VIRGO

Earth Sign *Earth Sign*
Ruled by Mercury *Ruled by Mercury*
- Organised
- Loyal

- Organised
- Loyal

- Precise
- Analytical
- Prudish

- Precise
- Analytical
- Prudish

In a Virgo-Virgo relationship, the element of Earth is common, however, it would not make the pair difficult to get along. In fact, since both the partners would enjoy following a regimen of sorts and also, be well-grounded people, they would be able to understand each other better. Both would refrain from being unreasonable, however, they would need to guard against fault finding and nitpicking.

Together, the two Virgos might frequently assess one another's actions, reactions and feelings. And would express their individual opinions on the same. This would be a big waste of time and energy. They should, rather, concentrate on realising and accepting their differences along with their similarities. Since they would have plenty in common, this wouldn't be a difficult task. Both of them would also, tend to be quite anxious about things and would be able to get used to their minor differences as well.

This happy and amicable relationship would continue forever, but not without a few tweakings here and there. How far would this relationship go depends mainly on how well would these two accept each others' shortcomings? If they do accept them, there is no reason why this union wouldn't be an eternally happy one. If they truly love and understand each other, this is one couple who would be totally in sync with one another. They would, indeed make conscious efforts to reach that level of empathetic understanding.

Their sexual union might be passionate to begin with, however, there exists the possibility that the fault finding habit might continue in the bedroom as well and this would cool the fire immediately. While the relationship would certainly not be based on sexual or physical attraction, sex would be able to give them a higher level of closeness and understanding. The lovemaking would be more gentle and sensitive than erotic and sensuous. There would be a reciprocal understanding and both would endeavor to give the other happiness and together they would be able to appreciate the beauty in their union.

Astro Advice
o Man should wear Emerald of six ratti on Wednesday.
o Woman should wear Diamond of one carat on Friday.

VIRGO & LIBRA

Earth Sign Ruled by Mercury	Air Sign Ruled by Venus
• Intellectual	• Insincere
• Through	• Kind
• Tactless	• Moderate
• Forceful	• Hair-splitting
• Neat	• Amiable

Two signs who have quite a few characteristic differences and yet, would be able to exist in peace and harmony with each other. While Virgo is quiet and polite; Libra is quick and razor-sharp. The sensitive, tranquil Virgo would accept the Libran rationale, sunny positivism and lengthy discourses with ease and patience. Virgo would cheerfully move through life in Libra's company and everything would be tuneful and synchronised.

In fact, it would be Virgo who would give up a lot and adjust many times for the sake of Libra's peace of mind and for the relationship to move to a higher level. However, this doesn't mean that Libra would take Virgo for granted. The Libra sense of fairness wouldn't ever allow that. Rather, Libra would be touched by the sacrifices Virgo makes and would try his/her very best to return them.

The calming presence of the Virgo would be like a breath of fresh air for the Libran, especially when he/she is sad or disturbed. Together this would be a couple who would do quite a bit of introspection and discard attributes which they feel are negative and fortify the ones they wish to develop. They, however, might be unduly worried about seemingly minor issues and this might rock the boat every now and then. They might also, not be able to express each and every sentiment at the appropriate moment and this might cause some confusions. But this means that they should be fairer and more tolerant of each other and see what lies beneath the surface when they assess and evaluate their partners.

The Virgo-Libra couple normally finds out an exceptional type of peace and satisfaction when they come together in a sexual union. The closeness that this gives them is at all levels, soothing and comforting.

Indeed, this is a relationship where the sexual aspect has many dimensions and every single dimension gives the relationship a uniqueness and happiness beyond description.

Astro Advice
o Man : your beloved needs emotional security.
o Woman : try to be honest and straightforward.

VIRGO & SCORPIO

| Earth Sign | Water Sign |
| Ruled by Mercury | Ruled by Mars |

- Truthful
- Voyeuristic
- Busy
- Tactless
- Wide-awake

- Magnetic
- Devious
- Power-tripper
- Strong-willed
- Over-sexed

The blending of Earth and Water would be quite positive in matters of the mind and day-to day life. However, as far as, matters of the heart go, it would leave much to be desired. While Virgo is more restrained and self-possessed with feelings, Scorpio tends to be passionate and fiery.

Highly pragmatic yet tender, Virgos tend to bring out the protector in the Scorpio who is indulgent with them and doesn't consider them a danger. The soothing aura that Virgo exudes tends to make the Scorpio feel rejuvenated and at the same time, calm. These two would have a fair enough understanding of their abilities and limitations and would never form unreasonable expectations from the other. Neither one of them would ever take the other for granted. There would exist at all times, a high level of mutual respect. After the relationship is formed and becomes firm, Virgo would cherish the unwavering dedication of the Scorpio immensely while Scorpio would value the Virgo's honesty and gentleness.

A Virgo-Scorpio couple would always, enjoy being able to give something of themselves to others. The desire to serve is strong in both. When saddened by something, they would sensibly resort to open communication and think with both their hearts and their heads. They share a mutual respect for honesty, uprightness, knowledge and a focused aim. More often than not, these two would be friends first and then lovers and would not be afraid of standing up for each other. However, it is unlikely that they would plunge headlong into a relationship with each other. The attraction is more likely to be built over a period of time rather than be instantaneous.

Sexually, since both would be somewhat hesitant and reticent, there could be a certain restraint in their demonstrations of love and affection. They would need to make a few adjustments and with the passage of time, there would be an intensity in their lovemaking that would definitely, bring them to a higher level of intimacy and sharing.

Astro Advice
o Women should wear any sort of head accessory it would be eye catching.
o Man should wear grey colour and preferably the neckline should have a V shape.

VIRGO & SAGITARIUS

Earth Sign
Ruled by Mercury
- Demanding
- Masochistic

Fire Sign
Ruled by Jupiter
- Restless
- Wasteful

- Thorough
- Complaining
- Sensible
- Practical
- Boorish
- Selfish

Although the two signs-Virgo and Sagittarius are temperamentally different, yet there is a thread of similarity that runs through their differences and tends to bring them closer to each other. Virgo is Earth and hence, logical, cautious, reserved and systematic. Sagittarius is Fire and therefore, swift, self-reliant, rash and somewhat of a spendthrift. Virgo is the kind who would handle one thing intensively and pay acute attention to the minutest detail to ensure that everything is in order. On the contrary, Sagittarius is the sort who would take on many things and would think more of how to conquer the future rather than tame the present. Both would tend to give expression to their dissimilarities in their own unique ways.

Although these two would speak a lot, their individual communication with each other would not be the best. However, if the stars are favourable, these two would be able to build a lasting and affectionate relationship. While the prim and proper Virgo would educate the footloose Sagittarius serenity, perseverance and even cultural etiquette, Sagittarius would, in return, teach the controlled Virgo how to be more relaxed, easy-going and liberal. Virgo's innocence and clear heartedness would touch the archer and together they would be able to overcome whatever hindrances to build a beautiful world together.

Although there is much that the Archer could admire in the Virgo and vice-versa, there would be some instances where they wouldn't always be in agreement and there could be some discord. However, with tenderness and the initial attraction between these two, there would be little difficulty in resolving whatever difference they may have hade. When the shy Virgo would seek refuge in

Sagittarius' arms, there would be no memory of any conflict and all misgivings and disapprovals would vanish. If the two learn to be more patient and understanding with each other, this bond would be one where passion and tranquility would merge beautifully.

The relationship has a distinct air of peace and quietness and this enables both of them to direct their love and passion for each other into a subtle and delicate expression. There could be instances when the Archer might not get the desired sexual response from the Virgo and be somewhat blunt about it. However, both would need to understand that it is only with tact, patience and profound love that they would be able to culminate their love for each other in a sexual union that would be transcendental and uplifting.

Astro Advice
o Man should wear a Yellow Sapphire of Eight ratti on Thursday.
o Woman should wear a Emerald of five ratti on Wednesday.

VIRGO & CAPRICORN

Earth Sign
Ruled by Mercury
- Analytical
- Down-to-earth
- Practical
- Tactless
- Quick-tempered

Earth Sign
Ruled by Saturn
- Mercenary
- Hard-working
- Self controlled
- Charitable
- Ego-tripping

Both Virgo and Capricorn are Earth signs and hence, both of them would be well-grounded people who would have a respect for realism in their relationships and careers. Diligent, reliable and dutiful, they would, however, need to learn to be a little laidback at times. Ruled by Mercury and Saturn, respectively, they would be quite compatible as far a professional endeavours go, yet emotionality would be another issue altogether. Virgo would be able to keep his/her composure at all times with the Capricorn and the latter would, quite admire, Virgo's organised, planned way of life.

These two have plenty in common, especially when it comes to practical issues. For instance, money would never be a bone of contention between these two. Both would be equally careful about how to spend and save it. They would also, have a sound sense of realism and matter-of-factness. Well-matched with each other, they would be able to have quite a good time with each other and would also, have the incredible capacity to overlook and forgive one another easily and swiftly.

Sexually, they are compatible as well. Just that they would need to build their emotional togetherness before they enter into a sexual union. The best gift that these two have is the ability to communicate with each other with honesty and intensity. They would enjoy their lovemaking and it would become more profound and meaningful with the passage of time. The intimacy between them would develop gradually and when they express their desire for one another, their individual loyalty, affection and integrity comes to the fore. The hesitation, gentleness, exquisite intensity would make their sexual union a momentous and integral part of their relationship. It would add to its warmth, solidity and intimacy.

Astro Advice
o Men: should avoid material disruptions.
o Women: should curb over-spending.

VIRGO & AQUARIUS

 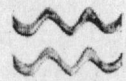

Earth Sign	*Air Sign*
Ruled by Mercury	*Ruled by Saturn*
• Prudish	• Broadminded
• Complaining	• Unpredictable
• Concentration	• Erratic
• Critical	• Negative
• Prissy	• Truthful

The alliance of Earth with Air shows the difference between the two. Moreover, the permutation of their individual rulers- Mercury & Uranus-highlights a rational and academic likeness, rather than a profound sentimental relationship. Virgo is logical and calm in approach and demeanor. Aquarius is aloof, unattached and unemotional in more ways than one. However, it is the Aquarian randomness, and eccentricity that tends to throw the placid Virgo off-guard and he/she finds it increasingly difficult to comprehend the Aquarian mystique.

This particular relationship can be quite a difficult task to handle. Since both enjoy observing the other from afar, they would need to be pushed towards each other to take the first step towards closeness. However, once they do form the bond, it would be filled with sparks and liveliness. The sharpness and logic of the Virgo is just what the imaginative and brilliant Aquarian needs.

Moreover, both are inherently gentle and sensitive and also, dream beautiful dreams deep within. They are independent yet related closely to one another. Theirs would have to be a unique and deep love.

Sexually, Aquarius would want gentleness and warmth and Virgo would be able to give the same. Virgo, however, would not be able to maintain an air of allure at all times and this may cause some dissatisfaction. Since both are not terribly oriented towards marriage, what would be the real direction of this relationship only time would tell.

Astro Advice
o Man : show your feelings by giving gifts and flowers.
o Woman wear gold bangle or bracelet.

VIRGO & PISCES

| Earth Sign | Water Sign |
Ruled by Mercury	Ruled by Neptune
• Analytical	• Apathetic
• Methodical	• Guilt
• Quick-tempered	• Cowards
• Fussy	• Humanitarian
• Prissy	• Lacking will power

The elements of Earth and Water have a natural bonding and thus, this implies that these otherwise opposite signs in the Zodiac actually, balance each other out. While Earthy Virgo is driven by logic, rationale and the like, Pisces is motivated by sentiments, perceptiveness and instincts. Together they make a wonderful pair travelling through Life with wide-eyed wonder and yet, an uncanny sense of knowing what comes next.

Both of them would have a well-established comfort level with each other and would be able to discuss practically everything under the sun. This would, also, help them to sort of any problem that might crop up along the way. Using a mix of reason, feelings and good conversation would enable them to figure out and overcome any hurdle that should ever stand in their way.

The tenderness of Virgo coupled with the compassion of Pisces would create a gentle and soulful love. They have a unique way of being able to know each other's mind and respond accordingly. Perceptive and gentle, they absorb and react to each other's vibrations with acuteness and accuracy. They share not just the good times but the sad times as well with the same amount of softness and wisdom. They are indeed well matched and well-suited. While Virgo is pure at heart, organised and sensitive, Pisces is sympathetic, intelligent and appreciative. Together they are magic.

However, there is a flip side. This, though, might be a rare occurrence. In most cases, this is a naturally compatible couple. They would combine and share everything they have-material and spiritual. Even finances, would never pose an issue with this pair.

Sexually, they would be just as compatible. Both would enjoy the act of love. Pisces' sensitivity and tact would win the gentle Virgo heart and he/she would participate with desire and sensuality. A deep love and respect for each other would merge perfectly with a strong sexual desire for each other and hence, there would be little that this relationship would ever lack. They would be partners in the true sense of the word and would be able to stand by each other through everything that comes their way. Truly, a couple that would be quite the example for many others.

Astro Advice
o Woman : telling a lie can create a problem.
o Man should wear Emerald of 8 ratti on Wednesday.

Libra–The Scales
(September 24 to October 23)
The Sign of the Statesman or Manager

How to Recognise Libra

Perhaps more than with any of the other signs of the Zodiac, the symbol for this sign, Libra-the balance-sums up very accurately the basic motivation and needs of the individual who has it emphasised in his or her birth-chart. Balance and harmony are crucial if Libra is going to function at all well, and it is the vital factor if they are going to live a fulfilled and satisfying life. Librans are not loners. They need to relate to other people in a well above average way and in all spheres of their lives, most importantly of course with a permanent partner. They have a great deal of love and affection to give to their lovers and it is only when a stable relationship is cemented that Librans become psychologically whole and function to the full. Sometimes, however, this need is so great that they will commit themselves prematurely, and as a result suffer very considerably when things go wrong. A peaceful existence is also an important priority and the theme of 'anything for a quiet life' is a recurring one. Interestingly, however, Librans need a great deal of reassurance that they are being loved, and it is not uncommon for them to go in for 'rocking the boat' tactics to get that particular reassurance. They will sometimes aggravate their partners and provoke a row-because it is so nice when they make up afterward.

Librans make easy-going parents, but will often pass the buck, A Urban mother will say 'See what Daddy says, dear' rather than come up with a straight answer, which can be more than annoying to anxious, enthusiastic children. Libran children will break down even the toughest adult defences and will wind the strictest teachers round their little fingers. Libra rules the kidneys, and those strongly influenced by this sign could be prone to slight kidney disorders. If they suffer from headaches this could be the cause. But their well- balanced lives-and the balance is so important to them-will usually ensure that they keep healthy. When it comes to choosing careers, Librans do well as agents or in any role in which they have to negotiate between two people or groups of people. They should aim always to work in partnership, and could do splendidly in the diplomatic corps.

Career and Finance

If a Libran is placed in a position of authority, which may for that reason be rather lonely, he or she may be less content than in a lower position, finding that responsibility brings stress and perhaps that decision-making does not come naturally. Librans who do get to the top should make sure that they have a team of experts or trustworthy colleagues to whom they can go for information and backing when decisions have to be made. Librans are at their best when they are working closely with other people for the good of a firm-in the way architects or lawyers work. In other words they like an atmosphere in which responsibility is shared and decisions are jointly made. Librans are usually considerate, kind, helpful and understanding. They are always ready to listen to suggestions from colleagues, which is a great asset. Their own decisions will be all the more effective if they have assimilated advice from others. Many people these days find themselves working under stress, with deadlines to meet and work constantly piling up at every moment of the day. Two things can happen to Librans under such circumstances. Either they will not survive the pace and will have to opt out, or they will keep their cool, calming down more flustered types and helping everyone to achieve a sense of balance and an overall view of the work to be done. Tact and diplomacy will probably be two of the Libra's greatest assets as far as their working lives are concerned, and very often we find them in jobs where these qualities are very much needed and can be most fully expressed.

Health and Food

On account of your having great recuperative power at the back of your constitution you are not likely to have much illness with the exception of having easily bruised flesh from which there may be some danger of tumours. In your early years you are likely to have inflamed tonsils and some trouble at the back of the tongue and throat. The kidney the back, the buttocks, generative organs are weak health zones. The nervous system is sensitive. Ugly environment and disturbed atmosphere could result in a health upset.

Suggested Food Options:

- Brown rice
- Peas
- Wheat
- Milk
- Strawberries
- Spinach
- Corn
- Avoid Sugar & starch

Your Love Life

First Decan of Libra: September 24 to October 2

Romance for you is lightness and beauty, pleasantness and happiness. Love should always be pure and bright.

These are some of the qualities that you would seek when in love and only if you find them would you have the inclination to move ahead in the relationship, else, you would merely turn away and keep looking till you meet the ideal partner.

The person, who would win your heart and keep it too, will be one who would be attractive in appearance and conduct. You would appreciate a person who spends considerable time and effort on the way he or she looks and also, the manner in which their home is kept. Neatness, beauty and freshness all appeal to you immensely. Despite the fact, that you appear frivolous and casual most of the time, when in love, you would be focused and serious only about the one you truly care for.

It is true that you would turn away and look for a more desirable partner if your current mate lets you down in any way. You would not be tied in an undesirable relationship and walking away doesn't seem difficult to you. This should not be termed as being fickle or hardhearted, it is just that you cannot give up your ideals for the sake of being with someone. You would rather be alone than be unhappy. Give yourself time and you would surely find a partner who would keep you happy for the rest of your life. It may be a long while, yet you would at the end of it all, have the most beautiful, ideal, love in your life.

Second Decan of Libra: *October 3 to October 12*

Romance for you, is an ideal state. It is above all others and what your heart truly desires is to be in love and be detached from all the mundane activities of your day to day life. Love entails flying high above all earthly restrictions and that is exactly what you would want to do when you meet the person who would make your heart sing beautiful songs. All that you would want to do then is make your retreat safe and secure from prying eyes and relax in the warmth of the affection that you receive.

When you fall in love with the right person, you soar high in the sky and enter your own dreamy, romantic world. The only hitch is that even your beloved would have slight difficulty in entering that world and hence, may have troubles in comprehending your actual depth of emotions.

When you enter the state of marriage, it would be with a lot of trust and hope. You would worship your partner and if this is reciprocated and your partner values you similarly, you would have a love that would be eternal and ethereal in quality. You are the kind who doesn't see any flaws in your beloved and the positive side to this is that your state of permanent attraction would lead to a state of lifetime bliss and contentment.

Third Decan of Libra: October 13 to October 23

All that you want from life is romance. And you would be willing to give up all that you possess for its sake. Even when you know that what your heart desires is unrealistic, you would not restrain from following it. Trusting and hopeful, you would base your love on these qualities and would not dream of questioning the motives of your beloved ever.

You desire a nice haven for your love to bloom in and you would make it more attractive by virtue of your abilities and the warmth of your love. It would give you immense happiness and contentment to be able to keep your home well kept and comfy for your beloved. You want a home where your children could be raised on love, attention and tenderness.

Peaceful and sober, you move through life at your own easy pace without disrupting anything or anyone. Your affection is calm and positive, adaptable and relaxed. Since you love in such a serene manner, you would always have an essentially affectionate and harmonious relationship with all those whom you interact with or meet.

You are generous and caring. You feel fortunate that you have been blessed with so much affection that you want to spread it all around and you would do so with grace and dignity, especially when you would play hostess to your circle of friends and also, those who you feel are deprived of this beautiful emotion.

Your Sex Life

First Decan, Venus ruled : September 24 to 2 October

Sex for you, must at all times, be sophisticated, even out of the ordinary and maybe a bit new, but what it should never be is gross or unsophisticated. Completely ruled by the planet Venus, you exhibit all the Venusian attributes-idealism, fondness for all things beautiful, opulent and stylish-in your approach towards sex as well as towards all other areas of life. You view sex as incredibly and uniquely, alluring and quite enjoy the prelude to the actual act itself. While you do have a strong desire for sex, it can decline rapidly when the scenario is boring, dull or your partner is highly straightforward or crass. These factors can reduce your sex drive immensely and instantly.

Second Decan, sub-ruled by Uranus : October 3 to 12 October

You are your own person and certainly do not conform to any pre-determined categories of sexual expression. You are interested in diversity and hence, would be attracted by anything that is novel or experimental. Just as you are attracted by variety, your reactions to sexual stimuli can also, be quite varied and erratic. You might be unmoved by stimuli that would have probably seduced other people. At the same time, you could be aroused by strange ideas, images, people, etc. though your desire for sex would be strong, it would also, be highly fickle and changeable. Truly individual and independent, it is a difficult task trying to predict what would be attractive or offensive for you and your sexual partners would have quite a tough job on their hands trying to please you and meet your standards at all times.

Third Decan, sub-ruled by Mercury: October 13 to 23 October

You are the kind of person who would enjoy debating the issue of sex more rather than indulging in the actual act. You are, also, fond of thinking about sex and enjoy the pleasure attached with the anticipation of and reminiscing about sex. Since you do have the essential Libran qualities of romanticism and fondness for opulence, these would play a significant role in determining your selection of a sexual partner and also, the situations where you would be comfortable expressing yourself sexually. Ruled by Mercury, partly, you would also, be affected by your own common sense and understanding of the real world while making your decisions about your sexual behaviour.

Libra Celebrities

Birth Date	Star	Vocation
2 October	Mahatama Gandhi	Political Leader
11 October	Amitabh Bachchan	Film Star
15 October	APJ Abdul Kalam	Scientist, Political Leader
21 September	Kareena Kapoor	Film Star
28 September	Lata Mangeshkar	Musician

Compatibility

LIBRA & ARIES

Air Sign
Ruled by Venus
- Harmonious
- Selfish
- Hospitable
- Reasonable
- Fastidious
- Escapist

Fire Sign
Ruled by Mars
- Charming
- Romantic
- Crude
- Sadistic
- Adventurous
- Optimistic

This is indeed, an interesting equation, since fire has an inherent closeness with air, yet both are opposite to each other in the zodiac, and therefore, they could both attract and keep away one another. At the start of the relationship, there is a high degree of attraction—physical or emotional between the two. However, in situations of disagreements, Aries would often gain the upper hand while Libra would feel emotionally drained and would walk away from the situation. While, most of the time,

Libra would maintain a steady and calm attitude, if fiery Aries becomes too bossy or domineering, there could be real fireworks. Libra gives the Aries bravery and a more objective and liberal motivation while Aries enthuses the Libran to become more decisive and firm with regards to his goals and aims.

In physical matters, Libra would depend on the feeling of romance and would have fun in love even when the relationship would culminate in marriage. He or she would, however, want his partner to reciprocate and therefore, Aries should be ready to be game for a long prelude to the actual act. This could range from a beautiful, candle lit dinner to a surprise vacation. What is important is that the magic should stay alive. When the relationship loses its thrill, Libra would become remote and disinterested. It is essential that any dreams that Libra has about Aries should be left as they are. Aries would need to keep up wooing the Libran with beautiful gifts and surprises. Once these minor adjustments are made, it would be smooth sailing for both.

For most part of the times, Libra would be the calming and soothing presence in this relationship, yet when the Arian pushiness becomes more than what he/she could possibly take, it would lead to trouble. Both would need to work together and learn to adapt to each other without trying to put the other one down. Since the Aries actually would value the Libran fairness and logic, he/she would try to top it. But what Aries needs to understand is that for the relationship to work, they would need to function as one unit and not rivals.

Astro Advice

o Man : avoid material disruptions and focus on your beloved.
o Women : should dress up in a white Sari with a golden border.

LIBRA & TAURUS

Air Sign Ruled by Venus	Earth Sign Ruled by Venus
• Harmonious	• Glutton
• Calculating	• Constructive
• Charming	• Sensual
• Unbalanced	• Generous
• Outgoing	• Self-centered
• Moody	• Tolerant

While the elements of Earth and Air have little in common, the ruling planet for both the signs- Venus produces a firm bond, that would thrive on shared love and liking for beautiful and comforting things. Both the signs value tranquility and synchrony and wouldn't create an atmosphere of disagreement and discord. Subtle Libra has the ability to adroitly manage the obstinate Taurus. Since both would want the pleasures of life, they would need a decent amount of money to run their household. On the whole, there wouldn't be many areas where these two would not be in accord with one another. For most part of the situation, they would learn to understand and appreciate the other's point of view.

The caring Taurus would not be the one to stir up a hornet's nest for trifling reasons. And for his/her part, Libra would be appreciative of the Taurean's ability to stay peaceful and placid in the face of all the chaos around them. Even when they do argue, the pair would be able to resolve it within next to no time and would on the surface of it be the picture of peace and harmony.

Both are ruled by the planet Venus and hence, would have little cause for concern on the sexual front. The act of love would be preceded by arranging the right tempo, atmosphere and using their creativity to the max. They would transcend the merely physical aspect and attain mental, emotional and even, spiritual fulfillment through the act of loving each other.

The strong and forceful attraction between this couple would add intensity to the sexual aspect of their affection. Emotional and tender, they would be able to mix the sensuous with the comfort of love and attain complete satisfaction, therein. This is a union of selfless love with an inherent inquisitiveness about sexual matters and along with other attributes, would lead to a powerful relationship, fulfilling and enjoyable for the partners and socially, an example to all those who are close to them. The calmness of the Taurean would pacify the impatience which Libra would often, feel and bond them together in eternal, lasting affection.

Astro Advice
o Man : curb your habit of over spending.
o Woman : impress your beloved by giving small gifts.

LIBRA & GEMINI

Air Sign *Air Sign*
Ruled by Venus *Ruled by Mercury*
- Charming
- Calculating
- Open-minded
- Intelligent

- Sociable
- Unrealistic
- Moderate
- Teases
- Gossips
- Communicative

Similarity of element along with a combination of Mercury with Venus, the Gemini-Libra relationship is indeed, one of taste, aesthetics and intelligence. A shared love of all that is pleasing to the senses, sophisticated, educative, it would involve many long discussions by the eager Gemini and received eagerly by Libra. Libra, in fact, wouldn't like being alone so the interesting new ideas and company of Gemini would prove to be perfect.

This relationship would have the quality of being blindingly brilliant and painfully whirly. Both have the knack of being incredibly fickle-minded so it would be next to impossible for one to know what comes next. The bright Gemini would enjoy a puzzle and Libra would often be one for them, so they would always remain interested and intrigued. They would, however, be much happier with themselves and their relationship if they learn to experience and enjoy the emotions more rather than merely analyse them and rationalise.

The amalgamation of exquisiteness, refinement, charisma, common sense, astuteness, radiance and mutual adulation makes them quite an irresistible couple. Spontaneous Gemini often makes a hasty choice and this for Libra is taboo. Libra can take forever when it comes to making up his/her mind and can even procrastinate about it for ages. However, it goes without saying that both are light rational beings who exist more in the head than the heart.

Sexually, they would have quite a satisfying relationship, especially since Libra is an extremely competent and sensitive lover with a fine intellect and would be able to stimulate Gemini mentally and even verbally. Sex would, however, need to go hand in hand with love and romance and life would turn into a real joyride for the two of them. Although it would be difficult to understand their relationship, yet they would have enough in it for them to feel at ease inside themselves and their physical expressions of love would have something fragile and vaguely aloof about them.

Astro Advice

o Man should wear white stone of ten ratti on Monday after Pran Pratishta (Prayer to Moon)
o Woman should wear Emerald of three ratti on Wednesday after Pran Pratishta (Prayer to Mercury).

LIBRA & CANCER

Air Sign	*Water Sign*
Ruled by Venus	*Ruled by Moon*
• Harmonious	• Shrewd
• Escapist	• King
• Moody	• Thrifty
• Loyal	• Helpless
• Balanced	• Masochistic

In spite of the fact that the elements of Water and Air are not in great harmony with one another, the planets that rule the signs-Moon and Venus, respectively are quite compatible and balance well together. Sensitive Cancer can bruise easily however; Libra is relatively calm and placid and would hardly ever hurt Cancer intentionally. Moreover, Libra would enjoy Cancer's warm affection at times, may take him/her for granted. Also, since Libra is indeed, more balanced in outlook than

Cancer, he/she might find Cancer extremely over-emotional.

This is an appealing and yet, demanding relationship. Both would need to comprehend and empathise with the other and that in itself would be a formidable task to accomplish. However, they should keep the end goal in mind and work towards it with perseverance and fortitude. Even though they are characteristically different from each other, yet they have the ability to be a wonderful couple together. With time and experience, they would learn to value each other and from then onwards, the relationship would a beautiful and expressive one. The composed Libra would be patient and understanding of Cancer yet wouldn't really go below the surface and see what lies beneath. That is something that Libra would need to develop-a deeper understanding of the seemingly hard-shelled but actually soft Cancer.

Finances would be yet another area where the two would not be able to see eye to eye. While the Cancerian would want money to gain a sense of security, the Libran would consider money earned to be money spent. While Cancer would gain maximum happiness from staying at home and keeping it warm and well-maintained, Libra would rather be out and about and socialise as much as possible. If they learn to balance their similarities and their differences in a seamless fashion, it would be a near-perfect relationship. However, if the differences crop up time and again, the stress would tell on both Cancer and Libra's mental health.

Together these two would enjoy uncovering new and fascinating things about the world and about one another. Their sex life would be understated and subtle, with good use of elements of romance, long forgotten by others. Although it might take ages for them to sort out their differences, yet in the end, it would be worth the effort and the time.

Astro Advice

- Man should wear white stone of seven ratti on Friday after Pran Pratishta (Prayer to Venus)
- Woman should wear Pearl of five ratti on Monday after Pran Pratishta (Prayer to Moon).

LIBRA & LEO

Air Sign Ruled by Venus	Fire Sign Ruled by Sun
• Harmonious	• Responsible
• Graceful	• Glory seeker
• Moody	• Cutting
• Fair-minded	• Vital
• Reasonable	• Popular

The natural affinity of Fire and Air would have a bearing on this relationship which would, of course, have many good things about it. Both Leo and Libra would have a common interest and liking for most of the finer things of life and would build many cheerful memories together. They would also, balance each other out. The level-headed Libra would help to keep the normally flashy and overgenerous Leo on an even keel.

The relationship would be a success mainly because there would be many channels of communication between the two. They would be friends and lovers, and hence, would share a natural and genuine bonding. They would take on life with all its ups and downs with vim and vigour. The usual development of understanding would have to be taken care of, though. The Leo would need to realise that when Libra wants to talk things out, he/she doesn't mean a yelling match. Similar adjustments would have to be made by Libra as well.

This is a relationship that could culminate in anything, from a strong friendship to a loving marriage or even, just a memorable affair. There is a great deal of common ground here so life seems much happier when they're together. They're both just and generous. Also, they have a fair amount of realism blended with their sunny optimism. Just that arrogant Leo's incessant demands might irk the sensitive Libra to the point of becoming really angry. Irrespective, Libra does admire Leo for all his/her good qualities-honesty, nerve, sense of humour and charisma. The adoring, stylish Leo will endearingly pay beautiful compliments to Libra which would heal any injury or hurt that the latter may have felt. With a smattering of tiffs, both would eventually realise that theirs is indeed a love that is meant to be. This is one relationship that can easily withstand the test of time.

Their compatibility extends to the sexual domain as well. The Lion is a sensuous and royal figure while the Libran is fascinating and enticing. Both make great lovers since they are expressive and emotional with each other. The intensity of their passions is well matched and their laidback approach would work wonders in this day of rush and haste. Each aspect of this relationship augurs well for both of them.

Astro Advice
o Men you should not lack motivation, ambition, or drive to face the challenges.
o Women you should sense the potential and look forward to what's ahead.

LIBRA & VIRGO

Air Sign *Earth Sign*
Ruled by Venus *Ruled by Mercury*

- Insincere
- Kind
- Moderate
- Hair-splitting
- Amiable

- Intellectual
- Thorough
- Tactless
- Forceful
- Neat

Two signs who have quite a few characteristic differences and yet, would be able to exist in peace and harmony with each other. While Virgo is quiet and polite; Libra is quick and razor-sharp. The sensitive, tranquil Virgo would accept the Libran rationale, sunny positivism and lengthy discourses with ease and patience. Virgo would cheerfully move through life in Libra's company and everything would be tuneful and synchronised. In fact, it would be Virgo who would give up a lot and adjust many times for the sake of Libra's peace of mind and for the relationship to move to a higher level. However, this doesn't mean that Libra would take Virgo for granted. The Libra sense of fairness wouldn't ever allow that. Rather, Libra would be touched by the sacrifices Virgo makes and would try his/her very best to return them.

The calming presence of the Virgo would be like a breath of fresh air for the Libran, especially when he/she is sad or disturbed. Together this would be a couple who would do quite a bit of introspection and discard attributes which they feel are negative and fortify the ones they wish to develop. They, however, might be unduly worried about seemingly minor issues and this might rock the boat every now and then. They might also, not be able to express each and every sentiment at the appropriate moment and this might cause some confusions. But this means that they should be fairer and more tolerant of each other and see what lies beneath the surface when they assess and evaluate their partners.

The Virgo-Libra couple normally finds out an exceptional type of peace and satisfaction when they come together in a sexual union. The closeness that this gives them is at all levels, soothing and comforting.

Indeed, this is a relationship where the sexual aspect has many dimensions and every single dimension gives the relationship a uniqueness and happiness beyond description.

Astro Advice
o Man : your beloved needs emotional security.
o Woman : try to be honest and straightforward.

LIBRA & LIBRA

Air Sign	*Air Sign*
Ruled by Venus	*Ruled by Venus*
• Beautiful	• Beautiful
• Loyal	• Loyal
• Indulgent	• Indulgent
• Vain	• Vain
• Selfish	• Selfish

Ruled by Venus-the planet which symbolises balance, synchrony and attractiveness and with the element of Air running through them, a Libra-Libra couple is indeed, one that would hardly see any disagreement or clash. For one, these disturbing situations tend to shake the Libran sense of equilibrium and moreover, it just goes against their basic temperament. Hence, their carefree and laidback attitude would ensure that there is no disruption for most part of the time. On the other hand, since they would both be laidback, there are fair chances that progress and growth would be relatively slow and laborious.

When two Librans get together, they would be a lot of communication flowing freely between them. Aside from their famed indecision and sense of justice, Librans have the touchingly sweet knack of being able to give the other one a feeling of serenity and quietness with just their presence. Their hearts would forever, have positivism and faith inside and they would move through life on their strength.

Librans of either sex would be aware of the fact that if their positive characteristics become stronger when they're together, the negative ones would also, be similarly affected. The green-eyed monster or envy is one such trait and since both men and women would be attractive and friendly, there would be many instances where this harmful feeling could come up. However, it would do both immense good, if they nip such feelings right in the bud and trust their partners implicitly.

Beautifully would they complement each other. While the Libra man would be prosperous financially, the Libra woman would make a graceful lady of the house and together they would spread warmth, cheer and exquisite taste through the home and family.

Physically, they would be dynamite and ever innovative. They would keep their partner wondering about what could be in store for them. The intellectual and emotional compatibility would definitely translate into sexual bonding and intimacy. Sex between them would always be exciting and new since they would ensure that it never loses its spark. They would be dedicated and adoring till the end of time.

Astro Advice
o Men : curb your habit of over spending.
o Woman : should wear light colour clothes.

LIBRA & SCORPIO

 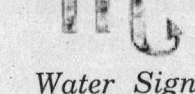

Air Sign	*Water Sign*
Ruled by Venus	*Ruled by Mars*
• Good-taste	• Creative
• Thoughtless	• Revengeful
• Tactful	• Positive
• Insincere	• Brave
• Vacillating	• Determined

While it may be true that the combination of Venus and Mars can result in a profound and intense attraction at many levels, it is also, true that the sensitive Libra may feel weighed down by the force and passion of Scorpio's feelings. The possible way that these two can attain bliss in each others' company is by giving each other a fair amount of happiness and since, both would be eager to do so, this would never be a problem. The magnetic attraction of Scorpio and the graceful appeal of Libra would come together to form an irresistible relationship.

Although, these two might be hesitant to get together yet there would be some crackling chemistry between them. It wouldn't be easy for the ever charming Libra to mould the tough Scorpio; however, the latter would definitely be tender and would feel quite desolate when neglected by the flirtatious Libran. The explicit preferences of Scorpio can sometimes, irk the more balanced Libran.

The fair, intellectual Libra would be quite intrigued by the Scorpio's passive expressions and would spend time deciphering them. Libra is, indeed, quick and sharp and this would be something that Scorpio would appreciate and respect. Both would have a strong intelligence and would want to help each other realise their dreams and ambitions. The cool, clear analysis of Libra would help Scorpio gain more focus and clarity while the Scorpio would strengthen Libran resolve with his/her dedication and integrity. Since both would be logical and would like to debate issues, disagreements would often stretch over hours and hours. There would, of course, be times when the determined Scorpio might seem somewhat revengeful, however, this would soon fade out and once they make up, life would be back to normal and everything would be forgotten.

Sexually, Libra would be sentimental, emotional and gently loving and all this would attract the Scorpio who does crave for deep love and gentleness. For his/her part, Scorpio would be an intense lover who would want to give Libra all the love, tenderness and fulfillment, emotionally, mentally and sexually.

Astro Advice

o Woman should wear Pearl of three ratti on Monday
o Man should trust his beloved.

LIBRA & SAGITTARIUS

Air Sign	Fire Sign
Ruled by Venus	Ruled by Jupiter
• Outgoing	• Tolerant
• Sympathetic	• Sloppy
• Escapist	• Dependable
• Jealous	• Sporting
• Unbalanced	• Disloyal

The elements of Air and Fire would be in harmony with each other in this relationship, since the planets that rule the signs-Venus and Jupiter are also, in harmony. The planets will bless the couple with affection, joy and prosperity throughout life. Even though Libra would want to spend more time with Sagittarius, he/she would be intelligent enough to respect the Archer's need to be free and unburdened. On the other hand, Sagittarius would be able to indulge and even pamper Libra to a fault.

Both Libra and Sagittarius are quick on the uptake and good conversationalists. They are also, immensely charismatic and can keep each other and even people around them captivated for hours. Whenever both are in a room, there would not be a single dull moment. They would have many good-natured arguments but at the end of it all, there would remain the old camaraderie and love for each other. Sadly, though, this relationship may appear ideal and idyllic, it would rarely if ever last for ever. Simply because both of them need change, novelty and movement in their lives and this would become difficult after a point. However for as long as it would last and even after, there would be many happy memories to cherish.

The gregarious Sagittarian dislikes being alone and hence, would appreciate the sweet and stimulating company of the Libran. Also, the Libran would enjoy being loved by Sagittarius since it would involve plenty of bright positivism and intelligent conversations. The fair-minded Libra values sincerity and optimism and hence, would relish the Sagittarius company. However, since both would be good-looking and friendly, there could be a few jealous moments now and then. Also, it is unlikely that this relationship would materialise into something permanent, since both have a tendency to link sex with love. What would happen would be that both would become good friends and their relationship would always, hold happiness and pleasant thoughts for both.

As a lover, the archer would cater beautifully to the Libran who would enjoy being wooed and appreciated. They would surely have something beautiful and remarkable with one another.

Astro Advice
o Man should wear yellow sapphire of seven ratti on Thursday.
o Woman should wear white stone of four ratti on Monday.

LIBRA & CAPRICORN

Air Sign Ruled by Venus	Earth Sign Ruled by Saturn
• Jealous	• Trustworthy
• Beautiful	• Calculating
• Considerate	• Hardworking
• Moody	• Limited
• Charming	• Manipulator

Since Air and Water do not blend easily enough, it is essential that this pair have a mutual goal in mind or that Fate smiles upon them, for a relationship to blossom and grow. Libra would want to be given love and appreciation and would wish to see these sentiments being demonstrated, however, Capricorn wouldn't be the sort who would really enjoy doing all these things and this would disappoint the gentle, sensitive Libran. Moreover, Libra would take pleasure in straightforwardness, comfort and the finer things of life. On the contrary, Capricorn would have a more solemn approach towards life and would be able to deal with a lack of financial resources and a life of simplicity without much trouble. To ensure that Libra doesn't wallow in pity, Capricorn would have to keep in mind, to display his/her love and affection for Libra every now and then.

Although, emotionally, they may need to build a stronger understanding, in most other areas of life, this partnership would be quite a dynamic one. Libra-Capricorn couples have a great deal of perseverance and are quite focused on their goals in life. They would strive determinedly to attain whatever they wished to and would be able to reach the pinnacles of success and glory. Together, they would be a powerhouse of energy, enthusiasm and electric vitality.

The Libran would be a picture of elegance, gentleness and melodious beauty blended together however, it is quite a possibility that a conservative, morose Capricorn might ignore all the attractiveness of Libra and be highly aloof.

Their sexual union can be brought about only by a series of tactful attempts by both of them. Their ruling planets- Venus and Saturn are powerful ones and it is possible that the fact that they are opposite, characteristically, might serve to bring them closer to each other. Both would want to take dissimilar directions and this could either build the sexual tension or thwart it completely. A great deal is dependent on their personal ambitions, wants and horoscopes. Temperamental, one would often find either one of them teetering on the line between happiness and sadness. This would be a challenging pair, indeed. Happiness would lie in their hands and they would need to make the necessary adjustments and compromises to keep the relationship going.

Astro Advice
o Woman should dress up in a traditional outfit with a matching bindi.
o Man should avoid dreaming.

LIBRA & AQUARIUS

 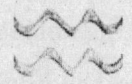

| Air Sign | Air Sign |
| Ruled by Venus | Ruled by Saturn |

- Considerate
- Jealous
- Good-taste
- Hospitable
- Fastidious

- Broadminded
- Eccentric
- Disruptive
- Inefficient
- Cowardly

The natural affinity between Air and Air brings these two signs in close proximity with each other and they would take pleasure in and even depend upon the company of one another. While Libra would symbolise the personal; Aquarius would signify the universal and together they would be able to create a relationship filled with tact, understanding, sharing and loving. Since Aquarius is somewhat erratic in disposition, Libra would need to demonstrate discretion and not annoyance, to handle the independent Water-bearer. Both would, as a matter of fact, give each other plenty of space and freedom and yet have a close bond filled with intimacy.

The two of them would enjoy honing their intellect and would engage in intelligent and meaningful discussions which would interest, enthuse and motivate them. The dreamy Libran would dream while the practical Aquarius would try to realise them or see their futility. While this could be amusing for sometime, after a point, it might tend to get on their nerves. However, whatever may be the case; it could always be resolved by a bit of compromise and adjustment. Also, Libra would always be able to forgive Aquarius and there wouldn't be any hard feelings.

Libra-Aquarius couples share many interests; especially in travel, the arts, children and even spirituality. They have an inherent compatibility and a strong appreciation for one another which would help them to actualise whatever they intend to. Both have a common interest in children, education, philosophy arts and foreign travel. The laidback Libra revels in opulence, ease and all the good things; this could well be in contradiction with the pragmatic Aquarian's desire to serve humanity and society. However, there is nothing that is grossly conflicting with these two and hence, can always be taken care of by cooperating and adjusting.

As far as their sexual relations go, Libra would want Aquarius to play the dominant part in bed and this could lead to frustrations and discord in the bedroom but in spite of all this, there would be a certain peacefulness and stillness whenever these two would make love.

It is quite a possibility that Aquarius with might not have given much importance to sex before this, however, one meeting Libra, he/she would definitely change this opinion. Libra is a spontaneous lover and would eventually win over the normally reticent Aquarian. Aquarius could also, learn how to be as innovative and inventive in bed as he/she is outside it. The simple truth of the matter being that both require each other immensely and hence, would try hard to please and satisfy the other. They are in perfect sync with each other and complete each other.

Astro Advice

o Men should avoid fickleness in love.
o Woman : your sweet words work like a magic cure on your beloved.

LIBRA & PISCES

Air Sign
Ruled by Venus
- Kind
- Selfish
- Vacillating
- Thoughtless
- Sociable

Water Sign
Ruled by Neptune
- Sympathetic
- Deceptive
- Creative
- Talented
- Psychic

Even though the elements of Air and Water are not terribly close, the natural bonding between their respective ruling planets enables this couple to enjoy each other. They would have some similar preferences, despite the differences in their personalities and would get pleasure from the finer things in life as also, the values and qualities of sensitivity, balance, love, companionship and the joys of being in love with someone. The Libran fair-mindedness and rationality would balance the Piscean indecisiveness, unrealism, and mental disarray.

This particular relationship is a calming and comforting one. Both would be unaware as to why they are where they are. They would, in all likelihood, be brought together by destiny and once together, they would want to explore the other person completely and interpret their personalities. How these two would conduct themselves and actualise their ambitions, inspirations and desires would have a deep impact on the people around them.

Although, Libra and Pisces might not fall in love instantly, once they do meet by chance or circumstance, they manage to combine their dissimilarities in a beautifully seamless fashion and make the best of what they have. They are intelligent and emotional, sensitive and tasteful. They appreciate tranquility and are not belligerent. Since Libra is nearly always attractive and alluring, it becomes easy for Pisces to be drawn to him/her at a mental, emotional and physical level. When Pisces returns the feelings of Libra, the former becomes intense and more devoted to the fish. As for Pisces, he/she would give Libra complete loyalty and dedication. Even though, this relationship may not run its full course, there are many chances that it would be filled with happiness, positivism and radiance.

Astro Advice

o Woman should respond vibrantly to the feelings and ideas of his beloved.
o Man should improve his tolerance power.

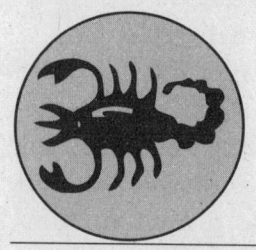

Scorpio–The Scorpion
(October 24–November 22)
The Sign of the King or President

How to Recognise Scorpio

This, the eighth sign of the Zodiac, is the strongest, offering the greatest resources of both emotional and physical energy. Those born with Scorpio prominently placed in their birth-chart must find ways of using these resources positively and in a fulfilling way. This is best achieved by expression in a career. No mere 'job' is good enough for a high-powered Scorpio-they should spend their working hours doing something they consider worthwhile as well as engrossing. Scorpio emotional intensity is terrific and this, too, needs positive direction and expression through a rewarding sex-life. However, the sexy element of this sign is often somewhat overstressed. It is vitally important to most Scorpios and probably in an above-average way, but there are many other ways in which their energy can be directed, and as I have hinted it is very often through the achievement of daunting objectives, It is also true that this drive and determination can sometimes become obsessive, and it is important that the individual realises that he or she may tend to become too involved. If this happens, other factors in life may be neglected, which might eventually lead to a kind of imbalance which is not healthy either physically or psychologically. However, this in itself is probably preferable to the reverse situation-inactivity caused by unemployment or some other reason not directly connected with the Scorpio himself, restlessness, stagnation and discontent are the greater evils.

Scorpios are the natural detectives of the Zodiac. They make superb researchers, working scientifically or in libraries. Many engineers are Scorpios, as are prominent members of the armed services. The wine and oil trades are also attractive to Scorpios. From a purely physical point of view this Zodiac type needs a lot of exercise, and many will enjoy demanding sports. Boxing, the martial arts in general, diving and underwater swimming are all rewarding and popular. The Scorpio body-area is the genitals, and it may well be this connection that has given Scorpio the sexiest image of all the twelve signs. There is a vulnerability to throat infections due to the influence of the Scorpio polar sign, Taurus. Scorpios make demanding but exciting partners. They have a great love of life and never do things by half. They need partners with a similar attitude to life. Although many are of a wiry build, more tend to put on weight, usually due to good living, and this is something that needs conscious controlling. Alas, Scorpios do not find it easy to cut down-in any way. Scorpios want their children to be as energetic and as fulfilled as they are themselves and will be demanding but inspiring parents.

Career and Finance

Power is extremely important in the Scorpio scheme of things, especially where the career is concerned. They cope easily with it and enjoy doing so. Sometimes they use their power mischievously to give themselves a little harmless fun, and occasionally they can, unfortunately, abuse it. But when Scorpios use power responsibly they can do so with great resoluteness, reaching decisions swiftly with the aid of knowledge that they have acquired over the years. When power is backed up with knowledge and experience in this way it can be a great force for good. As to the abuse of power, Scorpios with Pluto in Leo should be particularly aware that they can be tempted in this direction and should make sure that they use any power they have justly and with a sense of responsibility. Otherwise they could become autocratic, and many negative facets of their personality could emerge. Tradition links iron with Scorpio, but today we also think of steel as a Scorionic metal, and this is borne out when we consider the sort of careers that Scorpios follow. Many are attracted to engineering, mining or the construction industry. Heavy armaments can also attract them, which may be the reason why so many Scorpios are drawn to the armed services. Although of course Scorpios are found in all sorts of careers, there does seem to be an emphasis of this sort.

Health and Food

You have a strong constitute with phenomenal stamina. You are short in breath. You will be liable to fever of all kinds high blood pressure and over strain of the heart. You will meet with many accidents chiefly those caused by machines, also from fire arms. You are prone to accident and likely to meet violent mobs who can create injuries on your head and brain. The sex organs, throats , tonsils are the sensitive health zones. Drugs and drinks should be avoided at all costs. Health seeking habits arc prominent. Your cell salt is Calcium sulphate used in the repair of tissues. In the diet make it a point to include onions, greens, cauliflowers and cereals.

Suggested Food Options:
- Onion
- Mustard
- Cabbage
- Fish
- Honey
- Radish
- Coconut

Your Love Life

First Decan of Scorpio : October 24 to Novemeber 2

You enjoy reminiscing about all the happy days gone by and relish the warmth the memories fill you with. This, perhaps, is one of the reasons why you do not feel isolated even when you are by yourself. Since you do have a naturally powerful and dominating personality, it might happen that your marriage would be a one-sided affair. You must learn to let your partner also, participate and enrich the relationship equally.

Give your partner the security that each individual craves in a relationship. Also, give your partner the feeling that he or she is wanted and needed. Display a genuine and keen interest in the lives and happenings of your mate. Though you are really hardworking and enjoy the pleasure that doing everything single-handedly gives you, you must not forget that by doing so, you are undermining the capabilities of your partner and that is something which no one would really like. Share your work and chores so that both of you feel equally valued and worthwhile. This would be crucial to filling your marriage with happiness and bliss.

Inherently strong-willed, you wouldn't really enjoy being told to change or made to do something that you don't like. However, if your partner uses the right combination of tact and persuasion, you could be moulded well. You would also, try to penetrate the thoughts and ideas of your partner yet would keep your own well guarded and hidden. Try not to do this, since it would give your partner the feeling that he really doesn't know you that well.

Don't always try to dominate and be the strong one in your relationship. Although your love and affection for your mate may be intense and profound, it cannot really negate the ill-effects of being too dominating. Seek a partner who would be highly understanding and would let you be the person you want to yet at the same time, do not be too overpowering and overshadowing in your relationship.

Second Decan of Scorpio: November 3 November 12

You are so deep and profound sexually that you tend to become emotionally involved as well with your sexual partner which implies that you might go through a string of relationships which wouldn't really hold much meaning for you. It would be in your best interests not to link romance and sex together too often, else you'd only end up getting hurt.

You crave excitement and novelty and consider that marriage would bring you only monotony. Hence, you try to build up a life other than your married life. This would only create problems. Try not to do this. You do enjoy having a partner to talk to and share your views, opinions, happiness and sorrows with. Hence, the relationship of marriage does hold meaning and value for you.

You appreciate a well maintained home and a family that would appeal to your intellect and aesthetic sense as well. When you would have these, you wouldn't want to lose them by indulging in any kind of immoral or illicit activity. You like to be looked upto and wouldn't really appreciate being relegated to the background by your partner. At the same time, you need to respect and honour your spouse's individualism and adjust, discuss and listen to each other. Just as you want to know your partner completely, so does he or she. Therefore, do not behave in a secretive manner, rather let there be openness and trust between the two of you.

The intricacies of the human mind intrigue you and you are also, interested in the secrets of the mystical and unknown. Mundane matters hold little interest for you and therefore, your partner must be one who would be able to relate to this interests and converse with you intelligently about them.

Third Decan of Scorpio: November 13 to November 22

In affairs of the heart, you tend to be very passionate. As a result, you become helpless and at risk of being hurt. You may get disappointed by minor things and you may feel distressed by imaginary causes. Only if you would curb your fantastic imagination and your tendency to doubt your partner would you be able to enjoy a happy and satisfying married life.

Your sexual inclinations make you quite determined and you wouldn't really let go of your partner. Neither would your mate want to do so considering that you would hold your partner quite spell bound with your magic. Though you wouldn't really give up your confidence in the power of love yet you wouldn't want to continue with a marriage which wouldn't let you exercise your power sexually in the manner you wish to.

You do have the tendency to hurt your beloved by twisting love in a distorted manner. However, you would also, feel bad and would try to make up for your behaviour so that the future would remain unsullied and not hold any ill will between you and your partner.

What you want is a happy marriage, however, your passion and sensitive temperament tend to pull you away from fulfilling this desire. You need to take control of yourself and calm your violent and powerful feelings so that life would be peaceful and balanced. Choose the words you say with caution and your expressions with care, give your partner the trust that he rightfully deserves and life wouldn't be dismal at all.

Your Sex Life

First Decan, Pluto-ruled: October 24 to November 2

Born under this powerful and enigmatic sign, you are bestowed with a strong and intense sex drive, yet, at the same time, this doesn't imply that you would be highly active sexually. In fact, your level of sexual activity may be a little low, particularly, if you are involved with something that takes up most of your time and energy. This sign of the zodiac is a sign which may swing to two polarities of the spectrum- at one time, you would have the greatest restraint on your sexual activity and at another, you would be the most sexually active person ever. Another factor that plays quite a significant role in your sex life would be your emotional state of mind and the strength and depth of your emotions.

Second Decan, sub-ruled by Neptune: November 3 to 13 November

Although you do possess the fundamental Scorpio traits and features, you have an extra amount of idealism and also, the inclination to indulge in a variety of sexual fantasies. While you may involve yourself in this, you would look for a realisation of the same in your partners. Deeply imaginative and creative, you extend your creativity to your sex life and enrich it by virtue of your vivid imagination. You are also, quite intense emotionally and have a fondness for sensual pleasures. More often than not, you would have a strong desire for sex and would look for novel ways of satisfying the same.

Third Decan, sub-ruled by the Moon: November 14 to 22 November

Yours is the sex drive that would be more often than not, satisfied in your married life. You would consider marriage, home and family as critical to your sex life and impulses. You would use sex as an essential means of creating new life and filling your world with affection, dedication and warmth for your partner and your family. While you do have a powerful sex drive, it would be integrally bound up with your emotional frame of mind, your temperaments, emotions, and the sense of security that you get from your relationship as such.

Scorpio Celebrities

Birth Date	Star	Vocation
1 November	Aishwarya Rai	Film Star
2 November	Shah Rukh Khan	Film Star
3 November	Amartya Sen	Economist
14 November	Pt Jawahar Lal Nehru	Political Leader
30 October	H J Bhabha	Scientist

Compatibility

SCORPIO & ARIES

Water Sign
Ruled by Mars
- Over-sexed
- Magnetic

Fire Sign
Ruled by Mars
- Headstrong
- Enjoys challenges

- Survivors
- Boastful
- Obsessed
- Dynamic
- Confident
- Brash
- Hot tempered
- Go getter

The fire-water alliance is, indeed, one which is filled with potential for both good and bad. Since both these signs are ruled by the planet Mars, there would exist a reciprocal recognition of the positive points of each other. While straightforward Aries wouldn't really be too aware and even, appreciative of the hidden ways of Scorpio, this partnership would benefit from their fondness for working as a team, as long as they agree upon the goals that they wish to achieve. Scorpio adds value to the relationship by his/her immense dedication and principled temperament. At the same time, these two would also, have the ability to ruin one another. Aries might show an inclination to become unusually quiet and subdued in difficult times. However, during more pleasant times, the Scorpio would be able to give energy to the relationship as long as he/she maintains a balanced and liberal attitude towards the Aries' casual and amiable outlook.

While the Scorpio is not the sort to bother too much about appearances, the Aries can be quite conceited about the way they as well their partners' look. Capable and brave, the Aries would value Scorpio's smooth, affectionate and somewhat erotic voice. While the journey of life with a Scorpio may not be a bed of roses, with time and patience, it would definitely be a mature and harmonious relationship.

When it comes to physical matters, the Scorpio's possessive temperament would become stifling at times for the liberal Arian. Scorpio has a high sex drive and is an extremely ardent lover and this would need to be accepted by the Aries, if problems are to be avoided. The physical magnetism between the two can be quite powerful and permanent. The combination of love with sex is something that both find mutually gratifying and personally exhilarating. Deep inside, the Aries is sincere, virginal and childlike and in the same way, Scorpio is unique, alluring and inexplicable. They would definitely have the ability to build with each other a relationship filled with conviction and clemency.

Astro Advice
o Focus on good habits and avoid intoxication.
o Maintain diets and fitness routines.

SCORPIO & TAURUS

Water Sign *Ruled by Mars*	*Earth Sign* *Ruled by Venus*
• Magnetic	• Good taste
• Jealous	• Tenacious
• Creative	• Avaricious
• Greedy	• Slow
• Positive	• Practical
• Resourceful	• Persistent

Even though the element of Earth is well-matched with Water, the signs of Taurus and Scorpio are conflicting signs. To start with, in affairs of the heart, this conflict might result in attraction between the two, but with the passage of time, the emotion of love might give way to negative feelings unless the pair shares mutual interests and likings. Both have an inclination to be over domineering and hence, would need to trust each other implicitly. Since the strength of their emotions would be great, they would need to guard themselves against getting pulled into a whirlpool of emotional turmoil. When it comes to similarities, both would be distant with strangers and wouldn't be too great when it comes to communicating. They would believe in saying just what they have to in an unelaborated, simple, straightforward fashion.

Taurus and Scorpio would, both, have an unwavering confidence in their ability to judge the good from the bad and right from the wrong. When it comes to religion, they would either believe in God truly or doubt His existence. This is, indeed, a relationship that would have plenty of sparks flying considering how different yet alike the two are.

Realistic Taurus is certainly not irrational, erratic, impetuous or vague. Once the Bull has made up his/her mind that the Scorpion is the love of his/her life, there would be no looking back. Both would be equally faithful and devoted in their affections for each other.

While Taurus is ruled by Venus-the planet symbolising tranquility and love, Scorpio is ruled by Mars-the planet symbolising volatile passions and secrecy. The sexual attraction between the two would also, be filled with wondrous and unknown revelations. Scorpio would, also, regard the experience of sex as a sacred and spiritual quest and hence, satisfy the Taurean with tenderness and genuineness. The act of love is one of passion-emotional, mental and spiritual and though they would gain much out of it, this wouldn't be a determining factor to sustain the relationship. Considerable compromises and changes would have to be made by both of them so as to live a life filled with admiration and deep love rather than with bitterness and anger.

Astro Advice

o Man should dress up in casual wear but remember that strips will suit you.
o Woman : dress up in a traditional outfit with a red bindi on your forehead.

SCORPIO & GEMINI

Water Sign
Ruled by Mars
- Fanatical
- Constructive
- Resourceful
- Proud
- Sincere

Air Sign
Ruled by Mercury
- Adaptable
- Charming
- Selfish
- Fanciful
- Sharp-tounged

Extremely different, this is one relationship that would be made up of markedly opposite souls trying to battle it out together. Gemini with its element of Air, does not have the depth and passion of Scorpio, with its element as Water and would feel weighed down by such compelling and mesmerising influences. Moreover, the freedom loving Gemini would feel suffocated by Scorpio's possessiveness.

Usually Gemini and Scorpio would never get together unless someone makes a deliberate effort of pairing them with each other. Their complete lack of similarities and shared interests doesn't really allow that. However, when they do get together, regardless of the differences, there is considerable dedication on the part of Scorpio and similar amount of mysterious fascination of the Gemini towards the scorpion and these qualities would enable to weave tender, vague dreams with each other and even work towards realising those dreams.

This union is a fine specimen of how a couple's sex life is affected by what happens beyond the four walls of the bedroom. They would definitely come closer to each other because of the act of love yet a nagging insecurity could lead to frequent tiffs due to which the intense Scorpio may find solace in alcohol and the like. However, if they are sure about their partner one hundred per cent, they would be fiercely passionate and profound when expressing themselves sexually. One must not overlook the fact that while Scorpio has a strong sex drive, for Gemini, sex is just yet another thing to be explored and not all that significant. Hence, it is Scorpio who would often play the wooer and pursuer. Gemini would be more influenced by the scorpion's intellect and charisma.

Astro Advice
o You both should need to develop faith in each other.
o Women should apply light colour mascara.

SCORPIO & CANCER

Water Sign *Water Sign*
Ruled by Mars *Ruled by Moon*
- Magnetic
- Greedy
- Power-tripping
- Healers
- Courageous

- Ambitious
- Protective
- Loving
- Tenacious
- Retiring

Although the element Water is common for both, yet compatibility might not exist naturally within this relationship. Particularly, during times of arguments and disagreements, one would find that emotions would run high and disturb the equilibrium that existed during peaceful times. Since the element of Water would give both the signs high emotionality, this would come into play more during the difficult times. However, when everything would be fine, this would be a fantastic team and would show each other great understanding, trust and respect.

The attraction between the two might be instant and nearly magnetic, especially for Cancer. Though this might seem like an unlikely relationship, more often than not, it has a happy ending. Both are intuitive and would have many qualities-good and bad, in common. Their profound understanding of each other would result in the formation of a strong support system for both of them.

Both, Cancer and Scorpio are fiercely devoted, intense and infinitely tender, hence, when they come together, the relationship radiates warmth, affection and security. The challenging Scorpio enjoys pulling the Cancerian leg a little and the easy going Cancer enjoys matching the Scorpio's steady gaze for as long as possible. Fun, tender and affectionate. That is precisely what this relationship would be.

However, it is not as if everything would always be hunky-dory. There can be times when the temperamental, exacting Cancerian can throw a tantrum or when intense, passionate Scorpio can be too focused on his/her own idea of love. That is when disagreements could occur and throw a spanner in the works. Scorpio would need to show greater understanding of gentle Cancer and Cancer would need to be more empathetic of Scorpio and his/her views and ideas.

As far as the sexual aspect of the relationship is concerned, Scorpio would definitely be more passionate than Cancer, who in turn, would be romantic and whimsical about love. This blend would create a blissful union which would have a mutual attraction and an encouraging note in it. Both would endeavour to fill the sexual union with gentleness and softness which would make it truly an act of love. Their deep-seated passion gives them a devotion to love akin to spiritual zeal. This particular bond would create beautiful things if both love and sex go hand in hand and the usual adjustments are made without any ado.

Astro Advice
o Both should understand each others feelings.
o Woman should be confident while speaking.

SCORPIO & LEO

Water Sign	Fire Sign
Ruled by Mars	Ruled by Sun
• Boastful	• Superior
• Determined	• Leader
• Venomous	• Inexperienced
• Revengeful	• Vital
• Healers	• Jealous

The merging of Fire and Water along with the coming together of two strong and determined signs, would, indeed, result in a relationship that could become earthshaking. A consequence that can be avoided only if both agree to give each other their space and also, respect each others' individuality. If they learn to live and work together, these two can achieve great things and have great times in each others' company. Yet there would be times when the straightforward Leo would disagree with the secrecy, and craftiness that Scorpio would employ to achieve his/her means.

When it concerns things that they have in common, both Leo and Scorpio have a genuine, deep-seated mutual reverence. When they come together, they have their own unique intimacy and bonding. Perceptive Scorpio would intuitively know when proud Leo is injured or disturbed and would try to soothe and calm his/her frayed nerves. However, in a relationship that lacks this profound understanding, the charm may wear off sooner than expected and nothing would materialise out of the relationship.

While Leo is sunny, gregarious and extroverted, Scorpio is more worldly wise and philosophical, yet with a bit of understanding; they would balance each other and exist in perfect harmony. Money matters would pose a problem, since the Lion enjoys spending while for Scorpio that would be sacrilege. If they feel strongly about the relationship, they would be able to live happily forever. Leo can spoil Scorpio with an abundance of unconditional love while Scorpio can give Leo a sense of stability and steadfastness. Though the Lion may seem teasing in nature, he/she would be incredibly devoted to the Scorpion.

Sexually, they could have both good days and not-so-good days. There would be times when passions would rage high followed by days of detached coolness. Sporadic is probably the best way to describe its nature.

Astro Advice

o Man should wear Pearl of six ratti on Monday.
o Woman : avoid being stubborn.

SCORPIO & VIRGO

| Water Sign | Earth Sign |
| Ruled by Mars | Ruled by Mercury |
- Magnetic
- Devious
- Power-tripping
- Strong-willed
- Over-sexed

- Truthful
- Voyeuristic
- Busy
- Tactless
- Wide awake

The blending of Earth and Water would be quite positive in matters of the mind and day-to day life. However, as far as, matters of the heart go, it would leave much to be desired. While Virgo is more restrained and self-possessed with feelings, Scorpio tends to be passionate and fiery.

Highly pragmatic yet tender, Virgos tend to bring out the protector in the Scorpio who is indulgent with them and doesn't consider them a danger. The soothing aura that Virgo exudes tends to make the Scorpio feel rejuvenated and at the same time, calm. These two would have a fair enough understanding of their abilities and limitations and would never form unreasonable expectations from the other. Neither one of them would ever take the other for granted. There would exist at all times, a high level of mutual respect. After the relationship is formed and become firm, Virgo would cherish the unwavering dedication of the Scorpio immensely while Scorpio would value the Virgo's honesty and gentleness.

A Virgo-Scorpio couple would always, enjoy being able to give something of themselves to others. The desire to serve is strong in both. When saddened by something,

they would sensibly resort to open communication and
think with both their hearts and their heads. They share
a mutual respect for honesty, uprightness, knowledge and
a focused aim. More often than not, these two would be
friends first and then lovers and would not be afraid of
standing up for each other. However, it is unlikely that
they would plunge headlong into a relationship with each
other. The attraction is more likely to be built over a
period of time rather than be instantaneous.

Sexually, since both would be somewhat hesitant and
reticent, there could be a certain restraint in their
demonstrations of love and affection. They would need
to make a few adjustments and with the passage of time,
there would be an intensity in their lovemaking that
would definitely, bring them to a higher level of intimacy
and sharing.

Astro Advice

o Women should wear any sort of head accessory it
  would be eye catching.
o Man should wear grey colour and the neckline should
  have a V–shape.

SCORPIO & LIBRA

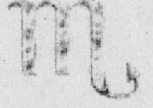 

Water Sign	Air Sign
Ruled by Mars	Ruled by Venus
• Creative	• Good taste
• Revengeful	• Thoughtless
• Positive	• Tactful
• Brave	• Insincere
• Determined	• Vacillating

While it may be true that the combination of Venus and Mars can result in a profound and intense attraction at many levels, it is also, true that the sensitive Libra may feel weighed down by the force and passion of Scorpio's feelings. The possible way that these two can attain bliss in each others' company is by giving each other a fair amount of happiness and since, both would be eager to do so, this would never be a problem. The magnetic attraction of Scorpio and the graceful appeal of Libra would come together to form an irresistible relationship.

Although, these two might be hesitant to get together yet there would be some crackling chemistry between them. It wouldn't be easy for the ever charming Libra to mould the tough Scorpio; however, the latter would definitely be tender and would feel quite desolate when neglected by the flirtatious Libran. The explicit preferences of Scorpio can sometimes, irk the more balanced Libran.

The fair, intellectual Libra would be quite intrigued by the Scorpio's passive expressions and would spend time deciphering them. Libra is, indeed, quick and sharp and this would be something that Scorpio would appreciate and respect. Both would have a strong intelligence and would want to help each other realise their dreams and ambitions. The cool, clear analysis of Libra would help Scorpio gain more focus and clarity while the Scorpio would strengthen Libran resolve with his/her dedication and integrity. Since both would be logical and would like to debate issues, disagreements would often stretch over hours and hours. There would, of course, be times when the determined Scorpio might seem somewhat revengeful, however, this would soon fade out and once they make up, life would be back to normal and everything would be forgotten.

Sexually, Libra would be sentimental, emotional and gently loving and all this would attract the Scorpio who does crave for deep love and gentleness. For his/her part, Scorpio would be an intense lover who would want to give Libra all the love, tenderness and fulfillment, emotionally, mentally and sexually.

Astro Advice
o Woman should wear Pearl of three ratti on Monday
o Man should trust his beloved.

SCORPIO & SCORPIO

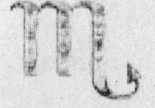

Water Sign *Ruled by Mars*	*Water Sign* *Ruled by Mars*
• Magnetic	• Magnetic
• Survivors	• Survivors
• Determined	• Determined
• Strong-willed	• Strong-willed
• Principled	• Principled

The potent blend of the element of Water with Water is one that would strengthen and fortify the existing intense sentiments, passions and longings in the hearts of the two Scorpios. Since, there is never anything insignificant about this particular sign, the relationship of two intense, motivated and powerful people creates many brilliant achievements, provided that they have common aims and ambitions. Just in case, they do not, then, there would be many altercations and much unpleasantness. This is one of those relationships which have a mix of both the good and the bad within it.

Both would be conscious of the strength and passion of the other. Even though, they would be happy to have someone who would appreciate and empathise with them, they would still be a little careful and wary of the other. It is never intentional; they just can't help being guarded. If one disregards the idea of two strong headed people coming together, one would be able to see the fantastic accomplishments that they would be able to produce. They would have their share of negative qualities such as, revengefulness, skeptical, aggressive yet they would also, be brave, direct and would have it within them to forgive the other. The last would, in fact, be the key to a strong and lasting relationship. If they manage to overlook their partner's faults and shortcomings, they would be able to love him/her till eternity.

Sexually, they would have an immensely satisfying and fulfilling life, since the relationship would have its basis in a powerful physical appeal. Moreover, their desires and passions would be mutual and would be reciprocated with intensity and fervour. They would have the ability to fill each others' senses completely and entice their partner's body, mind and soul. Sex would be an integral part of their relationship and would be firmly entwined with the emotional aspect. They would communicate with their expressive eyes and speak volumes without saying a word. The best part would be that it would be understood by the person who means the most to them. This would most definitely be a relationship to be reckoned with and looked upon with wonder and even, awe.

Astro Advice
o Man : cunningness and falsehood must be kept at bay.
o Woman : don't compare your beloved with anyone.

SCORPIO & SAGITTARIUS

Water Sign	Fire Sign
Ruled by Mars	Ruled by Jupiter
• Profound	• Earnest
• Ruthless	• Tolerant
• Constructive	• Sporting
• Healers	• Boorish
• Venomous	• Devoted

The relationship of Water and Fire is a problematic one, unless both the partners agree consciously to make a fair share of compromises and adjustments. Since Sagittarius would crave independence and openness, Scorpio would tend to feel somewhat insecure and even, envious. Scorpio is, in itself, quite a demanding sign and would want the complete attention and devotion of Sagittarius. However, Sagittarius is not the sort who would give into Scorpio easily and would chafe against too many restrictions and demands. The good part being that the infectious eagerness of Sagittarius would be able to motivate the Scorpio to scale great heights. The inherent evasiveness of the Scorpio, on the other hand, could irk as well as intrigue the innately blunt and straightforward Sagittarius

One of the strongest traits in common with both of them would be their curiosity. Sagittarians would always want to know something or the other and would ask questions in a direct manner. The Scorpio on the other hand, would probe for knowledge and information in a more discreet fashion but with the same amount of dedication. They would at all times, make concerted efforts to discover all that there is to each other. Another thing in common is that both would enjoy competing. Yet losing is a different issue, altogether. While the Scorpio would hate losing, the cheerful archer would be able to show him the values of good sportsmanship, positive thinking and truthfulness. The Scorpio could show the Sagittarian how to be assertive and self-confident at all times. Together they could embark on a journey of learning and discovery.

Scorpio would be responsible, focused, and determined but Sagittarius would be laidback, cheerful and spontaneous. There is no doubt that changes would have to be made and it would need to be done by both of them. They would need to show each other compassion and thoughtfulness at all times.

While Scorpio is quiet, understated, subtle and strongly passionate, Sagittarius is enthusiastic and ebullient. The latter would need to appreciate the Scorpion's love and emotions in order to make the relationship work. The openness of the Sagittarian would appeal to the Scorpio who would reciprocate with tenderness and intense feelings.

Although the two are markedly distinct from one another, they could make it together, provided they learn to be patient and dedicated to each other and to their love. It is then that they would not only cherish and love each other but also, respect each other's individuality and independence without a thought.

Astro Advice
o Man should wear yellow sapphire of six ratti.
o Woman should wear Pearl of four ratti.

SCORPIO & CAPRICORN

| Water Sign | Earth Sign |
| Ruled by Mars | Ruled by Saturn |

- Magnetic
- Creative
- Over-sexed
- Secretive
- Power tripping

- Social climber
- Limited
- Earthy
- Charitable
- Hard-working

The natural affinity of Water and Earth is indeed, a critical factor in this relationship, however, since the ruling planets, Mars and Saturn are strong, the journey ahead wouldn't be a mere bed of roses. Both, Scorpio and Capricorn, would have the attributes of diligence, dedication and determination and would be quite a partnership when pursuing a common goal of some significance. However, if they disagree, then there would be really troubled waters, since both would not give in without a fight. It would be silly to think that they would be able to make up quickly. Arguments and conflicts would stretch on endlessly, till either one of them sees reason and decides to make peace.

This couple would spend quite a lot of time talking about their personal and combined ambitions, aspirations and desires. While it is possible that the two might be in concurrence about the ambitions, they just might disagree about how to realise these aspirations. At the same time, both would want to be valued and appreciated and hence, might understand that the final result is more important than the ways adopted to achieve it.

Capricorn would be somewhat possessive and would want to give the relationship some sort of status, however, Scorpio might not return the sentiments. These two would not only share goals but also, personality traits, such as the habit of concealing their actual emotions and their ability to be restrained and regimented. Since they would have a certain amount of similarity between them, they would be attracted towards each other. Yet their companionship would have a tinge of isolation in it. They would love each other and give each other the warmth they need but would be cool and controlled once the wave of emotion has washed away.

As far as the sexual aspect of the relationship is concerned, Scorpio and Capricorn would both enhance and deepen the entire experience of love making. The intense Scorpio would arouse unknown emotions in Capricorn. They would share unique warmth in their lovemaking and would have a stable rapport with one another. However, Capricorn might hold back a little which could affect the experience and Scorpio could do with a bit more expressiveness. On the whole, though, both would have a good relationship with a fair amount of ups and downs, especially when both decide to stick to their individual guns and not budge. Patience, tolerance and logic are attributes they would really need to rely upon in order to reach a point where they attain bliss in each others' company forever.

Astro Advice
o Man : Avoid material disruption that hinder enjoyment.
o Woman : Keep no secret if you share a problem you will find a solution.

SCORPIO & AQUARIUS

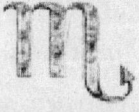 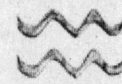

Water Sign
Ruled by Mars
- Courageous
- Hypersensitive
- Survivours
- Healers
- Arrogant

Air Sign
Ruled by Saturn
- Visionary
- Broadminded
- Critical
- Disruptive
- Negative

Since there is a tremendous disparity between the elements of air and water, these two signs would also show differences even in their similarities. Despite the fact that both are equally strong-minded and resolute and can bring about great results if they decide to pool their resources, the two are also, characteristically different. While Scorpio is deeply passionate and possessive, Aquarius is inclined to be liberated and absolutely his/her own person. If intense Scorpio attempts to rein in the eccentric Aquarian, there would be an endless conflict that shall affect the relationship severely.

In the event that there occurs a severe disagreement, Aquarius would try and get over it smoothly and with the least pain. However, Scorpio would be affected deeply. Both view the emotion of love in different perspectives. For Scorpio it is a profound emotion that must be felt completely. On the other hand, Aquarius has a wider definition of the same and it spans all humanity at an impersonal level. Both would need to be more understanding of each others' viewpoints and accept their differences along with their similarities. If the two decide to give the relationship a permanent status, there might be some teething difficulties; however, these could always be resolved by gaining an understanding of each other and by the use of astrology. This would be a enriching and illuminating experience for both of them.

It is indeed interesting to think about the consequences of putting a Scorpio and an Aquarian together. While the relationship may have quite a few adjustment problems, it could work out well if both the partners are mature enough to realise the significance of making those adjustments. Despite all their differences, they would be able to form a bond that is intriguing and innovative.

Sexually, Scorpio would have a stronger desire than the Aquarian which might cause the former to feel a little isolated and neglected. This would be one of the areas where they would need to work out their differences so that instead of a long drawn conflict situation, they are able to achieve a comfort level that warms their hearts and lives.

This would surely be a relationship that would demand a lot from both the partners. They would need to understand that togetherness is more essential than individuality and at the same time, should not sacrifice everything for the sake of being together. This is a delicate balance and with patience and determination, everything should work out in their favour. It would be filled with plenty of arguments, confusions and compromises, but the end result would be worth it all.

Astro Advice
o Man : your beloved expects much from you; so get ready for it.
o Woman : be tactful and laconic.

SCORPIO	PISCES

Water Sign   *Water Sign*
Ruled by Mars   *Ruled by Neptune*

- Determined
- Brave
- Profound
- Greedy
- Obsessed

- Ambitionless
- Dreamer
- Escapist
- Good-natured
- Idealistic

Water and Water. These two signs would have a unique and intense affinity and when they would come together, they would create pure magic. Scorpio would want to be the controller and wield the upper hand; and while Pisces is not really passive, it would yield and be the controlled. The tranquility that Pisces would radiate would help to calm and pacify the intensity and passion of the Scorpio. Both would be able to sense each others' fears, hopes and desires and would be emotional about sensitive issues.

Together, these two would be able to give each other companionship, and share a healthy camaraderie that would make the good times better and the bad times good. Both would have a profundity which would help them to communicate even in perfect silence. They would be able to give the experience of Life a whole new meaning, a meaning that would be rich, intense, insightful. This would be the wonderful quality that this particular couple would bring to their relationship.

They would have their share of conflicts and disagreements yet they would be able to make up and sort out their differences in next to no time. In any case, there is no doubt that with the two of them, the sunny days would be more than the cloudy ones and happiness would always be an integral part of their lives.

The two are constantly attracted towards each other by unknown and unforeseen forces. And they share a strong empathy with each other which only serves to forge the bond more closely than ever. Their powers of intuition would be strong and wondrous. Despite its apparent calmness, whenever there would be a clash, it would be Pisces who would take the stronger position.

The sexual aspect of the relationship is also just as emotional and dramatic. Scorpio's possessive streak would be subdued and soothed by the Piscean tact and empathy. Both would express their sexual desires and feelings in the most subtle yet intense fashion. A communication that would hold a great deal of meaning and passion hidden within it. This is, indeed, a relationship that has a bright future and good things in store for both the partners.

Astro Advice
o Men should practice flattery.
o Women : give extra attention to your beloved.

Sagittarius–The Archer
(November 23–December 21)
The Sign of the Sage or Counsellor

How to Recognise Sagittarius

Challenge and a need to feel free to express themselves in their own individual way are the two most important requisites for those who have this sign emphasised in their birth-charts. They cannot function satisfactorily without either. Put a lively Sagittarian in a situation where he or she has work that is repetitive or makes no demands on them and they will crumble. But many, of course, have to cope with such dreary circumstances, and then it is important that they should work out ways to divert their attention from what is basically an unrewarding set-up.

Usually Sagittarius is resilient enough to find interesting alternatives, and it is vital that they do so, otherwise the psychological suffering they will have to endure will be nearly intolerable. Sagittarius is a Fire sign, and this element makes its presence felt through a high level of enthusiasm for life and individual interests. To this it is possible to add that Sagittarians are keen to enjoy all aspects of life in a very positive way, and as they do so they will also inspire others to get as much out of life and their abilities as they do themselves. But challenge must be there; if it is not then Sagittarians must create it by presenting ideas to those who matter, and by showing others precisely what they are made of. It is important though that in the pursuit of many varied and diverse interests they do not lose out on the full development of what they can do best. It is also a good thing for those of this sign to express their versatility in a controlled way-by doing many different things, but making quite sure that one project is completed before another is started, so that when a year's work is assessed there will be a feeling that a great deal has been achieved in a variety of fields. Sagittarian make exhilarating partners in spite of their need for freedom, and will always encourage their lovers to develop their individual interests. They need an energetic, lively sex-life and will get very bored indeed with a partner who has no sense of fun or who is too pessimistic in outlook. If they keep busy and active they are usually very healthy, but the hips and thighs-the Sagittarian body-areas-are vulnerable, and it is here that most Sagittarians (Sun-and Rising-sign types) put on weight very easily.

The liver is also Sagittarian ruled, hence slight 'liverishness' and hangovers can be a problem. Sagittarians also make extremely lively and somewhat demanding parents-no bad thing, as they will certainly get a great deal out of their children because of their ability to encourage them in just the right way. Children of this sign must be given a lot of positive encouragement, but may need controlling in a gentle but firm way so that their exuberance does not become too overwhelmingly boisterous.

Career and Finance

A great deal has been written about the two types of Sagittarian-one whose energy is physically expressed and the other who tends to be intellectual by nature. There is a great deal of validity in the division, but what is often ignored is the fact that the 20-year-old sporting Sagittarian can develop into the 45-year-old intellectual Sagittarian, having understood and nurtured the growth of the mind. There does seem to be something of the eternal student about Sagittarians, and they should take this into consideration when choosing a career. They will probably think of their job, consciously or unconsciously, as a developing and creative aspect of life. They will tend not to think in terms of a career which will bring its rewards if they work hard. They will prefer to seek advancement by studying in their spare time, often contenting themselves with a menial position while they do so, believing that this scheme will lead them to better things. There will be an element of excitement, tinged by their liking for adventure and the unknown, in their approach to their career. In this sphere of life, as elsewhere, Sagittarians will create challenges for themselves and not only be ready to accept them as they occur in the natural order of things. There is also the possibility of restlessness, which should not be allowed to get out of hand. When contemplating a change of course, Sagittarians should ask themselves whether it will be a progressive and constructive one or whether they are not simply feeling fidgety and wanting change for its own sake. Although they are versatile, members of this sign like to get to grips with one job before passing on to the next. Too many changes could lead to dissatisfaction, a state of mind which is more lethal to Sagittarians than to others.

Health and Food

Generally you people have splendid physical constitutions and suffer very little from illness of any kind upto the age of about sixty. As you cross this age a change generally begins to show itself and if you do not lessen your responsibilities, the nervous system will begin to break down in many cases bringing on some form a paralysis affecting the spine, arms, hand and brain. You should avoid over- work and focus on complete rest and spiritualism.

Suggested Food Options:
- Raw eggs
- Raw Vegetables
- Fruits
- Tomatoes
- Beans
- Corn
- Avoid Spicy food & smoking

Your Love Life

First Decan of Sagittarius : November 23 to December 2

Happiness fills your heart when your beloved is pleased by the same small things that give you joy. It could be a song, a sight, a possession, just about anything under the sun. What is essential that you feel the bond of togetherness and oneness within your relationship. This would light the embers of romance in your life and give you a strong sense of security. It is, indeed, essential for you that there exist a sharing of interests other than mere sexual ones. Intellectual, emotional, social and other interests are what you would want to share with your partner.

Since you do have high standards when it comes to the feeling of being one in a relationship, it may be sometime before you find your partner. However, it is beneficial eventually since you would be sure that the person you find would be one who would be able to talk to you and interest you when the initial hue of romance wanes away. You would be mature and wise about marriage and would take everything involved in it with utmost seriousness. Despite the fact that you would approach marriage with sobriety, you would attract many people simply by being the naturally friendly person that you are.

Although there is no way that you could be called sycophant-like, you just enjoy doling out words of praise and appreciation to your near and dear ones. You would be elated when you find the one who suits you perfectly and would shower your spouse with immense love and affection. At the same time, you would understand and respect their need for independence and would blend it perfectly with your love to create an ideal marriage.

Second Decan of Sagittarius: December 3 to December 12

You are the kind who would build pleasing and enjoyable alliances with a variety of people and would endear them to you by virtue of your witty and intelligent conversation and good humour. Mostly, you would have transitory rather than lasting relationships since you enjoy change and variety and would move on quickly from one alliance to the other.

However, once you fall in love, you would be transformed and would become quite a different soul. You would now be sober, mature and attentive towards your loved one. Also, you would become quieter than before since now you wouldn't really feel the need to be verbose or garrulous. Quiet understanding is what would reflect the profundity of your love and affection.

You are not the one who would bear to listen to anything derogatory about your spouse or partner and would be extremely dedicated. However, you might feel hurt and let down by your partner because of your intensely sensitive nature. You would, nevertheless, forgive easily and also; realise that it is you who is being unreasonable. The more patience and understanding you show, the more would be the happiness in your marriage.

It would help you and your relationship if you would fill it with additional charm and grace. Accept the fact that most of your romantic experiences are but short-lived, yet hold on to their memories. Do not take love with only seriousness else it would become staid and stiff. Fill it with humour, lightness and laughter and you would have a relationship which is happy and harmonious.

Third Decan of Sagittarius : December 13 to December 21

You have been bestowed with an extremely high sense of morality. You also, have the habit of leading a virtuous and pure life which would win you the respect and honour of all those who know you. You would certainly never lower your standards and resort to unbecoming ways and mannerisms. For you, marriage is an eternal bond and you would have a sacred and deferential admiration for true and lasting love, which you feel is the basis of any marriage.

Marriage would imply devotion and genuineness in all aspects and you wouldn't deviate from the standards by even so much as an inch. You would understand your partner with sympathy, love and an acute intelligence. And you wouldn't be afraid of adjusting, co-operating and compromising to fill your marriage with peace, happiness and contentment.

Happiness should always exist in a marriage and you would leave nothing undone to ensure that this happens. You would have the ability to face all odds with strength and hence would be able to see your marriage sail through all of life's difficulties with ease.

Gifted with an intensity of discernment and powers of observation, you would display caution and care with your words and would never deliberately hurt your beloved. You would enjoy living a good life and hence, would have an active social life to add spice to your personal life. Secrecy and distrust would have no place in your relationship. You would consciously create the atmosphere of openness and honesty so that your love becomes an example for all others.

Your Sex Life

First Decan, Jupiter-ruled : November 23 to December 2

You have an enthusiastic and balanced approach towards sex. In fact, it is quite similar to your general approach towards life. An extrovert with bubbling confidence and good humour, you don't try too hard in your sexual exploits. Yet you are the kind of person who wouldn't leave his or her sexual partners filled with resentment. All that they would have would be happy thoughts about the time spent with you. Routine and monotony turn you off and you enjoy innovating and being spontaneous. Even though you may have a powerful sex drive, it certainly would not be your prime area of interest and occupation.

Second Decan, sub-ruled by Mars : December 3 to 12 December

You have an inherent restiveness which is shown even in your sexual life and your approach is one of extremes. You could move between plenty of sexual behaviour followed by absolute abstinence. You have an immense storehouse of physical energy however, you would utilise it in other ways than sex. But when your sex drive is in full form, you would want to spend it with aggression and passion. Thoughtful and understanding, you would always keep your partner's interests and feelings in mind. And even if you do happen to overlook them occasionally, you would ensure that you make up for it later. However, you are not the kind to put too much of importance on the issues of sex, most of the time.

Third Decan, subruled by the Sun : December 13 to 21 December

For you, sex is important however you would approach it in a balanced manner. What you do have is a healthy and decent outlook towards sexual behaviour and would often unite it with your emotional fulfillment. You fill your sex life with your characteristic good nature and have a sense of confidence about your sexual performance. You are quite traditional though and would often prefer a single partner relationship rather than exploring multiple partners, even though you do have the ability to keep many sexual relationships happy and satisfying.

Sagittarius Celebrities

Birth Date	Star	Vocation
1 December	Udit Narayan	Musician
11 December	Vishwanathan Anand	Sports Star
11 December	Dilip Kumar	Actor
14 December	Raj Kapoor	Actor
27 November	Arjun Rampal	Film Star

Compatibility

SAGITTARIUS & ARIES

Fire Sign
Ruled by Jupiter
- Honest
- Restless

Fire Sign
Ruled by Mars
- Strong
- Zestful

- Forthright
- Earnest
- Selfish
- Immoral
- Adventurous
- Independent
- Youthful
- Energetic

While two fire signs wouldn't exactly negate each other, they would need to give each other a fair amount of independence and space. Aries values the archer's positive approach and truthfulness while Sagittarius also, motivates the high-energy Aries. It is indeed a relationship which has a high level of enthusiasm and activity, hence the levels of calm and restfulness are relatively lower. Both wouldn't quite appreciate being pushed around. Aside from this, they would have lots more in common. They would enjoy being occupied-physically and mentally. That would give them a lot of joy. Though they might have the usual tiffs and spats, the Sagittarius character would always be touched by the straightforward attitude of Aries and similarly, the Archer would be able to show the Ram the importance of being affectionate and sympathetic impulsively.

A free soul, Sagittarius feels completely at home and at peace with himself when he is involved in more than one affair at a time and the Aries would need to deal with this. He would also, be quite a performer in bed and would always be able to satisfy the Arian. Hence, this particular aspect of their relationship would be both amazing and pleasing. They adapt to each other sexually almost, instinctively. Their ardour is tempered with their profound love for each other. They would be tender towards each other and hence, their relationship would be close and loving.

The two signs share quite a few traits and hence, are quite compatible. For instance, both have a fair degree of optimism and also, a liking to passionately argue out their point. Hence the attraction between them would be nearly instantaneous. Generous, confident and amicable, the affection would never cool, since they share a common enthusiasm for novelty and innovation. Their tendency to get involved with a cause also, brings them closer to each other.

Both Aries and Sagittarius know that cooperation and mutual give and take is the ideal approach there is to take care of all arguments and squabbles. Hence, this commonness enables them to accomplish a unique synchrony in emotional, sexual and mental matters.

Astro Advice
o Men should trust their beloved
o Woman should opt to wear dress with stripes or checks.
o Wear Coral of five carat

SAGITTARIUS & TAURUS

Fire Sign
Ruled by Jupiter
- Immoral
- Optimistic
- Lively
- Careless
- Restless
- Lawless

Earth Sign
Ruled by Venus
- Earthy
- Reliable
- Fruitful
- Persistent
- Kind
- Honest

The alliance of Taurus and Sagittarius is indeed, one with marked differences. The earthy stability of the Taurean contrasts sharply with the fiery Sagittarius's need to be liberated and on his/her own. The bull likes to be settled at one place whereas the archer wants nothing but to float about from place to place. Forever on the move, craving novelty and searching for the meaning of life in unknown places, the archer needs his/her space to flourish in. This would, in all likelihood, be quite unsettling for the stable, sedate Taurus. Yet if the emotion that they feel is sincere and deep enough, they would be able to overcome all their difficulties and differences to create a lasting and loving bond.

The spontaneous, flighty Sagittarian may feel a little bogged down by the slow pace of the doctrinaire Taurus. The calmness of Taurus can at times, irk the cheerful and emotionally volatile archer. However, both of them would share a sharp intellect and be able to see through the veneer of people with ease and clarity. They would also, share a respect for honesty and straightforwardness. Moreover, if they work together they would be able to put together a neat packet and give each other the comforts of life.

The Sagittarius lover gives the Taurean all that he would want in his relationship-happiness, intelligence, imaginativeness and an astute business sense. The archer is also, incredibly faithful and devoted. And if he gets all the love and attention that he wants, he would prove to be a strong, loyal and dedicated lover and life partner. The Taurean can complement the Sagittarian knack of dreaming up wild ideas by thinking them over and letting the Sagittarius see rationale before plunging headlong into anything. By giving the Sagittarius a patient ear, the Taurean would be giving him the respect and the attention that he so wants. The level-headedness and sensibility of the bull would be a happy foil for the impulsiveness of the archer.

To start with the two would be drawn to each other and the Sagittarius's directness would lead the Taurean to respond fully and with complete love and gentleness. Earthy and loving, the Taurus would put his/her feelings into words through the magic of touch and let the love flow through his/her gestures and caresses. He/she wouldn't be very communicative during the act of love and would try to express all the feelings through touch. However, for the Sagittarius, expression should be creative and dreamy, something that would add to the magic of the moment and give it greater depth.

The differences don't just end there. The Sagittarian enjoys a healthy debate and would never give up an opportunity to exercise and sharpen his wit. For the Taurean, on the other hand, this signifies mere wasting of time and energy. If they enter into marriage with each other, it would be filled with a combination of dedication and annoyance. Not the best thing, yet it would have its good moments as well. If the two manage to adjust well with each other and find their own unique rhythm, they would be able to create magic together.

Astro Advice

- Woman : should wear modern clothes to impress her lover.
- Man : avoid fickleness in love for the sake of personal gains.

SAGITTARIUS & GEMINI

Fire Sign
Ruled by Jupiter
- Generous
- Disloyal

Air Sign
Ruled by Mercury
- Artistic
- Erratic

- Optimistic
- Devoted
- Immoral
- Flirtatious
- Communicative
- Intelligent

The combination of Air and Fire is, indeed, an extremely exciting one however, not without its own set of flaws. As both these signs are in opposition to each other, they have the knack of being able to be drawn both towards and away from each other. Gemini would have its own individuality which would go well with the Sagittarius trait of wanting to be free and on their own. Since they are both inherently energetic and desire to lead eventful lives, they would keep themselves occupied with a multitude of interests and activities and hence, would have plenty to talk about.

Each time a Gemini and a Sagittarian enter a relationship, they normally follow one of the two modes of behaviour. They would either hero-worship one another and try and inculcate the qualities of the other one or they would feel insecure and jealous about the other's admirable characteristics. It is only due to the fact that they feel, and rightly so, that the other one has the attributes that they would like in their personality. So they would either work on developing those or they would resent their presence. However, since both are good communicators with each other, they would often be able to talk things out and realise that although they are markedly different, they have their own unique similarities and these would see them through all the difficult days.

They share a particular intellectual bonding which makes a good base for the culmination of their relationship in the act of love. They would make good use of their expressive eyes and other gestures to begin the physical expression of their love.

Both would enjoy a sex life that would be characterised by its adaptability and the constant element of novelty. This would make it highly interesting and fascinating for both the partners. Their desire to be reckless, adventurous, and flamboyant balances out any differences that they may have. The archer is mystified by the twins' sophistication and elegance and together, their mutual admiration for each other would ensure that their relationship is forever filled with an intense physical attraction. Since both also want to become more like the other one, they would endeavour constantly to grow and keep an element of change alive in the relationship.

The only potential drawback that their love as well as sex life could face would be the emotions of envy and temperamental swings taking over every now and then. They should learn to avoid these and be more adjusting with one another so as to be perfectly compatible.

Astro Advice
o Woman should share responsibilities of her lover.
o Man : avoid fickleness in love.

SAGITTARIUS & CANCER

Fire Sign
Ruled by Jupiter
- Honest
- Open
- Careless
- Indulgent
- Trusting

Water Sign
Ruled by Moon
- Secure
- Good-memory
- Sympathetic
- Depressive
- Unambitious

The blend of Water with Fire displays the stark contrast in the temperaments of the two signs. Unless the relationship is characterised by perfect communication, it is a difficult alliance with many challenges. While Cancer is a home bird, the archer is a complete extrovert with one foot always on the move. Moreover, Sagittarius has a high level of emotional, physical and intellectual independence and this can make the naturally timid Cancerian somewhat more anxious. Cancer has the desire to hold on while this would make the freedom loving Sagittarius feel stifled and claustrophobic.

However, it is not as if all is lost. Both have plenty in common and this is a relationship that would have many advantages for both, more so for Cancer. Because Cancer can inculcate the trait of being emotionally stronger and self-confident, while the Sagittarian can learn to appreciate the empathetic and gentleness of the Cancer. Together they can produce some brilliant ideas and do plenty of logical thinking. There could be a difference of opinion as far as money is concerned, yet as with everything else, they would manage to sort this one out as well.

The inquisitive Sagittarian would be intrigued by the mystery that Cancer would hold for him/her and also, be attracted by the powerful yet subtle sex appeal of the crab. And these factors would compel the normally ebullient archer to conduct himself/herself in an unusually calm and sedate fashion.

The crab would show his/her love in an understated yet erotic fashion and would give himself/herself to Sagittarius who would, return the feelings with equal ardour and passion. Sexually, they would be in harmony with each other and would carry their goodness of nature with them into their sexual union. Their genuineness, honesty and sensitivity would make their sex life a warm and fulfilling one. The gentleness and deep love of the Cancerian holds a promise of happiness for the Sagittarian and this would surely be an alliance of love and bliss.

Astro Advice

o Woman should wear yellow Sapphire of five ratti on Thursday after Pran Pratishta (Prayer to Jupiter)
o Man should wear pearl of seven ratti on Monday after Pran Pratishta (Prayer to Moon).

SAGITTARIUS & LEO

Fire Sign *Ruled by Jupiter*	*Fire Sign* *Ruled by Sun*
• Lawless	• Extravagant
• Gambling	• Stubborn
• Earnest	• Charming
• Restless	• Organised
• Tolerant	• Materialistic

The alliance of two fire signs ruled by Sun and Jupiter respectively is, of course, a favourable one. Primarily, for the reason, that their planets endow them with advantageous characteristics, which make them into well-rounded personalities, who are naturally compatible with one another. Both of them are straightforward, benevolent and sincere and hence, can very easily complement each other. Free and liberal Sagittarius would chafe and sulk if Leo attempts to be more domineering or possessive than necessary. On the other hand, Leo would feel ignored if Sagittarius leads a carefree and footloose lifestyle.

This is, however, a relationship that would witness, probably some of the most memorable disagreements and confrontations. Most of the conflicts though would be quite amicable and genial in nature, without a hint of malice or spite. The smarter ones realise that there wouldn't ever be a consensus and so decide to go with the flow of events. Irrespective of what their individual thoughts might be, as long as these two are together they would radiate energy and enthusiasm all around. They would unknowingly fill their own and the lives of others' with cheerfulness, brightness and optimism.

The Lion would exercise his/her opinions with wisdom and thought which would enable the normally forthright Sagittarius to also, learn restraint and hence, develop him/her into a better person.

Since Leo needs quite a lot to be made happy and feel loved, the archer would be quite the one with gifts, flowers, compliments, and the works. He/she would be a devoted, warm and thoughtful lover who would endeavour in all earnestness to fill Leo's life with immense love and caring.

The emotion of love would be demonstrated sexually through gentle, subtle yet passionate acts of love. There would be a sophisticated air along with the sensual ambience when these two indulge in sexual relations. In fact, when they unite sexually, it is quite a transcending experience.

They are one of those rare partners who manage to merge their love and their desire for each other in the most beautiful manner. The Leo-Sagittarius couple is one that is created for the purpose of love and affection. They move through life with an essence of innocence and worldliness, romance and erotica, realism and fantasy and spread joy wherever they go.

Astro Advice
- Man should try to be warm and soft.
- Woman : carry a bunch of flowers with you while going to meet your beloved.

SAGITTARIUS & VIRGO

Fire Sign Ruled by Jupiter	Earth Sign Ruled by Mercury
• Restless	• Demanding
• Wasteful	• Masochistic
• Practical	• Thorough
• Boorish	• Complaining
• Selfish	• Sensible

Although the two signs-Virgo and Sagittarius are temperamentally different, yet there is a thread of similarity that runs through their differences and tends to bring them closer to each other. Virgo is Earth and hence, logical, cautious, reserved and systematic. Sagittarius is Fire and therefore, swift, self-reliant, rash and somewhat of a spendthrift. Virgo is the kind who would handle one thing intensively and pay acute attention to the minutest detail to ensure that everything is in order. On the contrary, Sagittarius is the sort who would take on many things and would think more of how to conquer the future rather than tame the present. Both would tend to give expression to their dissimilarities in their own unique ways.

Although these two would speak a lot, their individual communication with each other would not be the best. However, if the stars are favourable, these two would be able to build a lasting and affectionate relationship. While the prim and proper Virgo would educate the footloose Sagittarius serenity, perseverance and even cultural etiquette, Sagittarius would, in return, teach the controlled Virgo how to be more relaxed, easy-going and liberal. Virgo's innocence and clear heartedness would touch the archer and together they would be able to overcome whatever hindrances to build a beautiful world together.

Although there is much that the Archer could admire in the Virgo and vice-versa, there would be some instances where they wouldn't always be in agreement and there could be some discord. However, with tenderness and the initial attraction between these two, there would be little difficulty in resolving whatever difference they may have had. When the shy Virgo would seek refuge in Sagittarius' arms, there would be no memory of any conflict and all misgivings and disapprovals would vanish. If the two learn to be more patient and understanding with each other, this bond would be one where passion and tranquility would merge beautifully.

The relationship has a distinct air of peace and quietness and this enables both of them to direct their love and passion for each other into a subtle and delicate expression. There could be instances when the Archer might not get the desired sexual response from the Virgo and be somewhat blunt about it. However, both would need to understand that it is only with tact, patience and profound love that they would be able to culminate their love for each other in a sexual union that would be transcendental and uplifting.

Astro Advice

o Man should wear Yellow Sapphire of eight ratti on Thursday.
o Woman should wear Emerald of five ratti on Wednesday.

SAGITTARIUS & LIBRA

Fire Sign Ruled by Jupiter	Air Sign Ruled by Venus
• Tolerant	• Outgoing
• Sloppy	• Sympathetic
• Dependable	• Escapist
• Sporting	• Jealous
• Disloyal	• Unbalanced

The elements of Air and Fire would be in harmony with each other in this relationship, since the planets that rule the signs-Venus and Jupiter are also, in harmony. The planets will bless the couple with affection, joy and prosperity throughout life. Even though Libra would want to spend more time with Sagittarius, he/she would be intelligent enough to respect the Archer's need to be free and unburdened. On the other hand, Sagittarius would be able to indulge and even pamper Libra to a fault.

Both Libra and Sagittarius are quick on the uptake and good conversationalists. They are also, immensely charismatic and can keep each other and even people around them captivated for hours. Whenever both are in a room, there would not be a single dull moment. They would have many good-natured arguments but at the end of it all, there would remain the old camaraderie and love for each other. Sadly, though, this relationship may appear ideal and idyllic, it would rarely if ever last for ever. Simply because both of them need change, novelty and movement in their lives and this would become difficult after a point. However for as long as it would last and even after, there would be many happy memories to cherish.

The gregarious Sagittarian dislikes being alone and hence, would appreciate the sweet and stimulating company of the Libran. Also, the Libran would enjoy being loved by Sagittarius since it would involve plenty of bright positivism and intelligent conversations. The fair-minded Libra values sincerity and optimism and hence, would relish the Sagittarius company. However, since both would be good-looking and friendly, there could be a few jealous moments now and then. Also, it is unlikely that this relationship would materialise into something permanent, since both have a tendency to link sex with love. What would happen would be that both would become good friends and their relationship would always, hold happiness and pleasant thoughts for both.

As a lover, the archer would cater beautifully to the Libran who would enjoy being wooed and appreciated. They would surely have something beautiful and remarkable with one another.

Astro Advice
o Man should wear yellow sapphire of seven ratti on Thursday.
o Woman should wear white stone of four ratti on Monday.

SAGITTARIUS & SCORPIO

Fire Sign	*Water Sign*
Ruled by Jupiter	Ruled by Mars
• Earnest	• Profound
• Tolerant	• Ruthless
• Sporting	• Constructive
• Boorish	• Healers
• Devoted	• Venomous

The relationship of Water and Fire is a problematic one, unless both the partners agree consciously to make a fair share of compromises and adjustments. Since Sagittarius would crave independence and openness, Scorpio would tend to feel somewhat insecure and even, envious. Scorpio is, in itself, quite a demanding sign and would want the complete attention and devotion of Sagittarius. However, Sagittarius is not the sort who would give into Scorpio easily and would chafe against too many restrictions and demands. The good part being that the infectious eagerness of Sagittarius would be able to motivate the Scorpio to scale great heights. The inherent evasiveness of the Scorpio, on the other hand, could irk as well as intrigue the innately blunt and straightforward Sagittarius.

One of the strongest traits in common with both of them would be their curiosity. Sagittarians would always want to know something or the other and would ask questions in a direct manner. The Scorpio on the other hand, would probe for knowledge and information in a more discreet fashion but with the same amount of dedication. They would at all times, make concerted efforts to discover all that there is to each other. Another thing in common is that both would enjoy competing. Yet losing is a different issue, altogether. While the Scorpio would hate losing, the cheerful archer would be able to show him the values of good sportsmanship, positive thinking and truthfulness. The Scorpio could show the Sagittarian how to be assertive and self-confident at all times. Together they could embark on a journey of learning and discovery.

Scorpio would be responsible, focused, and determined but Sagittarius would be laidback, cheerful and spontaneous. There is no doubt that changes would have to be made and it would need to be done by both of them. They would need to show each other compassion and thoughtfulness at all times.

While Scorpio is quiet, understated, subtle and strongly passionate, Sagittarius is enthusiastic and ebullient. The latter would need to appreciate the Scorpion's love and emotions in order to make the relationship work. The openness of the Sagittarian would appeal to the Scorpio who would reciprocate with tenderness and intense feelings.

Although the two are markedly distinct from one another, they could make it together, provided they learn to be patient and dedicated to each other and to their love. It is then that they would not only cherish and love each other but also, respect each other's individuality and independence without a thought.

Astro Advice
o Man should wear yellow sapphire of six ratti.
o Woman should wear Pearl of four ratti.

SAGITTARIUS & SAGITTARIUS

Fire Sign
Ruled by Jupiter
- Forthright
- Tolerant
- Lively
- Wasteful
- Selfish

Fire Sign
Ruled by Jupiter
- Forthright
- Tolerant
- Lively
- Wasteful
- Selfish

The double presence of Fire in this relationship has a positive influence, bringing about plenty of energy, enthusiasm and excitement for both the partners. Both might spend a lot of time deliberating and contemplating but when they do grasp the matter, they are capable of creating the best possible things and reaching great heights. While the male Archers are direct and positive, the female Archers are warm and merry; together they make cheery, bright, interesting couples. It is a relationship that is filled with positive vibes and even if they decide to go their separate ways, they would never be bitter with each other. It is next to impossible for Sagittarians to be resentful and vindictive. They are the sort who would easily forgive and then, forget.

There could be occasions when the two would fight minutes after display of great affection. It is not that they are crazy; it is just that they are extremely spontaneous and would always give into the emotion that overtakes them. However, just as quickly as they erupt, they cool as well. Therefore, they would make up quickly and go about life blissfully. Theirs is a partnership that would grow better with time and their closeness would definitely increase. There would be many hugs and kisses that are exchanged along with the trifling arguments and all of these would only serve to make the relationship stronger than ever.

Whenever two Sagittarians would decide to team up, whether romantically or otherwise, there would be plenty of introspection and analysis that takes place. They would also stand by each other at all times and give each other plenty of space and support. They would have mutual interests that would keep the spark alive and activities like reading, travelling, dancing, the arts, would all bring them to a higher level of intimacy. Their lovemaking would also have an element of spontaneity blended with intensity of passion and a streak of innovative fun.

Astro Advice
o Man should wear yellow sapphire of six ratti on Thursday.
o Woman should wear Coral of five ratti on Tuesday.

SAGITTARIUS & CAPRICORN

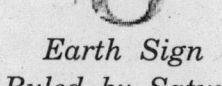

Fire Sign
Ruled by Jupiter
- Trusting
- Sporting
- Intelligent
- Escapist
- Undisciplined

Earth Sign
Ruled by Saturn
- Manipulator
- Materialistic
- Self-controlled
- Charitable
- Loyal

The stark contrast between the elements of Fire and Earth affects this relationship significantly. While Sagittarius is enthusiastic, positive, spontaneous and liberal, Capricorn is careful, reserved, orthodox, somber and even, cynical. Moreover, even the planets that rule them are conflicting. While the adage is that opposites attract, in this case, the temperamental and characteristic differences are too strong to be ignored. The open-minded, imaginative Sagittarius would not want to be tied down by the traditional Capricorn. Also, the latter would not be able to comprehend the Archer's inherent desires, ambitions and idealism. They would need to approach each other with more openness and cooperation if they want the relationship to be a satisfying one.

There is no doubt about the fact that the two are irresistibly drawn towards each other, irrespective of their differences. However, they would need to work out these differences so that peace and happiness may prevail. Especially when money and finances are concerned, they would have absolutely conflicting ideas and opinions. As far as similarities are concerned, the hardy Capricorn would be able to stomach the tactless straightforward nature of the Archer with relative ease.

There would be quite a few adjustments that would have to be made, as far as their attitude towards romance is concerned. There would be times when Sagittarius would want to play the seducer but Capricorn wouldn't be interested at all. This could lead to some amount of hurt and anger in both. However, it shouldn't indicate that they wouldn't be able to have a healthy sexual relationship; it just means that they would have to work out and sort out their differences in this area as well. Their sexual life would be negatively affected if they do not learn to solve their problems and adjust to each other's perspectives.

Since Sagittarius is spontaneous and warm, he/she may perceive Capricorn as being isolated and aloof. This could lead to problems in their sexual behavior. Capricorn would need to loosen up a little and give in to the impulsive nature of love instead of being rigid and regimented about the whole affair. Also, Sagittarius should understand that while lovemaking can be enjoyable and impulsive, it shouldn't ever interfere with the values of Capricorn; rather it should encourage him/her to be more expressive and effusive.

If they overcome their dissimilarities, they would have a sex life that would be stable and secure. They would need to trust each other implicitly and give each other gentle love and affection so as to reach the depths of intimacy.

Astro Advice
o Man : while going to meet it would help if you put on a white shirt with black trousers.
o Woman : remember that your hair is your crowning glory.

SAGITTARIUS & AQUARIUS

| Fire Sign | Air Sign |
Ruled by Jupiter	Ruled by Saturn
• Procrastinating	• Progressive
• Easy-going	• Unpredictable
• Open-critical	• Humanitarian
• Good-natured	• Considerate
• Practical	• Zealous

The elements of Fire and Air are closely linked to each other and so are their planets Jupiter and Saturn. Both the signs have a profound influence on each other and at the same time, have the maturity to give each other their own space, when needed. Since, both Sagittarius and Aquarius have a strong desire to be free and independent, they would understand each others' desire to be on his/her own every once in a while. Idealistic and philosophical, they would also, be pragmatic in their own way. Both would also, be amicable and warm and hence would have a wide circle of friends with the ability to share their lives and interests with a diverse group of people. At the same time, they would manage to bring a unique closeness into their relationship with each other and give each other the importance that is due.

This is a relationship which has a great amount of compatibility, especially when it comes to the fundamentals of a relationship. The Sagittarius's natural straightforwardness doesn't hurt the Aquarius who is quite comfortable handling the truth and has the intellect to deal with it in a sensible manner.

They would have the ability to give the relationship a life of its own by filling it with their affection, emotion, imagination. Love would be a whole new experience with these two. It would be humorous, inspiring, volatile; and at the same time, calm and soothing.

The truth loving Sagittarius would be quite comfortable with knowing the reality, irrespective of how hurting it might be. Also, the Archer happens to be somewhat spiritual yet analytical and may even lose his/her temper every now and then. But at the same, he/she would be able to cool down just as quickly and bring things back to normal. If both the partners really love each other, things would be quite wonderful and would have quite a touch of magic about them. They would have the amazing quality of being friends and lovers at the same time.

Sexually, this relationship would see a lot of interactive behaviour and innovativeness. Both Sagittarius and Aquarius would want to give one another their genuine, sincere love and yet not make it boring and monotonous. Variety and newness would keep the fire alive throughout for both. They would treat lovemaking like a fun activity and with tenderness, affection and an infectious amicability would love each other and demonstrate their passion for each other. They might be a bit possessive but at the same time, would be comfortable giving each other a lot of space and room to develop and grow. Therefore, the relationship would be a constant journey of evolution and discovery for both of them.

Astro Advice
o Woman should trust her beloved.
o Man : don't be dramatic or disloyal with your beloved.

SAGITTARIUS & PISCES

Fire Sign *Water Sign*
Ruled by Jupiter *Ruled by Neptune*
- Forthright
- Broad-minded
- High-principled
- Friendly
- Dependable

- Lazy
- Dreamers
- Receptive
- Talented
- Compassionate

The union of Fire and Water holds a great deal of intricacies and a lot of potential. There would be a degree of similarity and compatibility, since the partners would share interests in travelling, spiritualism, altruistic works and similar idealistic pursuits. There would also, be contrasts and conflicts as the pair experiences indecision, perplexity and doubts. There could also, be couples who might continue to exist in individual worlds, aloof and detached from one another. The Sagittarius desire to be free could arouse some fears and insecurities in the imaginative Pisces. Despite the fact that the Archer is an affectionate and warm being, he/she does not possess the softness that the Pisces craves for. Also, the Piscean knack of being irresolute, unrealistic and unsystematic could well, irritate the Sagittarius who is a stickler for doing things speedily and effectively, with the maximum decisiveness, optimism and energy.

When this couple decides to stay together and keep an atmosphere of peace prevailing, it is essential that they learn to keep a tight rein on their tempers. When they do that, calmness would automatically fill their lives. Also, the fact that both would be intrigued by spiritualism which would bind them together. The more they focus on their similarities and the less on their differences, the better and happier would be their relationship. These two might have to undergo many tough times, but if they learn to remain cool and balanced, life would be pleasant and peaceful.

Sexually, they would be compatible and would be drawn closer to each other as a result of their lovemaking. Both enjoy sex and would take a healthy interest in the same. However, if the sole basis of the relationship is sexual, it would not last for long, since both would want the company of someone who would please them intellectually, emotionally, mentally as well as sexually.

If all other criteria are met, Sagittarius would be drawn towards Pisces like a magnet and they would enjoy a satisfying and emotionally rich sexual life.

Astro Advice

o Man : should look glamorous and charming while going to meet beloved.
o Woman should remember not to put financial security in jeopardy.

Capricorn—The Goat
(December 22–January 20)
The Sign of the Priest or Scientist

How to Recognise Capricorn

Capricorn is the sign of the Goat. Here we have someone who is sure-footed and negotiates every obstacle with care but with a lively step. But what of the other half of Capricorn? Remember that the creature of the sign is only half goat. It has a fish's tail. Is this the 'wet fish' side of Capricorn? Or the poor domestic goat forever tethered to a post in the valley, and in no position to 'scale the mountain top?' Both, I think, for in essence they are similar. A negative, hopeless attitude can make its presence felt with those of this sign. Many feel that they will never 'get on' in life because there is so much against them. When this is the case, their friends and lovers must do their best to reassure them. As I have said, there are two distinct types of Capricorn. Our lively 'giddy' mountain goat, and our 'wet fish', or if you prefer it, our 'domestic animal'. Basically it is not difficult to decide which category our Capricorn friends fall into, but what is interesting is the fact that they will from time to time reverse their roles, so that unexpectedly we will find the lively, positive, aspiring mountain goat making its presence felt than someone who grumbles and moans a sure-footed trait of our, ambitious Capricorn friends. One of this sign's most endearing qualities is its off-beat sense of humour. We find the most dour, serious-minded Capricorn suddenly making the most unusual and witty remark-natural to them and a delight to others. Very often at such times they themselves will smile a grimacing kind of smile-the corners of their mouths turned down rather than up-an instantly recognisable characteristic. The Capricorn body-areas are the knees and shins; these are vulnerable, as are the teeth, skin and bones. Capricorns make good athletes, and long-distance running and rock-climbing are sports that could well appeal. Individual effort can be more fulfilling than participation in team games; Capricorns do well on their own and can cope with loneliness far better than many Zodiac types. Aquarius as Sun-sign Aquarius is the individualist of the Zodiac. Show two people with this sign prominent in their birth-charts a list of characteristics of the sign, and the only thing they will agree on is the fact that they share none of them. This sign bestows a great need for independence, which very often emerges in the building of a rather special and somewhat different lifestyle. Here, too, are some of the kindest, most helpful and friendly people of the Zodiac. They have a happy knack of knowing when help is needed and will give it freely without ulterior motives. However, although we may know them extremely well, if we think seriously about it they are in many way extremely private people. This could well be because of their need to be independent, and while having the capacity to give much of themselves to others they do not want to get too emotionally involved or find themselves in a situation which is at the most cloying or heavy.

Career and Finance

The potential for getting to the top is an integral part of every Capricorian character, and the sign is motivated by deep and powerful drive. Capricorn is an Earth sign, and while we find Capricornians in all kinds of careers (like every Sun-sign), they tend to gravitate to occupations with an 'earthy' quality-surveying property, farming, architecture, geology or geography, for instance. But politics and local government can attract them also, and so can the ultimate jobs at the top of their chosen profession-chairman of the board, headmaster or principal. Those of this Sun-sign can cope very well with the loneliness of a commanding position when, perhaps over the years, they have succeeded in getting to the top. They will stay there in perfect security, happily accepting ultimate responsibility, making final decisions, and in short be perfectly happy that the buck stops with them. Discipline and routine offer no problem, either, though sometimes they can tend to get stuck in a rut and be somewhat inflexible in their working methods.

Health and Food

In health sudden and unexpected illness are likely to happen. Stoppages and strictures of the internal organs and operations may be expected, but against that there will be long periods of good health.

You should study all questions of diet more than the average person and not allow yourself to live for any length of time in damp low-lying districts.

You are liable to have injuries to the lower limbs, weakness or turning of the ankles, injuries to the spinal column caused by falls or by accidents. Though the Saturnine influence indicates Virgoes constitution and good physical stamina but your tendency to depression may cause complicated health problems. You should cultivate optimism and cheerful disposition in order to keep in good health.

Suggested Food Options:
- Figs
- Green Vegetables
- Cow's milk
- Oranges

- Lemons
- Egg yolk
- Cheese
- Fish
- Food grains

Your Love Life

First Decan of Capricorn: December 22 to December 31

What you really want is the respect and affection of everyone around you and would shower those who love you with your own love and affection. This could be a slightly selfish approach and you might want to change it so as to avoid a potential partner from running away from you. No one would want to feel judged and evaluated all the while and hence, would want to look at more equable relationships.

The alliance of marriage for you is one which would satisfy your emotional wants and at the same time, would take care of the elements of romance and sexuality in your life. You would want the very best for your partner and would be quite critical even when loving your spouse.

You are very striving and motivated, however you need to stop coupling your personal and emotional ambitions together. Refrain from committing the grave error of pushing your spouse too hard to meet your own desires. After a while, your loved one would cease to see your love and look for it in another.

Although you might be pleased and content with your marriage, yet you wouldn't have the ability to see what all your partner would do for you and would only want things to be done in your own particular way. Your spouse would need plenty of patience and love to be able to overlook all your moods and tempers and give you the sense of importance that you so desire.

Second Decan of Capricorn: January 1 to January 10

You could be quite domineering in love, take your own good looks and charisma very seriously, and be inclined towards haughtiness of speech when wooed by someone who wants to know you well. In fact, you could well turn away your ideal partner by your behaviour and hence would need to be more careful about how you carry yourself.

In reality, you desire the emotion of love quite deeply. So deeply, that you want to deny its existence in your life. However, the fact remains that you want love and romance and no matter how hard you try to stomp it out using wisdom and pragmatism, it would always be there.

Your spouse or partner would need to have a lot of strength to be able to deal with your high ambitions and your emotions of bitterness which would engulf you when you feel that you are not making the desired progress and that you are being held back or thwarted by other people. Hence, you wouldn't be the easiest person to live with, and so should make a conscious attempt to better yourself.

You would be a dedicated and sincere partner when married to the right person. You need someone who would fulfill your sexual and emotional needs, be a motivating and supporting force in all your professional and social endeavours. It is then that you would give your very best to the relationship and hold on to it with tenacity and resolution.

Third Decan of Capricorn: January 11 to January 20

You have such a multifaceted personality that it becomes hard even for you to handle it completely. Affairs of the heart make things even more complex and at the same time, love is something that you truly value. When you're disillusioned or distressed with your love life, you can become unfaithful and indulge in extra marital relationships. You lack the ability to be positive about failure or the success of another person. As a result, you often tend to wallow in self-pity.

When in love with someone, you may be possessive, dominating and doubting. What you do want is to be married and that the marriage should make a difference to your lifestyle. If, perchance, your spouse doesn't give you the high life that you desire, you could well become contemptuous. Your spouse would have a tough job ahead in trying to meet your standards in all spheres of life.

You are extremely critical about how a person should look or dress and you wouldn't appreciate anyone who would be less than your expectations. Once married, you would want your partner to look his or her best at all times. The thoughts and opinions of your partner should also, be in keeping with your own and if they aren't you wouldn't hesitate from walking out of your marriage. Difficult to please and nearly mercenary, you wouldn't have many people who would be able to satisfy you and keep you content.

Your Sex Life

First Decan Saturn-ruled : December 22 to 31 December

Although you would have the powerful sex drive, so characteristic of Capricornians yet due to your attributes like determination to achieve a goal, restraint and patience, your interest in sex wouldn't be so obvious. Though your interest in the issue of sex might arise later in life, yet it wouldn't ever be a drawback. Fond of system and order, your sexual behaviour and expression would also, reflect the same. You would have immense energy for sex and also, an equally large repertoire for giving it expression.

Second Decan subruled by Venus: January 1 to 10 January

While you do have a pronounced romantic feature in your personality, it is not powerful enough to make you give up your inherently practical temperament. This would also, play an important role in your sexual behaviour as well. Although your naturally strong sex drive may take you towards many relationships, you wouldn't let this be the sole criterion when deciding about the permanence of a relationship. You would be good at planning for the future and this would influence your sexual expressions at the same time.

Third Decan, subruled by Mercury: January 11 to 20 January

For you, sex holds an important place, yet it isn't so vital that you would sacrifice everything else. Despite the fact that you have a powerful sex drive, you are not the kind to respond in an impulsive or reckless manner. You wouldn't hesitate from using sex to get what you want and your own ethics would determine how far you would go. You would make good use of your intelligence and practicality to attain a satisfying and gratifying sexual life style.

Capricorn Celebrities

Birth Date	Star	Vocation
6 January	A R Rahman	Musician
10 January	Hrithik Roshan	Film Star
11 January	Rahul Dravid	Sports Star
25 December	Atal Bihari Vajpayee	Political Leader
30 December	Sabeer Bhatia	Industrialist

Compatibility

CAPRICORN & ARIES

Earth Sign
Ruled by Saturn
- Stable
- Over-critical
- Determined
- Limited
- Social-climber
- Ambitious

Fire Sign
Ruled by Mars
- Weak
- Charming
- Hostile
- Trail-blazer
- Fickle
- Over-confident

Blending fire with earth can be quite a demanding composition, more so, since the ruling planets-Mars and Saturn, respectively, bestow contrasting characteristics on the two. While Aries' planet, Mars makes it impulsive, raring to go and burning with energy; Capricorn's ruler Saturn is vigilant, solemn, sedate and purposeful. Capricorn likes to be prepared for the future and can easily wait for results to show. However, Aries is restless and would need to see immediate results. The two would need to practice a great deal of patience and ensure that their differences don't create resentments. Aries might often get subdued by the Capricorn and might feel that the latter lacks understanding. This however is not really true, since Capricorn is capable of showing a great deal of sympathy when they want to do so.

Sexually, Capricorn desires to be romanticised before the act itself and Aries would need to ensure that this aspect is catered to, else Capricorn would lose interest and sex could become bereft of magic and love. Even though the Capricorn does not have a strong sex drive, he does enjoy the experience and would feel hurt if he/she isn't accepted easily. When hurt, Capricorn would retreat and Aries would need to bide his/her time till the former is willing to emerge once again and join in physical expressions of love. Sexually, like emotionally, their ruling planets play a significant role. While Aries is ruled by Mars-the planet of desire and sex, and hence would make the first move, frequently; Capricorn's planet is the steady Saturn which would give it the inclination to resist rather than reciprocate. Once these barriers are overcome and adjusted to, life would be relatively smoother and enjoyable for the two.

Capricorn would be pleasantly surprised and enchanted with the profundity of the love that he/she would receive and hence, this could play an important role in making their relationship rewarding, enduring and enjoyable.

Their sexual relationships would benefit greatly from paying heed to what they feel deep inside and by not repressing their desires and needs. This is true, especially for Capricorn who could spoil the spontaneity of the relationship by being too staid.

Take care, nourish and nurture your relationship with freshness and love and don't let the passions cool down. Only then would you be able to enjoy a mutually satisfying relationship that would stand the test of time.

Astro Advice
- Man should pursue surroundings with a positive force.
- Let your beloved handle any situation himself; do not interfere.

CAPRICORN & TAURUS

Earth Sign
Ruled by Saturn
- Stable
- Depressive
- Materialistic
- Trustworthy
- Depressive
- Generous

Earth Sign
Ruled by Venus
- Bibulous
- Temper
- Fertile
- Tolerant
- Selfish
- Tamper

This particular pairing is quite well-matched and attuned since the Taurean with his/her love of stability would value the Capricorn's realism, persistence and motivation. They would also, share attributes of patience, a certain level of orthodox values and most importantly, an adjustable attitude with an openness to share responsibilities. Since they would both place more emphasis on the deeper meanings and real pleasures of life rather than shallow ones, life could be a bit somber. However, their high level of compatibility would make up and they would manage to have a fair amount of fun as well.

Irrespective of when these two decide to get together, what they would want from each other and themselves would nearly always be similar. Practical and astute, they would be perturbed only by their own internal fears and anxieties. Though they would have a deep yearning for love and attention, they would hardly ever voice their feelings. So strong is their mutual respect and love for each other, that even when they would have the occasional tiff, they would find it hard to stay annoyed with one another for long. They would reason out with each other and make up within next to no time. Satisfied and happy, indeed, their union is a special one.

These two seem to be able to steer their relationship in the right direction and hence, their love affair would be free of unpleasant bumps and obstacles. Their relationship would be marked with fidelity, trust and love- the three essential ingredients for any successful relationship. The Taurean's sense of humour and impressive voice would be one of the sources of attraction for the Capricorn.

Taurus because of his/her highly developed senses is, in a way, better equipped and more ready for the sexual part of the relationship. This would help him/her to express the physical gestures of affection in a more expressive and sensitive manner.

For Taurus, the emotion of love when expressed physically is a profound and strong one. This would propel Capricorn to also, be more liberal and passionate in his/her quest for gentle, warm expressions of love.

Regardless of whatever minor differences they may have, these two are sexually just as compatible as they are emotionally and intellectually. Both have the ability to rouse the other to the heights of passion and sensuality. Their sexual union would have a firm foundation in the emotion of love which would, therefore, make it more meaningful. Both during and after the act, they would share a unique feeling of companionship and warmth that would bring them closer than ever before. They are, indeed, lucky because they would have a love that would last till the sun sets forever in the distant horizon.

Astro Advice

o Man should respond vibrantly to the feelings and ideas of his beloved.
o Woman should wear Blue Sapphire of five ratti on Saturday after Pran Pratishta (Prayer to Saturn).

CAPRICORN & GEMINI

Earth Sign Ruled by Saturn	Air Sign Ruled by Mercury
• Stable	• Intellectual
• Patient	• Communicative
• Reliable	• Open-minded
• Over-critical	• Ego-tripping
• Greedy	• Teases

Even though the elements of air and earth lack many similarities from one another, they still have the ability to give each other a sense of fulfillment. The youthfulness of Gemini complements the maturity of the Capricorn and they would spend many happy moments together as long as they learn to let each other know their thoughts and ideas verbally. There would be times when they would argue and debate, especially when Gemini would want to quit from something while Capricorn would want to take it through till the end. Moreover, the stable and balanced Capricorn would find it hard to comprehend the erratic, emotionally excitable temperament of Gemini. Yet, more often than not, they would be able to give each other a lot of mental and emotional satisfaction by their unique types of common sense and even, material gifts.

Theirs is a relationship that would be marked by their ability to accommodate and adapt. Somber but tender Capricorn would have the ability to soothe and direct the reckless, impulsive Gemini. he/she would have the capacity to give Gemini a place to seek refuge in and fill their souls with a feeling of tranquility.

As far as the physical aspect of the relationship goes, they would be able to bring the intuitive understanding of one another into this particular domain as well. It is not as if their sex life would be filled with fireworks, it would be more like a warm winter fire. For them, sex would be more a means of relaxing than anything else. Not the sort to be emotionally demanding they would enjoy feelings of companionship and bonding during sex.

Being able to express themselves sexually is critical and important for them and the relationship, particularly since both would attract and tempt each other infinitesimally. Although these two signs are considered to be quite cool emotionally, however, they do have a considerable amount of warmth concealed within them and at more than one level; this relationship has the quality of being rock solid and enduring.

It is indeed, a wonderful relationship and would have plenty of good moments to hold onto as warm memories.

Astro Advice
o Man : to impress your beloved show your good sense.
o Woman : wear any sort of dress with matching head accessory.

CAPRICORN & CANCER

Earth Sign   *Water Sign*
Ruled by Saturn   *Ruled by Moon*

- Social-climber
- Manipulator
- Limited
- Ambitious
- Materialistic

- Self-pitying
- Secure
- Tearful
- Cloying
- Helpless

While the elements of Water and Earth are indeed, compatible, the positioning of the signs in the Zodiac is such that they can not only be harmonising but also opponents to each other. The thin-skinned Cancer may feel wounded and uncared for if Capricorn is too ambitious and power-driven. While Cancer would appreciate and value the Capricorn's conscientiousness and dependability however, he/she would want Capricorn to be more emotional and warm since this would make a tremendous difference to the crab.

They have their share of similarities. Both are crusty outside but soft and mellow inside. They have a depth of emotion and would always like to be at the front. However, one of them would have to make more adjustments than the other and in all likelihood, it would be Cancer. Their similarities in conjunction with their differences would create a union that would be strong and supporting. It is a well-known fact that Cancer craves and seeks someone who would take care of his/her needs- emotional, mental and material. Therefore, the Capricorn is perfect because he/she is a motivated, prosperous, somewhat orthodox and slightly dominating go-getter. Initially, Cancer would give into Capricorn's authority for the sake of tranquility, however, at the end, it would be beneficial for both of them. The reticent Crab would be alluring and maybe a little too possessive while the Goat would be careful, genuine and protective. Together they would be sincere and wise about everything that they do.

Sexually as well, they would be sensitive and sensuous and even candidly erotic. The devotion and strength of Capricorn would motivate the Cancerian to be innovative and imaginative sexually. They would be as earnest about their sex life as they are with everything else. Deep, enriching and enlivening, they would give meaning and insight to their love and sex lives at all times.

Astro Advice
o Man should wear Blue Sapphire of six ratti on Saturday after Pran Pratishta (Prayer to Saturn)
o Woman : try to sort out of differences of opinion.

CAPRICORN & LEO

Earth Sign	Fire Sign
Ruled by Saturn	Ruled by Sun
• Narrow minded	• Ambitious
• Neglectful	• Popular
• Earthy	• Self-confident
• Loyal	• Restless
• Social-climber	• Elitist

The glaring differences between the element of Fire and Earth are further enhanced when one considers the éclat of the Sun with the orthodoxy of Saturn. When in a long-term intimate relationship, there is always the risk that the ebullient Leo would feel restrained and controlled by Capricorn. On the other hand, Capricorn could well think that Leo is way too much a spendthrift or even, physically demonstrative. The differences don't just end there. Leo would want to live life to the hilt while the careful Capricorn would want to plan and chart out everything to the minutest detail. Since Capricorn is not the kind to show his/her feelings in public, there would be times when Leo would feel isolated, ignored and abandoned. The Lion under all circumstances needs to be lavished with attention, care and recognition.

Since these two are so different from one another, they have an inherent inquisitiveness about the other one. This can result in one of two things. Either they would make each other get all awkward and nervy or they could bond together and learn to use their differences to the best possible advantage. It is, indeed, possible that Leo would learn stability and emotional security from Capricorn while the latter could adopt the Lion's optimism and ambition.

However, in all likelihood, this would be quite a tumultuous relationship with a fair amount of ups and downs. Particularly, because, Capricorn would find it difficult to be drawn towards a leonine personality. It is a personality that thrives on appreciation, attention and the element of drama. Capricorn would always find such a persona to be proud, arrogant and egotistic while Leo would consider Capricorn to be detached, aloof and cold-hearted. At the bottom of it all though, the fact remains that Leo would be able to mould Capricorn as per his/her likings, yet he/she would need to work really hard for the same.

Sexually, they can be quite incompatible. However, it does rest on the aspects of the planets in their individual horoscopes. Incompatibility could result in detachments and even, breaking away of ties. At the same time, if the planets are placed favourably, the sexual relations could be quite passionate and enduring.

All in all, this is a relationship that does not really stand on rock solid ground. It has an infirm basis and that could be its undoing.

Astro Advice
o Man should wear Blue Sapphire of six ratti on Saturday after Pran Pratishta (Prayer to Saturn)
o Woman should wear Ruby of six ratti on Sunday after Pran Pratishta (Prayer to Sun).

CAPRICORN & VIRGO

Earth Sign *Earth Sign*
Ruled by Saturn *Ruled by Mercury*

- Mercenary
- Hard-working
- Self-controlled
- Charitable
- Ego-tripping

- Analytical
- Down-to-earth
- Practical
- Tactless
- Quick-tempered

Both Virgo and Capricorn are Earth signs and hence, both of them would be well-grounded people who would have a respect for realism in their relationships and careers. Diligent, reliable and dutiful, they would, however, need to learn to be a little laidback at times. Ruled by Mercury and Saturn, respectively, they would be quite compatible as far a professional endeavors go, yet emotionality would be another issue altogether. Virgo would be able to keep his/her composure at all times with the Capricorn and the latter would, quite admire, Virgo's organised, planned way of life.

These two have plenty in common, especially when it comes to practical issues. For instance, money would never be a bone of contention between these two. Both would be equally careful about how to spend and save it. They would also, have a sound sense of realism and matter-of-factness. Well-matched with each other, they would be able to have quite a good time with each other and would also, have the incredible capacity to overlook and forgive one another easily and swiftly.

Sexually, they are compatible as well. Just that they would need to build their emotional togetherness before they enter into a sexual union. The best gift that these two have is the ability to communicate with each other with honesty and intensity. They would enjoy their lovemaking and it would become more profound and meaningful with the passage of time. The intimacy between them would develop gradually and when they express their desire for one another, their individual loyalty, affection and integrity comes to the fore. The hesitation, gentleness, exquisite intensity would make their sexual union a momentous and integral part of their relationship. It would add to its warmth, solidity and intimacy.

Astro Advice
o Men : avoid material disruptions.
o Women : curb over-spending.

CAPRICORN & LIBRA

Earth Sign *Air Sign*
Ruled by Saturn *Ruled by Venus*

- Trustworthy
- Calculating
- Hardworking
- Limited
- Manipulator

- Jealous
- Beautiful
- Considerate
- Moody
- Charming

Since Air and Water do not blend easily enough, it is essential that this pair have a mutual goal in mind or that Fate smiles upon them, for a relationship to blossom and grow. Libra would want to be given love and appreciation and would wish to see these sentiments being demonstrated, however, Capricorn wouldn't be the sort who would really enjoy doing all these things and this would disappoint the gentle, sensitive Libran. Moreover, Libra would take pleasure in straightforwardness, comfort and the finer things of life. On the contrary, Capricorn would have a more solemn approach towards life and would be able to deal with a lack of financial resources and a life of simplicity without much trouble. To ensure that Libra doesn't wallow in pity, Capricorn would have to keep in mind, to display his/her love and affection for Libra every now and then.

Although, emotionally, they may need to build a stronger understanding, in most other areas of life, this partnership would be quite a dynamic one. Libra-Capricorn couples have a great deal of perseverance and are quite focused on their goals in life. They would strive determinedly to attain whatever they wished to and would be able to reach the pinnacles of success and glory. Together, they would be a powerhouse of energy, enthusiasm and electric vitality.

The Libran would be a picture of elegance, gentleness and melodious beauty blended together however, it is quite a possibility that a conservative, morose Capricorn might ignore all the attractiveness of Libra and be highly aloof.

Their sexual union can be brought about only by a series of tactful attempts by both of them. Their ruling planets- Venus and Saturn are powerful ones and it is possible that the fact that they are opposite, characteristically, might serve to bring them closer to each other. Both would want to take dissimilar directions and this could either build the sexual tension or thwart it completely. A great deal is dependent on their personal ambitions, wants and horoscopes. Temperamental, one would often find either one of them teetering on the line between happiness and sadness. This would be a challenging pair, indeed. Happiness would lie in their hands and they would need to make the necessary adjustments and compromises to keep the relationship going.

Astro Advice
o Woman should dress up in a traditional outfit with a matching bindi on your forehead.
o Man should snap out of his dreamland.

CAPRICORN & SCORPIO

Earth Sign	*Water Sign*
Ruled by Saturn	*Ruled by Mars*
• Social-climber	• Magnetic
• Limited	• Creative
• Earthy	• Over-sexed
• Charitable	• Secretive
• Hard-working	• Power-tripping

The natural affinity of Water and Earth is indeed, a critical factor in this relationship, however, since the ruling planets, Mars and Saturn are strong, the journey ahead wouldn't be a mere bed of roses. Both, Scorpio and Capricorn, would have the attributes of diligence, dedication and determination and would be quite a partnership when pursuing a common goal of some significance. However, if they disagree, then there would be really troubled waters, since both would not give in without a fight. It would be silly to think that they would be able to make up quickly. Arguments and conflicts would stretch on endlessly, till either one of them sees reason and decides to make peace.

This couple would spend quite a lot of time talking about their personal and combined ambitions, aspirations and desires. While it is possible that the two might be in concurrence about the ambitions, they just might disagree about how to realise these aspirations. At the same time, both would want to be valued and appreciated and hence, might understand that the final result is more important than the ways adopted to achieve it.

Capricorn would be somewhat possessive and would want to give the relationship some sort of status, however, Scorpio might not return the sentiments. These two would not only share goals but also, personality traits, such as the habit of concealing their actual emotions and their ability to be restrained and regimented. Since they would have a certain amount of similarity between them, they would be attracted towards each other. Yet their companionship would have a tinge of isolation in it. They would love each other and give each other the warmth they need but would be cool and controlled once the wave of emotion has washed away.

As far as the sexual aspect of the relationship is concerned, Scorpio and Capricorn would both enhance and deepen the entire experience of love making. The intense Scorpio would arouse unknown emotions in Capricorn. They would share unique warmth in their lovemaking and would have a stable rapport with one another. However, Capricorn might hold back a little which could affect the experience and Scorpio could do with a bit more expressiveness. On the whole, though, both would have a good relationship with a fair amount of ups and downs, especially when both decide to stick to their individual guns and not budge. Patience, tolerance and logic are attributes they would really need to rely upon in order to reach a point where they attain bliss in each others' company forever.

Astro Advice

o Man : Avoid material disruption that hinder enjoyment.
o Woman : Keep no secret if you share a problem you will find a solution.

CAPRICORN & SAGITTARIUS

Earth Sign
Ruled by Saturn

- Manipulator
- Materialistic
- Self-controlled
- Charitable
- Loyal

Fire Sign
Ruled by Jupiter

- Trusting
- Sporting
- Intelligent
- Escapist
- Undisciplined

The stark contrast between the elements of Fire and Earth affects this relationship significantly. While Sagittarius is enthusiastic, positive, spontaneous and liberal, Capricorn is careful, reserved, orthodox, somber and even, cynical. Moreover, even the planets that rule them are conflicting. While the adage is that opposites attract, in this case, the temperamental and characteristic differences are too strong to be ignored. The open-minded, imaginative Sagittarius would not want to be tied down by the traditional Capricorn. Also, the latter would not be able to comprehend the Archer's inherent desires, ambitions and idealism. They would need to approach each other with more openness and cooperation if they want the relationship to be a satisfying one.

There is no doubt about the fact that the two are irresistibly drawn towards each other, irrespective of their differences. However, they would need to work out these differences so that peace and happiness may prevail. Especially when money and finances are concerned, they would have absolutely conflicting ideas and opinions. As far as similarities are concerned, the hardy Capricorn would be able to stomach the tactless straightforward nature of the Archer with relative ease.

There would be quite a few adjustments that would have to be made, as far as their attitude towards romance is concerned. There would be times when Sagittarius would want to play the seducer but Capricorn wouldn't be interested at all. This could lead to some amount of hurt and anger in both. However, it shouldn't indicate that they wouldn't be able to have a healthy sexual relationship; it just means that they would have to work out and sort out their differences in this area as well. Their sexual life would be negatively affected if they do not learn to solve their problems and adjust to each other's perspectives.

Since Sagittarius is spontaneous and warm, he/she may perceive Capricorn as being isolated and aloof. This could lead to problems in their sexual behaviour. Capricorn would need to loosen up a little and give in to the impulsive nature of love instead of being rigid and regimented about the whole affair. Also, Sagittarius should understand that while lovemaking can be enjoyable and impulsive, it shouldn't ever interfere with the values of Capricorn; rather it should encourage him/her to be more expressive and effusive.

If they overcome their dissimilarities, they would have a sex life that would be stable and secure. They would need to trust each other implicitly and give each other gentle love and affection so as to reach the depths of intimacy.

Astro Advice

- Man : while meeting it would help if you put on a white shirt with black trousers.
- Woman : remember your hair is your crowning glory.

CAPRICORN & CAPRICORN

Earth Sign
Ruled by Saturn
- Stable
- Patient
- Practical
- Earthy
- Charitable

Earth Sign
Ruled by Saturn
- Stable
- Patient
- Practical
- Earthy
- Charitable

Two Capricorns together means a couple who would be doubly traditional, practical, and careful as they move through the different phases of life. It would be essential that both interact and mingle with a variety of people else, they would become too staid and monotonous. if both the partners are pursuing the same goals, they would be able to realise them since their concerted efforts would definitely bring success. On the other hand, if either one of them tries to be manipulative, the other would become bitter and aggrieved. Those who are laidback and exploratory would tend to find this couple a bit too somber and strict, bordering on being stiff and distant.

The best part about this relationship would be the fact that neither Capricorn would run the other one down, especially since it would imply running oneself down. Rather they would smoothen troubled waters by amiably appreciating each others' qualities. Another reason for not being critical is simply that quite a few Capricorns tend to perceive their drawbacks as their strengths and would try and remove every possible shortcoming from their characters. When they decide to work together, they can bring about brilliant prosperity from the most meager of resources. Also, both wouldn't place too much importance on money and finances.

This couple wouldn't be the sort who would fall in love instantly. Mainly because both are too sensible to give in to the first rush of emotion. They would start out maybe, as friends and then, when they see the affection, warmth and tolerance being reciprocated, fall in love with each other. These virtues are essential since they would ensure that the relationship be a strong and stable one.

Both would have a healthy interest in sex and lovemaking, yet they would need to loosen up a little, otherwise, there is the possibility that they would be missing out on this essential aspect of a relationship. One of them, at least, would need to be more lighthearted and fun so that sexual activity continues without any problems.

Two Capricorns together would tend to be in perfect control of their emotions and hence, would be in a better position to direct the course of their relationship than other couples. If they work on being more demonstrative emotionally and affectionately, the relationship could be a happy and fulfilling one in all aspects.

Astro Advice

o Man should avoid junk food and focus on exercise.
o Woman : best to observe silence over heated discussion.

CAPRICORN & AQUARIUS

 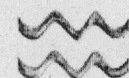

Earth Sign
Ruled by Saturn
- Limited
- Ego-trapping

Air Sign
Ruled by Saturn
- Fanatical
- Erratic

- Neglectful
- Self-controlled
- Ambitious
- Visionary
- Caring
- Loyal

The elements of Earth and Air do not have much in common; neither do the ruling planets of these signs-even though both signs have Saturn as ruling planet. This would be a relationship which would be affected by temperaments, opinions and personalities. Both the partners would have to make a lot of compromises and this could pose some problems, since the liberal, obstinate Aquarius would be stuck on his/her own ideals while the Capricorn would be just as rigid about his/her beliefs and opinions. Capricorn would find it difficult to understand why the Water bearer tends to become erratic and whimsical. This would have a negative impact on Capricorn's desire to achieve steadiness and stability in his/her life and relationship. What the Capricorn fails to see is that the intelligent, innovative Aquarian enjoys novelty and risks, irrespective of the results.

When a Capricorn and an Aquarius decide to join forces, one can never be sure of what would be the final result. The steady, realistic Capricorn cannot comprehend the Aquarian's point of view on most things and for the Aquarian dreams are just an extension of reality. The latter would dream of the most impossible things as per the Capricorn but then, would also, work hard at achieving them. The Aquarian is not satisfied treading the beaten path and would blaze his/her own trail wherever he/she goes.

As far as their physical relationship is concerned, it wouldn't be all smooth sailing. Capricorn would have a tendency to be gloomy and Aquarian would tend to be occupied with one of his/her many pursuits. In fact, Capricorn could have to face quite a few difficulties in getting the Aquarian to take a keen interest in lovemaking. The sober, calm and stable Capricorn could find the Aquarian quite a strange being and would need to look at him/her through a wider perspective. The Aquarian approach towards sex and lovemaking could extend from an avid inquisitiveness to an aloof approval while the Capricorn would view it more as an obligation of being in love. The one thing that is for sure is that neither one would overestimate or underestimate its importance. They would eventually participate and practice sexual activities but without any intensity of emotion or passion. This aspect of their relationship could have quite a few problems and both would need to work together in order to resolve them.

This would be a union which would gain meaning and insight with the passage of time. Both partners would learn to accommodate and adjust. They would have a better way of looking at the other's point of view and this could create a sense of harmony in an otherwise disturbed equation.

Astro Advice
o Man should wear black stone of five ratti on ring finger.
o Woman should wear Blue sapphire of four ratti on Saturday.

CAPRICORN & PISCES

Earth Sign *Water Sign*
Ruled by Saturn *Ruled by Neptune*
- Social-climber
- Inhabited
- Dependable

- Peaceful
- Guilt
- Diffuse

- Over-critical
- Limited
- Unreliable
- Idealistic

The elements of these two signs- Earth and Water respectively have a natural bonding with each other and despite their dissimilarities; they do tend to harmonise with one another. Capricorn is the very personification of stability and steadiness. Pisces, on the other hand, is quite comfortable adjusting to such kind of people. However, the tender and romantic Pisces may feel injured at times, when the serious Capricorn doesn't demonstrate his/her affection. Both would, in most cases, work in tandem with one another. Pisces is not the sort who is overly ambitious and hence, would be supportive of Capricorn's desire to grow and rise in life and society. Moreover, the steady Capricorn's realism and ability to administrate would protect the Piscean from the difficulties that life may present in front of them.

The astute Capricorn would give the sensitive and gentle Pisces a warm sense of security and faithfulness which would illuminate and enrich his/her life and bring the relationship to a new dimension altogether. As far as their sexual relationship is concerned, both would give it a practical yet romantic touch. The Capricorn would express himself/herself in a straightforward way and also, be attentive to the Piscean needs and wishes. Their lovemaking would be marked by the strength and intensity of their emotions for each other. Since both wouldn't be extremely communicative, their silence, itself, would speak volumes. The sexual bonding of these two souls would be sensitive, ideal and would bring them together in perfect intimacy; filling their hearts and minds with tranquility, softness and completeness.

Astro Advice
o Man should wear Blue sapphire of four ratti on Saturday.
o Woman : focus on good habits.

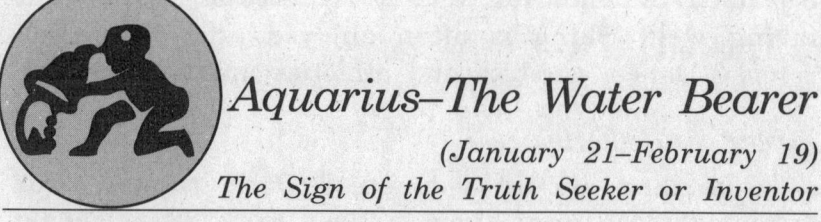

Aquarius–The Water Bearer
(January 21–February 19)
The Sign of the Truth Seeker or Inventor

How to Recognise Aquarius

Aquarians have great originality and real flair, which can be used in a variety of fields, and should be allowed full expression. They often do well in the so-called glamourous professions-theatre, television, the beauty trades, or anywhere where their originality can be expressed freely and rewardingly. Many carve successful careers in science, and interestingly it is very often the case that Aquarians are fascinated by the remote past and the equally remote and distant future-archaeology and geology at one end of the scale and space fact and fiction at the other. This too can colour the choice of spare-time interests. Aquarians make excellent forward-looking parents, and will sympathise with their children when they become involved with the concerns and crazes of their generation. But, surprisingly, Aquarians can be very stubborn and extremely unpredictable, and it is their children, as much as their friends and partners, who will become aware of these particular, and to all intents and purposes somewhat unexpected, traits. Parents of Aquarian children must respect their tremendous need for independence, and learn to accept it and the fact that while they may appear somewhat zany there is probably more common sense in their personalities than may appear on the surface. Interests that are way out or wild must not be discouraged - here is a young Aquarius expressing his or her originality. The Aquarian body-area is the ankles. These are vulnerable. The circulation is also ruled by Aquarius, and it is necessary to keep it moving well. Sking is often enjoyed, and is a good exercise. Dance, aerobics and athletics are all excellent.

Career and Finance

Aquarians should not waste their capacity for conceiving ideas in relation to their work. They should think them through properly and put them to their employers, for they have a talent for invention and may well come up with some excellent suggestions. They should apply themselves to thinking how work can be made quicker, more efficient and more interesting. If they are working, say, on a factory assembly line with no outlet for their inventiveness, they might do as well to turn their attention to the social life of their firm. They would find a great deal of satisfaction discovering common areas of interest among their workmates and setting up societies and clubs. Alternatively they might put their energies into union affairs and become hard-working shop-stewards. Such activities greatly enliven their working days. Often when a human problem is involved the Aquarian is there to help, whether by visiting a sick colleague in hospital or making sure that a retired employee is not forgotten. Aquarians are not usually too concerned about the atmosphere in which they work. They can concentrate in a noisy room, and are good at shutting off their minds from any squabbles or arguments going on in the office. If promotion comes to them they will accept it with pleasure, and usually with the conviction that they can handle any additional responsibility. If someone behaves offensively to them Aquarians tend to rise above any personal feelings of injury and bid their time until everything is forgiven and forgotten, or the conflict is resolved in some other way. Aquarians usually hate to waste time on any form of petty distraction from the job in hand. They will enjoy their coffee-breaks or business luncheons, but they will be equally happy to fill the entire day with work.

Health and Food

Persons born in this sign give the appearance of being more healthy than they really are. They get little or no warning about illness, they often suddenly collapse from heart failure or a clot of blood in the brain.

Suggested Food Options:
- Fish
- Pear
- Lemon
- Oranges
- Radish
- Grapes
- Peach

Your Love Life

First Decan of Aquarius: January 21 to January 30

You have a tendency of being quite serious and difficult as far as the affairs of the heart are concerned. You deem yourself superior to the rest and have a nearly irrational wish to have all the aspects of your life to be absolutely perfect and ideal. Hence, you would be prone to disappointment and disenchantment. Despite the fact that you are an air sign, your criteria for judging the love in your relationship would be quite earthy and realistic.

You would have a somewhat self-centred approach towards relationships, wanting to take more than what you, yourself, are willing to give. You would also, have high standards and would expect more than a hundred percent from your partner. Broken promises, insincerity and the like would freeze you completely and you may reconsider the relationship. Even when married, if your spouse doesn't live up to your standards, you could become highly aloof and isolated.

While you may get married and even stay married, you would still be able to travel beyond the romantic emotions of love and affection and exist in a world of your own making, devoid of illusions and idealism. This would, unfortunately, isolate you from those who truly care for you and can also, cause you to wander from place to place in search of the true meaning of life. Try not to be too harsh and demanding and give your partner some leeway. This would help you to build a harmonious and happy relationship which would withstand the test of time and turmoil.

Second Decan of Aquarius: January 31 to February 9

You have quite an idealist's view of romance and the way you react in situations of the heart is quite delicate and airy, typical of your sign. You fit the role of a dreamer perfectly and your love could remain unfulfilled if you don't learn to accept and care for people as they are, with the good and the bad in them. It is essential that you keep in mind that love entails being able to accept one's loved ones with all their shortcomings and flaws and not using these to judge them harshly.

While you may float on cloud nine when in love, you could also, become aloof and isolated when you detect something that is not to your liking. In states of irritation and anger, you could use harsh and cutting words with the one you love and may even be difficult to understand since more often than not, you would be in a world of your own.

You do have good chances of being happy and content in your love life, if you learn to be more conversant about what makes you anxious or annoyed and also, if you learn to be a little easy on people. With understanding, warmth and love you would indeed be able to enjoy a love that would stay sparkling forever and would radiate its tenderness and glow throughout your life for all the days to come. Just learn to give people a chance and not be highly critical of the one you love. Let them be who they are for that is the reason you fell in love with them in the first place.

Third Decan of Aquarius : February 10 to February 19

Born in this decan of the zodiac, you could have the maximum amount of trouble with affairs of the heart than any other sign. Though you regard the emotion of love as a boon to humanity, you are quite hard to please and also, the most likely to walk away from a relationship. The person who cares for you should in every case, value your independence, your individualism, your radical thinking and you, completely.

The person who would love you and stay with you through all the tests of time would be one who is highly selfless and at the same time, self-respecting. Since you are the kind who would have a wide circle of friends from both sexes, it is easy for anyone to become possessive and jealous and that is something you wouldn't appreciate. Hence, it would take a person who truly trusts and respects you to be able to stay with you forever.

When you are in a promising and stable relationship which has the necessary elements of love, trust and security, you would be filled with a lot of happiness and would cherish your beloved deeply. Although you are not the kind to indulge in public displays of affection, your small gestures would speak volumes. Profoundly devoted and sincere, you wouldn't stand a single instance of disloyalty or unfaithfulness. This doesn't mean that you cannot forgive; just that you have high standards as far as fidelity in marriage or a relationship is concerned.

Your Sex Life

First Decan, Uranus-ruled: January 21 to 30 January

You would, in all likelihood, have a sex life that would swing between periods of hectic sexual activity and absolute indifference. Erratic and fickle, you would be the same in your approach towards sex as you are with other things. While your outlook may seem illogical to others, you would be able to justify it completely. Ruled by the planet Uranus, you are somewhat excitable and edgy and can be attracted by unusual relationships. You would also have a nonchalant irreverence for the current traditions and principles. Though you would have a powerful sex drive, it could be slightly sporadic and would be quite a reflection of your actual personality.

Second Decan, sub-ruled by Mercury: January 31 to February 9

You have the wonderful knack of being able to use the power of words to get out of or into any situation you want. This extends to sexual situations as well, where you sometimes might get caught in the heat of the moment and then realise that it is not what you wanted. Essentially, your mental approach plays a more critical role in your sexual behaviour than mere physical attraction. Hence, your sex life and behaviour could easily be a result of the way the sexual stimuli act upon your mind and how you make use of the powers of imagination and creativity. Your mind would be a powerful determinant of your sexual expression.

Third Decan, sub-ruled by Venus: February 10 to February 19

As you are quite the romantic dreamer and aren't afraid of exploring the new and unknown, you would be quite drawn towards the strange, fascinating and other intriguing aspects of sex. This would further imply that your sex life would be a myriad collection of exotic experiences. Though many astrological factors, such as your birth chart factors, and other personality attributes would play a critical role in determining your sexual behaviour, it is quite obvious that you would have an extremely exciting sexual life and it would be filled with many striking sexual escapades.

Aquarius Celebrities

Birth Date	Star	Vocation
1 February	Ajay Jadeja	Sports Star
4 February	Birju Maharaj	Dancer
8 February	Jagjit Singh	Musician
25 January	Kavitha Krishnamurthy	Musician
31 January	Preity Zinta	Film Star

Compatibility

AQUARIUS & ARIES

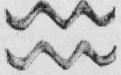 

Air Sign
Ruled by Saturn
- Cowardly
- Truthful
- Sympathetic
- Progressive
- Caring
- Honest

Fire Sign
Ruled by Mars
- Enjoys challenges
- Reckless
- Bossy
- Optimistic
- Diligent
- Adventurous

While Fire and Air do tend to gel quite well with each other, the planets that rule them tend to create a huge amount of power and influence which would need to be dealt with in a positive manner.

The unique Aquarius would not ever want to put a wet blanket on the natural freedom and inventiveness of Aries, while Aries would welcome the presence of a companion in Aquarius. The innovative methods of the Aquarian would appeal to Aries, who in turn would appreciate anything with a touch of novelty. However, the erratic behaviour of the Aquarius could throw the Aries off and make him/her irritated. Both signs would, in any case, get along quite well simply because both are quite often misconstrued and think out of the box. There would be the occasional instances when Aquarius wouldn't be able to comprehend the Arian's fiery temper and the Arian would feel as if the Water bearer exists on a different planet. Yet, aside from these minor issues, the two would share an inimitable connection with each other.

Aquarians would hardly, if ever, overdo him/herself in the sexual department. Primarily so, because they would be more involved in other activities and hence, would engage in sex only when they feel like, which could make them somewhat selfish in this area.

Fundamentally, the two signs share a lot of similarities and hence, would understand and respect each other greatly. While there could be fireworks since both can get somewhat forceful at times, the level of harmony would be much greater. Aries and Aquarius would be drawn towards each other because of their emotional and intellectual similarities. All this would ensure that the relationship is rewarding and beneficial to both the parties involved and the occasional tiffs would only add to the magic between the two. With time and practice, the two would learn how to create the beautiful music of

AQUARIUS

While Fire and Air do tend to gel quite well with each other, the planets that rule them tend to create a huge amount of power and influence which would need to be dealt with in a positive manner.

The unique Aquarius would not ever want to put a wet blanket on the natural freedom and inventiveness of Aries, while Aries would welcome the presence of a companion in Aquarius. The innovative methods of the Aquarian would appeal to Aries, who in turn would appreciate anything with a touch of novelty. However, the erratic behaviour of the Aquarius could throw the Aries off and make him/her irritated. Both signs would, in any case, get along quite well simply because both are quite often misconstrued and think out of the box. There would be the occasional instances when Aquarius wouldn't be able to comprehend the Arian's fiery temper and the Arian would feel as if the Water bearer exists on a different planet. Yet, aside from these minor issues, the two would share an inimitable connection with each other.

Aquarians would hardly, if ever, overdo him/herself in the sexual department. Primarily so, because they would be more involved in other activities and hence, would engage in sex only when they feel like, which could make them somewhat selfish in this area.

Fundamentally, the two signs share a lot of similarities and hence, would understand and respect each other greatly. While there could be fireworks since both can get somewhat forceful at times, the level of harmony would be much greater. Aries and Aquarius would be drawn towards each other because of their emotional and intellectual similarities. All this would ensure that the relationship is rewarding and beneficial to both the parties involved and the occasional tiffs would only add to the magic between the two. With time and practice, the two would learn how to create the beautiful music of love with each other. They do have the capacity to enrich each other's lives and would do so, once they overcome the minor hurdles in their path.

Astro Advice
o You are advised to keep porcelain figures of Venus and Jasmine in the South-West corner of your bedroom.
o Man should wear Yellow Sapphire of seven carat on index finger
o Woman : it may be necessary to accept a stronger point of view.

AQUARIUS & TAURUS

Air Sign	Earth Sign
Ruled by Saturn	Ruled by Venus
• Honest	• Distrusting
• Negative	• Philosophical
• Critical	• Boring
• Rebellious	• Artistic
• Cowardly	• Slow
• Truthful	• Fruitful

These are two signs who are two opposite poles and hence, have little in common with each other. Different in temperament, they would find it difficult to understand and adjust with one another. While the earthy Taurus would find it hard to accept Aquarius's erratic ways and desire for freedom along with openness to spread love and affection with all and sundry, the liberal Aquarian would find Taurus' inability to share love with everybody difficult to digest. For Taurus, feelings and emotions are meant to be shared only with those who hold any significance. Moreover, they would also, differ socially. The Aquarian would be able to make acquaintances if not friends in next to no time while for the Taurean it would take ages to be able to bond with another. Taurus is practical and realistic, taking in to account the present and preparing for the future while the Aquarian is just the opposite, living in an ideal world and more in the future than in the present. All things said and done, if the two want to make the relationship work, they would be able to do so only if they learn to communicate with one another and also, compromise and adjust with each other. If they do so, there is plenty that they could learn from each other and it would be an extremely enlightening experience for both of them. Talking things out and learning to deal with their differences would bring them closer emotionally and also, give them greater insight into each others' souls.

For the Taurus, love is an emotion that needs to be taken seriously and rarely if ever, would one find the Taurean plunging headlong into love. However for the Aquarian, love happens mostly at first sight. For the Taurean, profound, sincere love happens over a period of time and is the most beautiful, soul-touching emotion of all.

Since both are tightly wound bundles of energy, there would be quite a few turbulent scenes. Yet they also, have the capacity to brave the odds and forge a bond filled with gentleness and understanding. Sexually, they wouldn't be compatible unless they learn to satisfy the other's needs and merge their desires with their imagination to be able to achieve sexual compatibility.

Astro Advice

o Man should show their feelings by giving gifts and valentine cards.
o Woman should wear modern clothes to impress her lover.

AQUARIUS & GEMINI

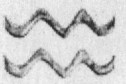

Air Sign Ruled by Saturn	Air Sign Ruled by Mercury
• Honest	• Ambitious
• Forthright	• Imaginative
• Erratic	• Bright
• Cowardly	• Impulsive
• Caring	• Temperamental

Although the combination of Air with Air is well-matched yet the planets that rule them-Mercury and Saturn endow them with diametrically opposite temperaments and thought processes. It would be this constant element of change and differences that would make the relationship enjoyable and appealing. The freedom-loving Gemini would be able to get accustomed to Aquarius's aloofness and unconventional behaviour and would also, be inspired by his/her innovativeness and uniqueness.

Despite the differences that their respective planets bestow them with, Gemini and Aquarius are usually quite compatible with one another. They have more or less the same way of looking at things, issues and opinions. They are not disturbed by each others' idiosyncrasies and variable moods. Together they can be entertaining, amusing and even, thought provokingly deep.

They have the habit of being either a wonderful source of happiness or an irritatingly complex enigma for others, yet for each other they would be plain, simple, easy to read as books. The areas they would need to tread with care would be the fact that both are equally complicated and although fits of rage would be rare, there could be plenty of arguing and heated debates. On the whole, this is one pair with an exceedingly strong compatibility. With relatively few areas of concern, they would sail through life and togetherness blissfully. They would make a good amount of money, however, even if they happen to lose it, they wouldn't be terribly perturbed. Their shared likes and dislikes in movies, books, travel, spiritualism and even animals would ensure that they always have something to talk about and discuss.

Since both of them would have a diverse range of interests and hobbies to keep them busy, they would often not feel the need to engage in sexual activities as often as others. Gemini might feel the lack at times, but on the whole, both would be occupied and engaged in a host of other things and wouldn't even realise that there is something missing.

Sexually, they wouldn't give a lot of importance to the act of loving. At the same time, they wouldn't neglect it altogether. It is just something that they would accept as being part of a relationship and deal with it. They would enjoy it whenever they indulge in it. It would be like everything else in their relationship-enigmatic, exhilarating, and elating. So entertaining is this pair that even the wrong moves they would make would be highly enjoyable.

They would be able to achieve better and more sexual satisfaction if Venus and Mars in their horoscopes are heavily afflicted. This is one relationship, where even if the partners do have some doubts about their sexual compatibility, as long as they are together, their sex life would be fantastic even if occasional.

Astro Advice

o Man should wear Black Stone of eight ratti on Saturday after Pran Pratishta (Prayer to Saturn).
o Woman should trust her beloved.

AQUARIUS & CANCER

| Air Sign | Water Sign |
Ruled by Saturn	Ruled by Moon
• Honest	• Lazy
• Impractical	• Fertile
• Erratic	• Good-memory
• Cowardly	• Dramatic
• Loyal	• Helpless

The elements of Water and Air as well as the ruling planets- Moon and Saturn have a great deal of differences. The emotional temperament and possessiveness of Cancer can stifle and smother the liberal and independent Aquarius. The water bearer is an aloof, impersonal lover who would radiate his/her love to the entire world rather than confine it to one single person.

While Cancer finds Aquarius intriguing and Aquarius finds Cancer cooperative, the two have very little in common, as far as personality traits are concerned. Cancer doesn't like the straightforward nature of the

Aquarian while the latter doesn't really appreciate the Cancerian habit of sulking. Together they would be highly volatile. The emotional Cancer would experience and express all the emotions under the sun but the practical Aquarian would muse about the essentiality of those emotions and the reasons for them. There could be times when they could get on each others' nerves and need to be away from one another so that the distance could make the heart grow fonder. However, if they are willing to adjust and make compromises, they would find happiness and love in each others' arms. The determination of the crab would win over the Aquarian while the idealism of the water bearer would strike a chord with the Cancerian.

Physically, the relationship would be quite harmonious. Cancer would have to tempt Aquarius, so that the latter doesn't get occupied with one of his varied interests. Intellectual stimulation works best with Aquarius. Both would use the power of gestures and eyes to communicate their feelings. Their sexual union would indeed be charged and dynamic which would enhance the quality of their relationship as well.

Astro Advice
o Man : do not be in the grip of false hopes.
o Woman : you need to take care of your body & health.

AQUARIUS & LEO

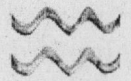 

Air Sign
Ruled by Saturn
- Honest
- Caring

Fire Sign
Ruled by Sun
- Rude
- Over-sexed

- Individualistic
- Zealous
- Rebellious
- Loving
- Creative
- Leader

Regardless of the fact that Fire and Water have an inherent attraction, the signs of Leo and Aquarius are placed opposite to one another in the Zodiac charts. At the beginning there could be a powerful attraction which could later, turn into equally intense antagonism. Both, Leo and Aquarius, have set ideas, strong wills and are intensely indomitable. Therefore, if one of them doesn't learn to adjust and give way, there could be big problems on hand.

Since Leo needs validation and attention at all times, he/she would find it difficult to digest that Aquarius intends on spending a considerable amount of time and attention on people in general. It would be hard for the Lion to get accustomed to the idea of Aquarius being independent and even aloof. The unpredictable, erratic nature of Aquarius would never cease to puzzle and confuse Leo. This could lead to some misunderstandings which would need to be dealt with in a mature fashion with communication and rationality.

It is not as if both of them are starkly different. They do have a fair deal in common and would often have great times in each others' company. Both are fond of being surprised and are liberal in their thinking. They are both givers and protectors of the weak and needy. Most of the values they believe in are common. Hence they would manage to generate an atmosphere of optimism, goodness and ambition around them. Both of them are also, logical and intelligent beings who would consciously make an effort to develop qualities of gentleness, patience, meekness which would ensure that the relationship moves on the right track at all times.

There would be instances when the fixated nature of their signs would make them adopt contradictory stances in a discussion resulting in a stand-off. The pride of the Lion would confuse and even irk, the relatively fuss-free Aquarius. The indifference of Aquarius, on the other hand, coupled with his/her changeableness would make Leo display his/her fiery temper. This would be one of the times when a logical, calm discussion would just not be possible. It would be best to let time do its work and when they cool down, both would be able to analyse and reflect on their actions and words in a sensible manner.

Sexually, Leo would be the one to take dominance, since he/she would have a powerful sex drive and would be able to use it well to enrich the relationship. In this area, Aquarius would cede gracefully and admire the Lion's excellence. Their lovemaking would be preceded by sweet words, gestures and even, gifts to please. The entire atmosphere would be one of tranquility and bliss.

Although, their individual needs from the relationship differ, yet their sexual bonding would bring them much closer and would give their relationship a wonderfully, interesting dimension.

Astro Advice
o Both are suggested to avoid getting caught in controversial issues.

AQUARIUS & VIRGO

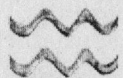

Air Sign
Ruled by Saturn
- Broadminded
- Unpredictable

Earth Sign
Ruled by Mercury
- Prudish
- Complaining

- Erratic
- Negative
- Truthful
- Concentration
- Critical
- Prissy

The alliance of Earth with Air shows the difference between the two. Moreover, the permutation of their individual rulers- Mercury & Uranus-highlights a rational and academic likeness, rather than a profound sentimental relationship. Virgo is logical and calm in approach and demeanor. Aquarius is aloof, unattached and unemotional in more ways than one. However, it is the Aquarian randomness, and eccentricity that tends to throw the placid Virgo off-guard and he/she finds it increasingly difficult to comprehend the Aquarian mystique.

This particular relationship can be quite a difficult task to handle. Since both enjoy observing the other from afar, they would need to be pushed towards each other to take the first step towards closeness. However, once they do form the bond, it would be filled with sparks and liveliness. The sharpness and logic of the Virgo is just what the imaginative and brilliant Aquarian needs. Moreover, both are inherently gentle and sensitive and also, dream beautiful dreams deep within. They are independent yet related closely to one another. Theirs would have to be a unique and deep love.

Sexually, Aquarius would want gentleness and warmth and Virgo would be able to give the same. Virgo, however, would not be able to maintain an air of allure at all times and this may cause some dissatisfaction. Since both are not terribly oriented towards marriage, what would be the real direction of this relationship only time would tell.

Astro Advice

o Man : show your feelings by giving gifts and flowers.
o Women : wear gold bangle or bracelet.

AQUARIUS & LIBRA

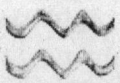 

Air Sign	Air Sign
Ruled by Saturn	Ruled by Venus
• Broadminded	• Considerate
• Eccentric	• Jealous
• Disruptive	• Good taste
• Inefficient	• Hospitable
• Cowardly	• Fastidious

The natural affinity between Air and Air brings these two signs in close proximity with each other and they would take pleasure in and even depend upon the company of one another. While Libra would symbolise the personal; Aquarius would signify the universal and together they would be able to create a relationship filled with tact, understanding, sharing and loving. Since Aquarius is somewhat erratic in disposition, Libra would need to demonstrate discretion and not annoyance, to handle the independent Water-bearer. Both would, as a matter of fact, give each other plenty of space and freedom and yet have a close bond filled with intimacy.

The two of them would enjoy honing their intellect and would engage in intelligent and meaningful discussions which would interest, enthuse and motivate them. The dreamy Libran would dream while the practical Aquarius would try to realise them or see their futility.

While this could be amusing for sometime, after a point, it might tend to grate on their nerves. However, whatever may be the case; it could always be resolved by a bit of compromise and adjustment. Also, Libra would always be able to forgive Aquarius and there wouldn't be any hard feelings.

Libra-Aquarius couples share many interests; especially in travel, the arts, children and even spirituality. They have an inherent compatibility and a strong appreciation for one another which would help them to actualise whatever they intend to. Both have a common interest in children, education, philosophy arts and foreign travel. The laidback Libra revels in opulence, ease and all the good things; this could well be in contradiction with the pragmatic Aquarian's desire to serve humanity and society. However, there is nothing that is grossly conflicting with these two and hence, can always be taken care of by cooperating and adjusting.

As far as their sexual relations go, Libra would want Aquarius to play the dominant part in bed and this could lead to frustrations and discord in the bedroom but in spite of all this, there would be a certain peacefulness and stillness whenever these two would make love.

It is quite a possibility that Aquarius might not have given much importance to sex before this, however, on meeting Libra, he/she would definitely change this opinion. Libra is a spontaneous lover and would eventually win over the normally reticent Aquarian. Aquarius could also, learn how to be as innovative and inventive in bed as he/she is outside it. The simple truth of the matter being that both require each other immensely and hence, would try hard to please and satisfy the other. They are in perfect sync with each other and complete each other.

Astro Advice

o Man : do not be fickle in love.
o Woman : your sweet words work like a magic cure on your beloved.

AQUARIUS & SCORPIO

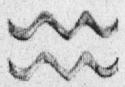

Air Sign	Water Sign
Ruled by Saturn	Ruled by Mars
• Visionary	• Courageous
• Broadminded	• Hypersensitive
• Critical	• Survivors
• Disruptive	• Healers
• Negative	• Arrogant

Since there is a tremendous disparity between the elements of air and water, these two signs would also show differences even in their similarities. Despite the fact that both are equally strong-minded and resolute and can bring about great results if they decide to pool their resources, the two are also, characteristically different. While Scorpio is deeply passionate and possessive, Aquarius is inclined to be liberated and absolutely his/her own person. If intense Scorpio attempts to rein in the eccentric Aquarian, there would be an endless conflict that shall affect the relationship severely.

In the event that there occurs a severe disagreement, Aquarius would try and get over it smoothly and with the least pain. However, Scorpio would be affected deeply. Both view the emotion of love in different perspectives. For Scorpio it is a profound emotion that must be felt completely. On the other hand, Aquarius has a wider definition of the same and it spans all humanity at an impersonal level. Both would need to be more understanding of each others' viewpoints and accept their differences along with their similarities. If the two decide to give the relationship a permanent status, there might be some teething difficulties; however, these could always be resolved by gaining an understanding of each other and by the use of astrology. This would be a enriching and illuminating experience for both of them.

It is indeed interesting to think about the consequences of putting a Scorpio and an Aquarian together. While the relationship may have quite a few adjustment problems, it could work out well if both the partners are mature enough to realise the significance of making those adjustments. Despite all their differences, they would be able to form a bond that is intriguing and innovative.

Sexually, Scorpio would have a stronger desire than the Aquarian which might cause the former to feel a little isolated and neglected. This would be one of the areas where they would need to work out their differences so that instead of a long drawn conflict situation, they are able to achieve a comfort level that warms their hearts and lives.

This would surely be a relationship that would demand a lot from both the partners. They would need to understand that togetherness is more essential than individuality and at the same time, should not sacrifice everything for the sake of being together. This is a delicate balance and with patience and determination, everything should work out in their favour. It would be filled with plenty of arguments, confusions and compromises, but the end result would be worth it all.

Astro Advice
o Man : your beloved expects much from you; so get ready for it.
o Woman : be tactful and laconic.

AQUARIUS & SAGITTARIUS

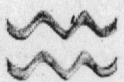 

Air Sign Ruled by Saturn	Fire Sign Ruled by Jupiter
• Progressive	• Procrastinating
• Unpredictable	• Easy going
• Humanitarian	• Open-critical
• Considerate	• Good-natured
• Zealous	• Practical

The elements of Fire and Air are closely linked to each other and so are their planets of Jupiter and Saturn. Both the signs have a profound influence on each other and at the same time, have the maturity to give each other their own space, when needed. Since, both Sagittarius and Aquarius have a strong desire to be free and independent, they would understand each others' desire to be on his/her own every once in a while. Idealistic and philosophical, they would also, be pragmatic in their own way. Both would also, be amicable and warm and hence would have a wide circle of friends with the ability to share their lives and interests with a diverse group of people. At the same time, they would manage to bring a unique closeness into their relationship with each other and give each other the importance that is due.

This is a relationship which has a great amount of compatibility, especially when it comes to the fundamentals of a relationship. The Sagittarius's natural straightforwardness doesn't hurt the Aquarius who is quite comfortable handling the truth and has the intellect to deal with it in a sensible manner.

They would have the ability to give the relationship a life of its own by filling it with their affection, emotion, imagination. Love would be a whole new experience with these two. It would be humorous, inspiring, volatile; and at the same time, calm and soothing.

The truth loving Sagittarius would be quite comfortable with knowing the reality, irrespective of how hurting it might be. Also, the Archer happens to be somewhat spiritual yet analytical and may even lose his/her temper every now and then. But at the same, he/she would be able to cool down just as quickly and bring things back to normal. If both the partners really love each other, things would be quite wonderful and would have quite a touch of magic about them. They would have the amazing quality of being friends and lovers at the same time.

Sexually, this relationship would see a lot of interactive behaviour and innovativeness. Both Sagittarius and Aquarius would want to give one another their genuine, sincere love and yet not make it boring and monotonous. Variety and newness would keep the fire alive throughout for both. They would treat lovemaking like a fun activity and with tenderness, affection and an infectious amicability would love each other and demonstrate their passion for each other. They might be a bit possessive but at the same time, would be comfortable giving each other a lot of space and room to develop and grow. Therefore, the relationship would be a constant journey of evolution and discovery for both of them.

Astro Advice

o Woman should trust her beloved.
o Man : don't be dramatic or disloyal with your beloved.

AQUARIUS & CAPRICORN

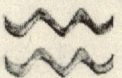

Air Sign *Ruled by Saturn*	*Earth Sign* *Ruled by Saturn*
• Fanatical	• Limited
• Erratic	• Ego-tripping
• Visionary	• Neglectful
• Caring	• Self-controlled
• Loyal	• Ambitious

The elements of Earth and Air do not have much in common; neither do the ruling planets of these signs-Saturn and Uranus respectively. This would be a relationship which would be affected by temperaments, opinions and personalities. Both the partners would have to make a lot of compromises and this could pose some problems, since the liberal, obstinate Aquarius would be stuck on his/her own ideals while the Capricorn would be just as rigid about his/her beliefs and opinions. Capricorn would find it difficult to understand why the Water bearer tends to become erratic and whimsical. This would have a negative impact on Capricorn's desire to achieve steadiness and stability in his/her life and relationship. What the Capricorn fails to see is that the intelligent, innovative Aquarian enjoys novelty and risks, irrespective of the results.

When a Capricorn and an Aquarius decide to join forces, one can never be sure of what would be the final result. The steady, realistic Capricorn cannot comprehend the Aquarian's point of view on most things and for the Aquarian dreams are just an extension of reality. The latter would dream of the most impossible things as per the Capricorn but then, would also, work hard at achieving them. The Aquarian is not satisfied treading the beaten path and would blaze his/her own trail wherever he/she goes.

As far as their physical relationship is concerned, it wouldn't be all smooth sailing. Capricorn would have a tendency to be gloomy and Aquarian would tend to be occupied with one of his/her many pursuits. In fact, Capricorn could have to face quite a few difficulties in getting the Aquarian to take a keen interest in lovemaking. The sober, calm and stable Capricorn could find the Aquarian quite a strange being and would need to look at him/her through a wider perspective. The Aquarian approach towards sex and lovemaking could extend from an avid inquisitiveness to an aloof approval while the Capricorn would view it more as an obligation of being in love. The one thing that is for sure is that neither one would overestimate or underestimate its importance. They would eventually participate and practice sexual activities but without any intensity of emotion or passion. This aspect of their relationship could have quite a few problems and both would need to work together in order to resolve them.

This would be a union which would gain meaning and insight with the passage of time. Both partners would learn to accommodate and adjust. They would have a better way of looking at the other's point of view and this could create a sense of harmony in an otherwise disturbed equation.

Astro Advice
- Man should wear black stone of five ratti on ring finger.
- Woman should wear Blue sapphire of four ratti on Saturday.

AQUARIUS & AQUARIUS

 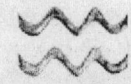

Air Sign
Ruled by Saturn
- Dithering
- Perverse
- Caring
- Zealous
- Tolerant

Air Sign
Ruled by Saturn
- Dithering
- Perverse
- Caring
- Zealous
- Tolerant

Ruled by the planet Saturn, the Air sign Aquarius is influenced immensely by the planet. Attributes of innovativeness, unpredictability, unconventionality, fickleness and many others are the gifts of the ruling planet. Aquarius never ceases to mystify and intrigue all those he/she comes into contact with. People find it difficult to get accustomed to Aquarian's streak of genius and madness. When two Aquarians get together, they are able to understand each other in a way that no one else can. A lot rests on which one of the numerous aspects do both of them have, however, one thing is for sure that the relationship would be impacted by the diverse circumstances brought about as a result of their temperaments.

The final result of a relationship between two Aquarians cannot be determined; the one thing that can be determined is that the level of empathy and understanding between the two would be high. Their life together would be filled with eccentricity but for an Aquarian that would be quite normal. When two Aquarians join forces, there is an overflow of intelligence, idiosyncrasies and innovativeness.

For the water bearer, male or female, the relation of friendship would take predominance over the relation of love. They thrive on acquiring and maintaining friends and the level of trust that they share with their friends is great. Most of them would establish a friendship before moving on to love and from thereon, to sex. The whole relationship of love and sex is something that intrigues them and once they achieve the perfect sexual union with their Aquarian partner, they would be able to reach fulfillment and completeness in each others' arms. Not one for being exquisitely communicative, they would demonstrate their love for each other through their eyes and through numerous small but meaningful gestures.

When two Aquarians bond and unite in love, they appreciate each other with the best of understanding, and a perfect matching of wavelengths. The sex could range from being volatile to purely tranquil. They would be just as compatible in bed as anywhere else. The relationship would be as unique as the two partners, themselves.

Astro Advice
o Men should put emphasis on spiritualism.
o Woman : avoid long term plans.

AQUARIUS & PISCES

Air Sign   *Water Sign*
Ruled by Saturn   *Ruled by Neptune*

- Impractical
- Considerate
- Broadminded
- Tolerant
- Fanatical

- Susceptible
- Compassionate
- Permissive
- Deceptive
- Guilt

This is one relationship which would be different and even, unprincipled, considering that the ruling planets of both the signs and the elements go beyond the limits of the ordinary world. This combination bestows the partners with exceptional and interesting attributes which affect the relationship in a variety of ways. Both feel like a fish out of water (pun intended!) in the company of others and it is this feeling that draws them towards each other. The couple would have many dimensions to their relationship with one another. For one thing they would have the supposedly normal appearance of a traditional relationship, but at the same time, there would be complexities and intricacies which would make the relationship more complicated than normal. Both would be able to see each other as being profound and astute and this attribute would remain even when they have been with each other for years at a stretch. They would be able to imagine, innovate, ideate, influence and inspire one another. Though they do have a great affinity with each other, yet there are also, a few oddities that separate the one from the other. For instance, Pisces' patience is one thing that the Water-bearer could inculcate while the Pisces could be more tolerant of the Aquarian peculiarities.

The Fish is artistic and has an acute vision of where he/she wants to be and would achieve the fame and luxury that is his/her goal. The Aquarian on the other hand, is more offbeat and would want to serve the cause of humanity rather than be completely self-centered and this might create some tensions. But even then, there is just about nothing that would keep the two away for long. They would come back together with greater understanding and intensity than ever.

Both would be fairly honest and wouldn't be the sort who would make false promises. They would believe in keeping their word and would not make a promise if they don't feel they could live up to it. Also, since both are sensitive and gentle, they could have to go through some painful and hurting experiences of life before they finally mature and learn to take the rough with the smooth.

Sexually, the Aquarius-Pisces couple would be innovative and experimental, willing to try out new things and make the sexual union more meaningful and deep than ever. They would take this to a higher level and the gentle process of lovemaking would become a revelation in itself.

Astro Advice
o A woman should sense the potential of her husband and look forward to what's ahead.
o Man : be confident while speaking and avoid flirtation.

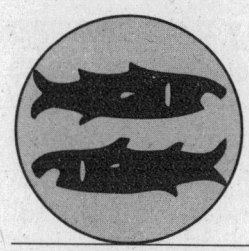

Pisces–The Fish
(Feburary 20–March 20)
The Sign of the Poet or Interpreter

How to Recognise Pisces

Pisces is the poet of the Zodiac. With signs of the Water element emotion is plentifully expressed at a moment's notice: the dilating pupils of the Piscean eyes will at once tell us when the individual is moved. Pisces is, of course, the sign of the fishes. But look at the symbol- two fishes swimming in opposite directions, with a cord in their mouth connecting them. This sums up Pisces beautifully. Here we have the kindest and most charitable of all the signs. Pisceans will make many sacrifices for other people, a trait they share with their polar or opposite sign, Virgo. Sometimes this tendency will get out of hand, and the marvellous potential present in most Pisceans is frittered away or comes to nothing because Pisces is otherwise occupied. But it might just be that Pisces will divert time and energy in some 'sacrificial' way because of an inherent lack of self-confidence. If they are busy caring for others or fulfilling a supportive role, then they do not have to fight to keep up with opponents in their field or cope with the rat race. Opting out, they find that a cloistered life gives them a sense of security, and this in a subtle way is a modern expression of the religious aspects of this sign, the 'monk-like' or 'nun-like' aspirations of the past, in essence very Piscean. They do particularly well in the caring or medical professions. But what of the Pisces poet? Of course not all Pisceans go dreamily around with notebook in hand composing verses, though when they do, they do it very well. There is, however, creative ability in most Pisceans. It needs tremendous support and encouragement from partners, as do all practical aspects of their lives. When this is available, their talent emerges strongly. They make excellent dancers and ice-skaters and enjoy swimming, and all these activities are physically good for them. But above all it is involvement in the fine arts that is particularly satisfying on all levels.

The Pisces body-area is the feet, Pisceans either have marvelously neat ones, and no trouble, or are in constant difficulty. Shoes will either be a perennial problem or a continual source of delight. There is a tendency to worry, which may cause stomach upsets. When troubled in this way, Pisceans should fall back on their ample intuition and their natural instinct.

Career and Finance

When assessing the Piscean potential in careers and financial ability we must consider not only the psychological motivation and mode of expression attributed to Pisces but also the thinking processes of Mercury, and how these two factors combined can be best used in both areas. Then there is the influence of Venus, a planet as strongly related to finance and possessions as to relationships. The latter aspect is also important in this sphere as it will affect how a person will get on with colleagues, in business partnerships, and so on. Mars may well give some hints as to the direction of energy and will most certainly influence the physical element - the drive and energy put into the day's work. As we shall see, the influence of the combined Sun and Rising-sign is interesting and very personal; but if your birth time is not available and you cannot find out your Rising-sign, do not be too disappointed; you should be able to gain plenty of information about this sphere of your life from the more general paragraphs. Pisceans are a fascinating study when it comes to careers because their needs in this area tend to be very individual. They are not easily fitted into pigeonholes. All Pisceans should therefore do some careful thinking before-choosing a career if they are to make the best of their lives.

Health and Food

This question largely depends on your outlook to life. As long as you can continue in active work you will keep well and in a healthy condition. If forced for any reason into inactivity you will become pleasure loving and indolent, inclined to put on flesh and let the reins of life easily drop from your hands.

Suggested Food Options:
- Egg Yolk
- Onions
- Food grains
- Lamb
- Pear

Your Love Life

First Decan of Pisces: *February 20 to February 29*

You have a profound interest in spiritual and such matters which are above the mundane issues of daily life. Your inclinations take you towards thoughtful and deeper topics. Your principles focus is on being of assistance to others in order to make their existence more enriched than before. There might even be the situation that you let matters of the heart pass you by since you would be deeply occupied in serving others. Although, you should take special note of the fact that love is really what you require in order to live your own life with happiness and contentment, therefore, you shouldn't let it pass you by rather you should try and bring it into your life as early as possible.

It would give you the greatest joy being able to make your partner happy and your benevolence would propel you into finding your happiness in the happiness of others. You would even put your needs away and be content with what you give to your mate.

You do need to be a little careful while choosing a partner for life. Take care not to get entangled with someone who would take you for granted rather find someone who would share your generous spirit and value it. When in a happy marriage, you would truly blossom and would work hard at making your home the happiest and warmest.

If perchance, your partner is self-centered and unkind, you would be the most miserable soul. Take care that your sentiments are not brushed aside or treated with cruelty. Rely on your keen perception and sixth sense while interacting with potential partners and though it may take time, you would soon, find the one person who would bring you all the happiness that you need in order to live your life with a calm contentment.

Second Decan of Pisces : March 1 to March 10

For you romance is the very essence of life and living and you cannot even begin to comprehend a world sans romance. You are the sort who would gladly chase rainbow coloured dreams and would give up all that you have to follow the music of your heart. Your love and likings have the capacity of being intensely passionate.

You do have an inclination of being a diehard passionate and idealistic individual who might never stay with any one person simply due to the fact that you would lose your heart many times over, so much so, that there would be a time when you wouldn't really trust your own self and your own feelings enough and would feel wobbly and uncertain about the entire issue of love.

What you would in reality, be looking for would be a perfect love, an everlasting love, a complete love.

Since your ideals and standards are rather exceptional, it is quite a tough task to gain your approval and even your friends find it a difficult task to make you happy. Therefore, it would be even more so for a lover. You do need someone who would be able to match these extraordinary qualities.

The one who would finally win your heart and your hand would be an individual with immense adaptability, tenderness and diversity. Not the one to look after the home and hearth with complete dedication you would want a partner who would enrich you life with varied experiences and also, shoulder domestic responsibilities with a smile. He would need to keep you interested at all times and not let you drift into monotony or else, you would just drift away from him or her.

Third Decan of Pisces: March 11 to March 20

Though you value the emotion of love greatly, you do have the tendency of being somewhat money-oriented, wanting wealth and objects which would make others envious of your status. You do have an incredible amount of talent and a keen discernment, therefore, it is not surprising that people are drawn to you and are intrigued by you.

Your beloved must be a receptive and astute individual. One who would be able to match your own sharp intellect and abilities. You are fond of the arts and would appreciate those who are adept in them. In fact, you would look for someone who would have something special and unique about him or her, a certain specialty that would make him/her stand out in the crowd. It is absolutely essential for you to admire the one you love. And if your partner's abilities match your own, the alliance would indeed be a pleasantly balanced one.

You have the special knack of putting your feelings into the most beautiful words and expressions, therefore, making the romance a delightful and vibrant journey. You would not tread the beaten path but blaze your own trail when keeping the magic alive in your relationship. You would experiment and explore new ways of filling your life with freshness and passion.

In restrained and understated manners, you may dominate the home front but would do so in such a sedate fashion that even you wouldn't realise that you are doing it. You do possess a certain aura about you that makes your entire character a powerful one. Your partner would value and cherish you deeply because of the strong, sensitive and sedate persona that you hold.

Your Sex Life

First Decan Neptune-ruled : February 20 to March 1

You maintain a fine balance between the sentimental and the aesthetic, are immensely romantic and receptive to sexual ideas. You do have a tendency to develop emotional bonds with your sexual mates and this can often lead to sadness and misery, if the latter are aloof or distant. Love and warmth stimulate you sexually and you do need these, at times, to respond completely during sex. Especially since your sex drive is highly influenced by your emotional temperament more than anything else and that is what would determine how you respond to various sexual stimuli.

Second Decan, subruled by the Moon : March 2 to 11 March

You possess the fundamental Pisces qualities of optimism, opulence, and a yearning for the love, warmth and attention of your partners - all these attributes are completely and firmly tied up with your sex drive. Your need for emotionality in a relationship is also greater and this would also, have an effect on your sexual behaviour. It would have either a positive or negative effect depending upon the situation. Like most other Pisceans you, too, would find that your satisfaction in your sex life is highly dependent on how well connected are you with your partner on an emotional level. The higher this would be, the better would be your sex life and expression.

Third Decan, subruled by Pluto : March 12 to 20 March

As compared to fellow Pisceans, your sex drive would be stronger and even, more forceful. At the same time, you would also, have the need to feel emotionally secure in your relationship to gain complete sexual satisfaction and complete expression of your sex drive. As you may consume a lot of energy in moving from one highly emotionally charged situation to another, you may experience a reduction in your energy level in the matter of sex. You must maintain a cheerful, carefree and happy outlook in life and towards everything, in general and this would definitely have a positive impact on your sex life as well.

Pisces Celebrities

Birth Date	Star	Vocation
7 March	Anupam Kher	Actor
9 March	Zakhir Hussain	Musician
10 March	Alka Yagnik	Musician
14 March	Aamir Khan	Film Star
18 March	Shashi Kapoor	Actor

Compatibility

PISCES & ARIES

Water Sign
Ruled by Neptune

- Cowards
- Deceptive
- Creative
- Trustworthy
- Guilt-ridden
- Escapist

Fire Sign
Ruled by Mars

- Strong
- Enthusiastic
- Active
- Selfish
- Insensitive
- Hot-tempered

Aries - ruled by fiery Mars and Pisces ruled by watery Neptune are poles apart in temperament. So great would be the difference that it would be extremely hard to find something that the two could possibly share. Optimistic, energetic Aries would not be able to understand the vague, mystifying character of Pisces who would further bother the Aries with his indecisiveness and pessimistic outlook.

They would be able to co-exist if they decide not to interfere with each other's attitude and outlook. There would be frequent heated arguments and cold wars, more so, when the blunt Arian would lose patience with the wily ways of the Piscean.

In physical matters, the fish is quite adjusting yet thin-skinned, which implies that he wouldn't be able to take any harshness in this aspect. He/she might display somewhat masochistic inclinations during sex by imagining that Aries is infidel. Yet these wouldn't be mentioned in the light of the day, since the fish would be quite scandalised by such talk. The fish would also, need to curb his need to be out of the house, socialising or drinking, which would only serve to make the Aries feel sad and exploited. On the whole, though, the two would enjoy a satisfying sexual relationship.

The partnership of Aries and Pisces is a gentle and pleasant one. Pisces would not be too opposing to Aries who in turn, would find them calming and soothing. The relationship would be gratifying for the two, if they learn to come to a common ground and adapt to each other's differences.

Astro Advice
o You are adviced to keep porcelain figures of Venus and Jasmine in the South-West corner of your bedroom.
o Man should wear Yellow Sapphire of seven carat on index finger.
o Woman : it may be necessary to bend to a stronger point of view.

PISCES & TAURUS

Water Sign *Earth Sign*
Ruled by Neptune *Ruled by Venus*
- Broad-minded
- Loyal
- Dreamer
- Diffused
- Drifting

- Tenacious
- Nagging
- Obstinate
- Kind
- Fruitful

This particular union of Earth with Water is a pleasantly satisfying one since the planets that rule the signs-Venus and Jupiter are not in opposition to each other. They would enjoy a relationship filled with plenty of companionship, affection and a common love for the finer things in life. They would help to provide harmony to each other. The realist Taurus would be able to bring the dreamy Pisces back to Earth gently and firmly.

While the Piscean would display greater and more creative powers of making and spending money, it would be the steady Taurean who would be able to educate the Piscean about valuing money and learning through experiencing reality more so than anything else. It is not as if everything would be smooth sailing with the two of them, they would have their share of arguments and quarrels. However, their sense of humour would save the day and they would be able to make up with a good laugh over things. It is a fact that they are inevitably drawn together since they both tend to value and appreciate the same things, such as calmness and tranquility, with a slight danger of becoming prone to sadness and negativity.

This is one couple who would be able to offset each others' attributes perfectly. Sexually as well, they would have a high level of compatibility and would be able to give themselves to the other without any questions. Taurus would be able to give plenty to the tender, creative Pisces. The Taurean sense of peace, gentleness, soothing presence and warmly gentle expressions of love would fill the Piscean with wonder and awe. Both of them would enjoy the sensuality and passions of love making and would be able to let the other know their true feelings and emotions. This in itself would make their union a pleasurable and happy one.

Astro Advice
o Man should be wary of beloved who suddenly presents you with unsolicited ideas for consideration.
o Woman should avoid junk food.
o Man : try not to go to meet your beloved in casual wear.

PISCES & GEMINI

Water Sign Ruled by Neptune	Air Sign Ruled by Mercury
• Cowards	• Youthful
• Compassionate	• Humorous
• Unreliable	• Conversational
• Apathetic	• Sharp-tounged
• Lazy	• Distracted

Glaring differences in the temperaments and attitudes of the two signs only confirms the influence that the difference in their elements exercises. While Gemini is decisive, analytical, realistic and inclined to think with the head, Pisces is fickle, vague, and thin-skinned and leads with the heart. However, they are quite adjusting by nature and would be quite patient with one another and even if they don't really understand each other they would not be critical of the other one.

Even if there may not always be smooth sailing with the two of them, it is possible for them to live happily, as long as they continue to make whatever minor adjustments are needed. If Gemini learns to communicate more expressively and Pisces learns to be a good listener, they would be quite content with each other. While Gemini would need someone who would value them, Pisces would want to feel wanted. So, if they learn to satisfy their individual expectations in the best possible way, they could well be happy and peaceful in this particular union.

As far as their sexual aspect of the relationship is concerned, they would be quite satisfied with it. Since both of them would want the emotional aspect of their relationship to be a part of the sexual expression. Also, both would be equally open to introducing newness in the relationship, so that monotony doesn't set in. Gemini's unconventional approach to sex would be appealing to the highly creative imagination of the fish. These two would also, share plenty of other likes and dislikes. Quite a good number of them make proficient lovers who admire loveliness and the finer aspects of life. At the same time, since both Air and Water do not really feel the need for sexual expression as strongly as other elements, this aspect might lack real meaning for them.

Theirs is a union which would have many happy moments. Their lives would move together and although there would be plenty of love, yet physically, it would be bereft of real warmth and closeness. It would have many other good things that would make up for this particular aspect.

Astro Advice

o Men should wear yellow sapphire of six carat on their index finger on Thursday after Pran Pratishta (after prayer to Jupiter)
o Women should use light colour lipstick and hair should be combed back in a bun.

PISCES & CANCER

Water Sign
Ruled by Neptune
- Cowards
- Depressive
- Nourishing
- Secure
- Maternal
- Cloying

Water Sign
Ruled by Moon
- Youthful
- Guilt
- Philosophical
- Ambitionless
- Confused
- Escapist

The joining of Water with Water symbolises a high level of emotionality, since Water is linked with sentiments and emotions. Therefore, the feeling aspect would always have dominance over reason and logic in this relationship. Pragmatism might get overlooked and even neglected. The intensity of emotions would bring you closer and increase the level of intimacy in your relationship without you making a conscious attempt. Both of you are incredibly romantic and yearn to be cared for and made a fuss of.

This is one alliance where everything would nearly always be peaceful and composed. Their sympathy and understanding for one another is nearly instantaneous. They have more similarities of character than differences. Both of them are equally temperamental, fickle, enigmatic and insightful. The one area where they could be differences would be finances and even here, adjustments and conciliations could be effected.

Since the crab is more overprotective, he/she would try to influence the fish into adapting more. Moreover, Cancer also, enjoys holding onto yesterdays and yesteryears.

However, since Pisces is considerably more adjusting and is also, an incredibly good listener, therefore, there would be many happy days together. This is in many more ways than one an elegant and blessed couple. Their differences are few and far between and the similarities make the journey a pleasant and enjoyable one.

Sexually the creativity of this couple would be at its height and they would use their intense love for each other to enhance and liven up their sex life. The element of romance would play a dominant role as would their individual imaginations. A satisfying sex life would only strengthen their already strong and dynamic relationship.

This is in nearly every way a perfect relationship. Physically, emotionally, mentally, Cancer and Pisces have a togetherness that is profound and at the same time, inspiring. Their life with each other would be full of intense love and sensitive love making signifying an ideal understanding, a perfect union.

Astro Advice
o Men : don't forget to carry a pack of chocolates with you.
o Women should remember your beloved believes in Spartan simplicity.

PISCES & LEO

Water Sign
Ruled by Neptune
- Dreamers
- Guilt-ridden

Fire Sign
Ruled by Sun
- Rude
- Creative

- Philosophical
- Idealistic
- Romantic
- Administrator
- Hospitable
- Loving

The disparity between Fire and Water just goes to show how unlike Leo and Pisces are from each other. While Leo is straightforward, gregarious and candid, Pisces is vague, profound, mystifying and can be quite an enigma for most whom they come in contact with. Leo can never quite figure out what makes Pisces tick however, Pisces does appreciate Leo and his/her characteristics such as perseverance and focus. Pisces frequently needs to be more planned and orderly and the Lion is the ideal teacher for the same.

As far as Pisces is concerned, he/she can fill Leo's life with a lot of gentleness and perceptiveness. And the Lion can further give Pisces a strong sense of security and stability. Yet for all the enrichment that they can do for each other, they lack the basic compatibility that is so essential for any successful relationship and they would, both, need to work really hard at bringing about any kind of equilibrium and synchrony in their lives. Once they learn to do that, they can focus on inspiring each other and helping one another towards self-development.

While Leo has a regal bearing and elegance, Pisces has an inherent philosophical superiority and this complements the leonine personality perfectly. Hence, with some work, they would be able to form a lasting and enduring relationship and give it their best.

There could be times when Leo would be unreasonable with the fish however, Pisces would realise that eventually Leo would be a warm and companionable partner who would loyally and passionately protect and love them. Sexually, there could be minor hitches. The mystery of Pisces could be too delicate to satisfy the Lion. On the other hand, the Lion could be too passionate and overbearing for the Fish. Their sexual relations would have their basis in a mutual admiration for each other more than anything else. And in order for sex to be there, the element of love must always be there.

When they overcome all their challenges, both would want to create an atmosphere of romance and sensuality preceding their lovemaking. Their intimacy would be characterised by plenty of tender, romantic moments. There does exist the possibility of envy creeping into the relationship since both have the capacity to tease and flirt. If they learn to get their expectations right from the relationship, they would attain a great deal of happiness. Leo would want to get generous amount of loving, appreciation and intense passion. Pisces would crave a fulfillment complete in all respects. Together, with compromises and adjustments, they would lead happy and delightful lives.

Astro Advice
o Men should show their feeling by giving gifts and cards.
o Women should wear yellow sapphire of six carat on her index finger.

PISCES & VIRGO

Water Sign *Earth Sign*
Ruled by Neptune *Ruled by Mercury*
- Apathetic
- Guilt-ridden
- Analytical
- Methodical

- Cowards
- Humanitarian
- Lacking will power
- Quick-tempered
- Fussy
- Prissy

The elements of Earth and Water have a natural bonding and thus, this implies that these otherwise opposite signs in the Zodiac actually, balance each other out. While earthy Virgo is driven by logic, rationale and the like, Pisces is motivated by sentiments, perceptiveness and instincts. Together they make a wonderful pair travelling through Life with wide-eyed wonder and yet, an uncanny sense of knowing what comes next.

Both of them would have a well-established comfort level with each other and would be able to discuss practically everything under the sun. this would, also, help them to sort out any problem that might crop up along the way. Using a mix of reason, feelings and good conversation would enable them to figure out and overcome any hurdle that should ever stand in their way.

The tenderness of Virgo coupled with the compassion of Pisces would create a gentle and soulful love. They have a unique way of being able to know each other's mind and respond accordingly. Perceptive and gentle, they absorb and react to each other's vibrations with acuteness and accuracy. They share not just the good times but the sad times as well with the same amount of softness and wisdom. They are indeed well matched and well-suited. While Virgo is pure at heart, organised and sensitive, Pisces is sympathetic, intelligent and appreciative. Together they are magic.

However, there is a flip side. This, though, might be a rare occurrence. In most cases, this is a naturally compatible couple. They would combine and share everything they have-material and spiritual. Even finances, would never pose an issue with this pair.

Sexually, they would be just as compatible. Both would enjoy the act of love. Pisces' sensitivity and tact would win the gentle Virgo heart and he/she would participate with desire and sensuality. A deep love and respect for each other would merge perfectly with a strong sexual desire for each other and hence, there would be little that this relationship would ever lack. They would be partners in the true sense of the word and would be able to stand by each other through everything that comes their way. Truly, a couple that would be quite the example for many others.

Astro Advice
o Woman : telling lie can create a problem.
o Man should wear Emerald of eight ratti on Wednesday.

PISCES & LIBRA

Water Sign	*Air Sign*
Ruled by Neptune	*Ruled by Venus*
• Sympathetic	• Kind
• Deceptive	• Selfish
• Creative	• Vacillating
• Talented	• Thoughtless
• Psychic	• Sociable

Even though the elements of Air and Water are not terribly close, the natural bonding between their respective ruling planets enables this couple to enjoy each other. They would have some similar preferences, despite the differences in their personalities and would get pleasure from the finer things in life as also, the values and qualities of sensitivity, balance, love, companionship and the joys of being in love with someone. The Libran fair-mindedness and rationality would balance the Piscean indecisiveness, unrealism, and mental disarray.

This particular relationship is a calming and comforting one. Both would be unaware as to why they are where they are. They would, in all likelihood, be brought together by destiny and once together, they would want to explore the other person completely and interpret their personalities. How these two would conduct themselves and actualise their ambitions, inspirations and desires would have a deep impact on the people around them.

Although, Libra and Pisces might not fall in love instantly, once they do meet by chance or circumstance, they manage to combine their dissimilarities in a beautifully seamless fashion and make the best of what they have. They are intelligent and emotional, sensitive and tasteful. They appreciate tranquility and are not belligerent. Since Libra is nearly always attractive and alluring, it becomes easy for Pisces to be drawn to him/her at a mental, emotional and physical level. When Pisces returns the feelings of Libra, the former becomes intense and more devoted to the fish. As for Pisces, he/she would give Libra complete loyalty and dedication. Even though, this relationship may not run its full course, there are many chances that it would be filled with happiness, positivism and radiance.

Astro Advice
o Woman should respond vibrantly to the feelings and ideas of his beloved.
o Man should need to improve tolerance power.

PISCES & SCORPIO

Water Sign
Ruled by Neptune
- Ambitionless
- Dreamer
- Escapist
- Good-natured
- Idealistic

Water Sign
Ruled by Mars
- Determined
- Brave
- Profound
- Greedy
- Obsessed

Water and Water. These two signs would have a unique and intense affinity and when they would come together, they would create pure magic. Scorpio would want to be the controller and wield the upper hand; and while Pisces is not really passive, it would yield and be the controlled. The tranquility that Pisces would radiate would help to calm and pacify the intensity and passion of the Scorpio. Both would be able to sense each others' fears, hopes and desires and would be emotional about sensitive issues.

Together, these two would be able to give each other companionship, and share a healthy camaraderie that would make the good times better and the bad times good. Both would have a profundity which would help them to communicate even in perfect silence. They would be able to give the experience of Life a whole new meaning, a meaning that would be rich, intense, insightful. This would be the wonderful quality that this particular couple would bring to their relationship.

They would have their share of conflicts and disagreements yet they would be able to make up and sort out their differences in next to no time. In any case, there is no doubt that with the two of them, the sunny days would be more than the cloudy ones and happiness would always be an integral part of their lives.

The two are constantly attracted towards each other by unknown and unforeseen forces. And they share a strong empathy with each other which only serves to forge the bond more closely than ever. Their powers of intuition would be strong and wondrous. Despite its apparent calmness, whenever there would be a clash, it would be Pisces who would take the stronger position.

The sexual aspect of the relationship is also just as emotional and dramatic. Scorpio's possessive streak would be subdued and soothed by the Piscean tact and empathy. Both would express their sexual desires and feelings in the most subtle yet intense fashion. A communication that would hold a great deal of meaning and passion hidden within it. This is, indeed, a relationship that has a bright future and good things in store for both the partners.

Astro Advice
o Men should practice flattery.
o Women : give extra attention to your beloved.

PISCES & SAGITTARIUS

Water Sign *Fire Sign*
Ruled by Neptune *Ruled by Jupiter*
- Lazy
- Dreamers
- Forthright
- Broad-minded

- Receptive
- Talented
- Compassionate
- High-principled
- Friendly
- Dependable

The union of Fire and Water holds a great deal of intricacies and a lot of potential. There would be a degree of similarity and compatibility, since the partners would share interests in travelling, spiritualism, altruistic works and similar idealistic pursuits. There would also, be contrasts and conflicts as the pair experiences indecision, perplexity and doubts. There could also, be couples who might continue to exist in individual worlds, aloof and detached from one another. The Sagittarius desire to be free could arouse some fears and insecurities in the imaginative Pisces. Despite the fact that the Archer is an affectionate and warm being, he/she does not possess the softness that the Pisces craves for. Also, the Piscean knack of being irresolute, unrealistic and unsystematic could well, irritate the Sagittarius who is a stickler for doing things speedily and effectively, with the maximum decisiveness, optimism and energy.

When this couple decides to stay together and keep an atmosphere of peace prevailing, it is essential that they learn to keep a tight rein on their tempers. When they do that, calmness would automatically fill their lives. Also, the fact that both would be intrigued by spiritualism would bind them together. The more they focus on their similarities and the less on their differences, the better and happier would be their relationship. These two might have to undergo many tough times, but if they learn to remain cool and balanced, life would be pleasant and peaceful.

Sexually, they would be compatible and would be drawn closer to each other as a result of their lovemaking. Both enjoy sex and would take a healthy interest in the same. However, if the sole basis of the relationship is sexual, it would not last for long, since both would want the company of someone who would please them intellectually, emotionally, mentally along with sexually.

If all other criteria are met, Sagittarius would be drawn towards Pisces like a magnet and they would enjoy a satisfying and emotionally rich sexual life.

Astro Advice

o Man : should look glamorous and charming while going to meet beloved.
o Woman should remember not to put financial security in jeopardy.

PISCES & CAPRICORN

Water Sign	Earth Sign
Ruled by Neptune	Ruled by Saturn
• Peaceful	• Social-climber
• Guilt	• Inhabited
• Diffuse	• Dependable
• Unreliable	• Over-critical
• Idealistic	• Limited

The elements of these two signs- Earth and Water respectively have a natural bonding with each other and despite their dissimilarities; they do tend to harmonise with one another. Capricorn is the very personification of stability and steadiness. Pisces, on the other hand, is quite comfortable adjusting to such kinds of people. However, the tender and romantic Pisces may feel injured at times, when the serious Capricorn doesn't demonstrate his/her affection. Both would, in most cases, work in tandem with one another. Pisces is not the sort who is overly ambitious and hence, would be supportive of Capricorn's desire to grow and rise in life and society. Moreover, the steady Capricorn's realism and ability to administrate would protect the Piscean from the difficulties that life may present in front of them.

The astute Capricorn would give the sensitive and gentle Pisces a warm sense of security and faithfulness which would illuminate and enrich his/her life and bring the relationship to a new dimension altogether. As far as their sexual relationship is concerned, both would give it a practical yet romantic touch. The Capricorn would express himself/herself in a straightforward way and also, be attentive to the Piscean needs and wishes. Their lovemaking would be marked by the strength and intensity of their emotions for each other. Since both wouldn't be extremely communicative, their silence, itself, would speak volumes. The sexual bonding of these two souls would be sensitive, ideal and would bring them together in perfect intimacy; filling their hearts and minds with tranquility, softness and completeness.

Astro Advice
o Man should wear Blue sapphire of four ratti on Saturday
o Woman : should focus on good habits.

PISCES & AQUARIUS

Water Sign *Air Sign*
Ruled by Neptune *Ruled by Saturn*
- Susceptible
- Compassionate
- Impractical
- Considerate

- Permissive
- Deceptive
- Guilt-ridden
- Broad-minded
- Tolerant
- Fanatical

This is one relationship which would be different and even, unprincipled, considering that the ruling planets of both the signs and the elements go beyond the limits of the ordinary world. This combination bestows the partners with exceptional and interesting attributes which affect the relationship in a variety of ways. Both feel like a fish out of water (pun intended!) in the company of others and it is this feeling that draws them towards each other. The couple would have many dimensions to their relationship with one another. For one thing they would have the supposedly normal appearance of a traditional relationship, but at the same time, there would be complexities and intricacies which would make the relationship more complicated than normal. Both would be able to see each other as being profound and astute and this attribute would remain even when they have been with each other for years at a stretch. They would be able to help imagine, innovate, ideate, influence and inspire one another. Though they do have a great affinity with each other, yet there are also, a few oddities that separate the one from the other. For instance, Pisces' patience is one thing that the Water-bearer could inculcate while the Pisces could be more tolerant of the Aquarian peculiarities.

The Fish is artistic and has an acute vision of where he/she wants to be and would achieve the fame and luxury that is his/her goal. The Aquarian on the other hand, is more offbeat and would want to serve the cause of humanity rather than be completely self-centered and this might create some tensions. But even then, there is just about nothing that would keep the two away for long. They would come back together with greater understanding and intensity than ever.

Both would be fairly honest and wouldn't be the sort who would make false promises. They would believe in keeping their word and would not make a promise if they don't feel they could live up to it. Also, since both are sensitive and gentle, they could have to go through some painful and hurting experiences of life before they finally mature and learn to take the rough with the smooth.

Sexually, the Aquarius-Pisces couple would be innovative and experimental, willing to try out new things and make the sexual union more meaningful and deep than ever. They would take this to a higher level and the gentle process of lovemaking would become a revelation in itself.

Astro Advice
o Woman you should sense the potential of her husband and look forward to what's ahead.
o Man : be confident while speaking and avoid flirtation.

PISCES & PISCES

Water Sign
Ruled by Neptune
- Confused
- Creative
- Loyal
- Good-natured
- Philosophical

Water Sign
Ruled by Neptune
- Confused
- Creative
- Loyal
- Good-natured
- Philosophical

Since this is a sign whose element is Water, when two Pisceans come together, the relationship is dominated by emotions, perception, reveries, creativity and an insightfulness that is unique. Both partners would have their own private space to retreat into when the troubles of the world become too much to handle. Intuitive and perceptive, they would be able to feel the vibes of each other and also, those around them with acuteness. They would also, have the tendency to be chaotic, confused, unsystematic and unsure, so there would be times when tasks are left undone and incomplete. Both the Pisceans would have the ability to show off their positive traits to the best of their abilities when they are together. They also, have the exclusive art of being able to accept people and situations as they are without wanting to change or modify them. This does not imply that they are passive, it is just that they realise that there is a reason for everything and do not like to interfere with that reason. Both Pisces men and women find their ways to win over the other, either by achieving their life's ambitions or by a display of emotions.

Sexually, they would be attracted towards each other and they would work hard at keeping the romance alive in their life. Their creativity and imaginativeness would extend to the bedroom as well and would ensure that the sparks keep flying. It is, in fact, quite a possibility that the two may get together purely on the basis of physical attraction and this could lead to only a short-term affair. They should understand and look for things other than sex appeal when aiming for a long-term relationship and also, once in a relationship, should commit to loyalty and faithfulness. If this is taken care of, their bonding would have intimacy, warmth and plenty of affection.

Astro Advice
o Men should dress up in casual wear but remember stripes will suit you.
o Women : you need to be punctual.